God and Meaning

God and Meaning

New Essays

Edited by
Joshua W. Seachris and Stewart Goetz

Bloomsbury Academic
An imprint of Bloomsbury Publishing Inc

B L O O M S B U R Y
NEW YORK · LONDON · OXFORD · NEW DELHI · SYDNEY

Bloomsbury Academic
An imprint of Bloomsbury Publishing Inc

1385 Broadway	50 Bedford Square
New York	London
NY 10018	WC1B 3DP
USA	UK

www.bloomsbury.com

BLOOMSBURY and the Diana logo are trademarks of Bloomsbury Publishing Plc

First published 2016

© Joshua W. Seachris, Stewart Goetz, and Contributors, 2016

All rights reserved. No part of this publication may be reproduced or transmitted in any form or by any means, electronic or mechanical, including photocopying, recording, or any information storage or retrieval system, without prior permission in writing from the publishers.

No responsibility for loss caused to any individual or organization acting on or refraining from action as a result of the material in this publication can be accepted by Bloomsbury or the author.

Library of Congress Cataloging-in-Publication Data
Names: Seachris, Joshua W., editor.
Title: God and meaning : new essays / edited by
Joshua Seachris and Stewart Goetz.
Description: 1st [edition]. | New York : Bloomsbury Academic, 2016. |
Includes bibliographical references and index.
Identifiers: LCCN 2016003585 (print) | LCCN 2016022882 (ebook) |
ISBN 9781628927597 (hardcover) | ISBN 9781628927627
(ePub) | ISBN 9781628927634 (ePDF)
Subjects: LCSH: Life. | Life—Religious aspects. | Meaning (Philosophy) |
God. Classification: LCC BD435 .G53 2016 (print) |
LCC BD435 (ebook) | DDC 202/.2—dc23
LC record available at https://lccn.loc.gov/2016003585

ISBN: HB: 978-1-6289-2-759-7
PB: 978-1-6289-2-761-0
ePub: 978-1-6289-2-762-7
ePDF: 978-1-6289-2-763-4

Cover design: Catherine Wood
Cover image © Walter Zerla/Getty Images

Typeset by Newgen Knowledge Works (P) Ltd, Chennai, India

*For William, Owen, and Evan Seachris
constant reminders of what really matters
and
Virginia Goetz
who in so many ways made life worth living*

Contents

Acknowledgments   ix

Introduction   1
Stewart Goetz and Joshua W. Seachris

Part 1   Clarifying the Question: Conceptual and Theistic Tools

1   The Meaning of Life and Scripture's Redemptive-Historical Narrative: Illuminating Convergences   13
Joshua W. Seachris

Part 2   Meaningfulness and God

2   What God Could (and Couldn't) Do to Make Life Meaningful   37
Timothy Mawson

3   Hedonistic Happiness and Life's Meaning   59
Stewart Goetz

4   Belief That Life Has Meaning Confirms That Life Has Meaning: A Bayesian Approach   81
Trent Dougherty

5   Can the Demands of the Perfection Thesis be Trivialized?   99
Nicholas Waghorn

Part 3   Meaningfulness, Time, and Eternity

6   Meaningfulness, Eternity, and Theism   123
John Cottingham

7   The Expansion and Contraction of the Meaning of Life   137
Charles Taliaferro

8   How God Makes Life a Lot More Meaningful   149
Richard Swinburne

Part 4 The Purpose(s) of Life

9 Affective Gethsemane Meaning for Life 167
   Paul K. Moser

10 St. Isaac's Dictum 185
   Terence Cuneo

Part 5 Meaning in Ecclesiastes

11 Wisdom and Meaning: Philosophy and the Theology of the Meaning of Life in Ecclesiastes 209
   Craig G. Bartholomew

12 "Meaningless, Meaningless, Says Qohelet": Finding the Meaning of Life in the Book of Ecclesiastes 231
   Tremper Longman III

Notes on Contributors 247
Bibliography 251
Index 263

Acknowledgments

We are grateful to a number of people without whom this collection would not have come to fruition. Thank you to the students who have enrolled in our meaning of life courses over the years. Through our interactions, you have helped us further understand this vast, important topic. Thank you to our contributors. It was a privilege working with each of you in the realization and completion of this collection. I (Josh) thank Michael Rea and Samuel Newlands at the University of Notre Dame's Center for Philosophy of Religion for my position's flexibility to work on projects such as this one. To Haaris Naqvi, Mary Al-Sayed, and the entire team at Bloomsbury Academic, thank you. We can say, without hesitation, that working with you on this project—start to finish—has been both a privilege and a pleasure. Your professionalism is exemplary. Finally, we owe deep gratitude to our families for your loving presence and support in our lives.

Joshua W. Seachris
Notre Dame, IN
(November 2015)

Stewart Goetz
Collegeville, PA
(November 2015)

Introduction

Stewart Goetz and Joshua W. Seachris

Within the last fifteen to twenty years, analytic philosophers (from here on, simply philosophers) have increasingly devoted attention to the topic often dubbed "the meaning of life."[1] With the demise of logical positivism (which

---

[1] Helpful surveys of this work are available by Thaddeus Metz, "The Meaning of Life," *Stanford Encyclopedia of Philosophy*, ed. Edward N. Zalta, http://plato.stanford.edu/entries/life-meaning/, "New Developments in the Meaning of Life," *Philosophy Compass* 2 (2007): 196–217, "Recent Work on the Meaning of Life," *Ethics* 112 (July 2002): 781–814, and by Joshua Seachris, "General Introduction," in *Exploring the Meaning of Life: An Anthology and Guide*, ed. Joshua Seachris (Malden, MA: Wiley-Blackwell, 2012), 1–20, "'Meaning of Life' Contemporary Analytic Perspectives." *Internet Encyclopedia of Philosophy*, eds. James Fieser and Bradley Dowden, http://www.iep.utm.edu/mean-ana/. Stewart Goetz has written a more theistically focused survey, "The Meaning of Life," in *The Routledge Companion to Theism*, ed. Charles Taliaferro, Victoria S. Harrison, and Stewart Goetz (New York: Routledge, 2013), 698–709. Beyond surveys, there is a steadily growing number of journal articles, including special journal issues devoted entirely to the topic of life's meaning, for example, *Philosophical Papers* 34:3 (November 2005) and *The Monist* 93:1 (January 2010). Significant work has been done, even since 2010 though. One will find new articles in top specialist and generalist philosophy journals including *Mind*, *Philosophy and Phenomenological Research*, *Australasian Journal of Philosophy*, *Religious Studies*, and *Ethical Theory and Moral Practice* among many others. A growing number of books are available, for example, Julian Baggini, *What's It All About? Philosophy and the Meaning of Life* (Oxford: Oxford University Press, 2010), John Cottingham, *On the Meaning of Life* (London: Routledge, 2003), and *The Spiritual Dimension: Religion, Philosophy and Human Value* (Cambridge: Cambridge University Press, 2006), Terry Eagleton, *The Meaning of Life* (Oxford: Oxford University Press, 2007), Stewart Goetz, *The Purpose of Life: A Theistic Perspective* (London: Continuum, 2012), Todd May, *A Significant Life: Human Meaning in a Silent Universe* (Chicago: University of Chicago Press, 2015), Thaddeus Metz, *Meaning in Life* (Oxford: Oxford University Press, 2014), Susan Wolf, *Meaning in Life and Why It Matters* (Princeton: Princeton University Press, 2010), and Nicholas Waghorn, *Nothingness and the Meaning of Life: Philosophical Approaches to Ultimate Meaning through Nothing and Reflexivity* (London: Bloomsbury, 2014). Several anthologies and collections of essays are also available on the topic, including David Benatar, ed. *Life, Death, & Meaning: Key Philosophical Readings on the Big Questions* (Lanham, MD: Rowman & Littlefield, 2004), Beatrix Himmelmann, ed. *On Meaning in Life* (Boston: De Gruyter, 2013), E. D. Klemke and Steven Cahn, eds. *The Meaning of Life*, 3rd edn (New York: Oxford University Press, 2008), and Joshua W. Seachris, ed. *Exploring the Meaning of Life: An Anthology and Guide* (Malden, MA: Wiley-Blackwell, 2012).

is, very roughly, the view that a statement is meaningful only if it is empirically verifiable/falsifiable), philosophers have warmed to the idea that treatments of the meaning of life are themselves meaningful—they make sense and are significant, worthwhile areas of inquiry. Other trends, especially in value theory, correlate with attention to well-being in general, and to the conditions under which meaningful life is possible. More often than not, those who have written on the meaning of life have been nontheists (naturalists, agnostics, and atheists). Perhaps surprisingly, theistic philosophers are late in recognizing the growing interest in the meaning of life, and are only now beginning to make more substantive contributions to the discussion of the topic. We hope that this collection of new papers will demonstrate that theists have interesting and important contributions to make to the burgeoning discussion about life's meaning.

For those coming to this discussion of the meaning of life for the first time, it is important to understand that not all participants are comfortable with talk about "the meaning of life." This is particularly the case for nontheists. As Susan Wolf, a nontheist, has noted, mention of the meaning of life commonly connotes or suggests the idea of the purpose of life.[2] Seeing a close connection between meaning and purpose is common among philosophers and nonphilosophers alike. However, because nontheists reject the view that human beings are artifacts created by God for a purpose, many of them believe it is important to distinguish between the meaning *of* life and meaning *in* life, where it is possible to have the latter without the former. In other words, these nontheists believe it is possible for persons to act for purposes that provide meaning in their lives while at the same time denying that these purposes have anything to do with a purpose of life provided for them by a creator.

Theists think the two senses of purpose are compatible—there can be many purposes in life while at the same time affirming a meaning or purpose of life. Not infrequently, nontheists question the idea of a purpose of life on the grounds that it is demeaning and degrading. Kurt Baier offers a version of this criticism:

> To attribute to a human being a purpose in [the sense of the purpose of an artifact] is not neutral, let alone complimentary: it is offensive. It is degrading for a man to be regarded as merely serving a purpose. If, at a garden party, I ask a man in livery, "What is your purpose?" I am

[2] Susan Wolf, "The Meanings of Lives," in *Introduction to Philosophy: Classical and Contemporary Readings*, 5th edn, ed. John Perry, Michael Bratman, and John Martin Fischer (New York: Oxford University Press, 2010), 794–795.

insulting him. I might as well have asked, "What are you *for*?" Such questions reduce him to the level of a gadget, a domestic animal, or perhaps a slave. I imply that *we* allot to *him* the tasks, the goals, the aims which he is to pursue; that *his* wishes and desires and aspirations and purposes are to count for little or nothing.[3]

Surely, however, Baier is overreaching here. While it is possible that a human being's having a purpose (similar to an artifact having a purpose) is degrading for that human being, it is not immediately obvious that it must be. It all depends upon what the purpose is. What if the purpose is that the individual be perfectly happy? Is that offensive and degrading for that individual? It is hard to see how it is, because such happiness seems to be in the person's overall or long-term best interest. And consider desire. Does having a purpose of life entail that an individual's desires count for nothing? Again, it is hard to see how that is the case, if the desire for perfect happiness can be satisfied.

Moreover, *desiring* perfect happiness hardly seems degrading. Perhaps Baier and others who make criticisms similar to his believe that a desire for perfect happiness is degrading because an individual does not have any choice about what he or she ultimately desires. A person is simply stuck with desiring perfect happiness and has no say in the matter. If one believes that not having ultimate control over what one desires is degrading, then the theistic view of life's meaning does have a strike against it. But then so does an atheistic view of life, because no one in an atheistic world has ultimate control over what he or she desires. We all come into this world with desires that we did not choose. In short, at first glance at least, Baier fails to make a convincing case for the view that a person's being an artifact and, thereby, having a purpose is necessarily degrading.

While the concept of the meaning of life is commonly associated with the idea of the purpose of life, there are other plausible ways to understand "the meaning of life." For example, when considering the meaning of life, one might be considering the idea of whether there is something that makes life worth living. On this approach, a meaningful life is one worth living, whereas a meaningless life is not. Without getting into the specifics of what constitutes a life worth living, if there is something that makes life worth living then it would likely be a great or intrinsic good. There is much discussion in the meaning of life literature about whether there is such a good, but it is sufficient to note at this juncture that a theist need have no objection to the

---

[3] Kurt Baier, "The Meaning of Life," in *The Meaning of Life: A Reader*, 3rd edn, ed. E. D. Klemke and Steven M. Cahn (New York: Oxford University Press, 2008), 101.

existence of such a good and to affirm that a person's possession or enjoyment of that good makes life worth living and therefore meaningful.

Talk of the meaning of life can also raise the idea of whether or not "things" ultimately fit together in the right way. In this way, the *meaning* of life is related to meaning in semantic contexts. After all, in such contexts, we say that individual semantic units that fit together in the right way form meaningful semantic constructions (e.g., the English letters and symbol—s, h, e, s, c, o, r, e, d, a, g, o, a, l !,—forming "She scored a goal!"), whereas those that fail to fit together in the right way do not, the resulting construction being meaningless. Talk of meaning in this way can be reasonably applied outside the domain of the strictly semantic. To illustrate this idea, one need only think of the traditional problem of evil. One way of parsing the objection is viewing it as the claim that things ultimately do not fit together in the right way: what fits with the existence of God (a being who is all-good, all-wise, and all-powerful) is a world in which there is much less or no evil of some or any kind. The presence of evil in a theistic universe does not ultimately make sense. It doesn't fit, so the argument goes. On the larger scale of life's meaning, one might say that if things ultimately fit together (according to some framework of intelligibility and value) then life is meaningful, whereas if things ultimately do not fit together, then life is meaningless.

An example of this way of understanding the meaning of life (a kind of *sense-making*) is to view the "meaning" under consideration as the overall explanatory account—perhaps even a *narrative* explanation—that illumines the cluster of issues which are part and parcel of the human condition. Such issues include ultimate origins, purpose, value, pleasure, pain, suffering, and evil, and how it is all going to end. The meaning of life in this case just is the *meta*-narrative that illumines these things. On this proposal, when we ask for the meaning of life we are in search of an ultimate narrative or narrative-like explanation that narrates across those aspects and accompanying questions of life of greatest existential import to human beings. The meta-narrative we seek helps us to make sense of these existentially salient portions of existence and provides a blueprint for how to live a flourishing life. Taking the idea of narrative seriously here, one might therefore think that life (on both personal and cosmic levels) is meaningful in virtue of having the right kind of narrative structure and content. Meaningful individual lives (and meaningful life in general) are, then, perhaps similar to good stories.[4]

---

[4] There is, of course, much debate about whether and how lives (and life) are like narratives. For example, see Jerome Bruner, "Life as Narrative," *Social Research* 54:1 (1987): 11–32; Anthony Rudd, "In Defence of Narrative," *European Journal of Philosophy* 17:1 (2007): 60–75; Bernard Williams, "Life as Narrative," *European Journal of Philosophy* 17:2 (2007): 305–314; Galen Strawson, "Against Narrativity," *Ratio* 17:4 (2004): 428–451;

There are a variety of ways, then, that "the meaning of life" can be understood. Perhaps the lesson here is that there is no single correct way to think about what is being queried when we ask "What is the meaning of life?" Perhaps something like the *amalgam* approach is correct, wherein the classic formulation of the question (What is the meaning of life?) stands for a multiplicity of questions and concerns that are distinct yet share family resemblances.[5] Regardless, asking about the meaning of life is a query that needs clarification. Because it can be understood divergently, careful work must be done to specify exactly what a person has in mind when asking about life's meaning.

In their essays, the contributors to this volume discuss issues related to each of the approaches to life's meaning just mentioned. One will find discussions of perennial meaning of life themes like purpose, worthwhile life, the problem of evil, futility, the role of meta-narratives, death, and, of course, God, among many others. Though most essays focus on overtly normative questions about whether and how meaningful life is possible, a few devote considerable space to interpretive issues about how best to understand the question, "What is the meaning of life?" All, however, bring to bear on the topic the unique conceptual, ontological, and normative resources found in Theism. Collectively, the authors agree that theistically informed views remain undertheorized in the discussion about life's meaning. One aim of the present collection is to spearhead such development, and in so doing add important interlocutors to the growing discussion.

Though readers will notice that all contributors are theists from within the Christian theistic tradition, it is worth noting the philosophical and theological diversity represented by the authors. The twelve authors of these new essays come from Roman Catholic, Eastern Orthodox, Anglican (Episcopalian), Reformed Protestant, and other Protestant theological traditions. And while most of the essays are written by philosophers, two are by biblical scholars with expertise in Hebrew wisdom literature. Overall, the disciplines of theology and biblical studies complement the perspectives of philosophy, giving the volume an important interdisciplinary dimension. The collection is not, nor is it intended to be, comprehensive in scope in terms of the theistic positions developed. Rather, it is better viewed as an invitation for others—theists, naturalists, and those from nontheistic religious traditions—to contribute to the weighty, yet under-researched, topic of life's meaning. All

---

and Alan Dershowitz, "Life Is Not a Dramatic Narrative," in *Law's Stories: Narrative and Rhetoric in the Law*, ed. Peter Brooks and Paul Gewirtz (New Haven, CT: Yale University Press, 1998), 99–105.

[5] Cf. R. W. Hepburn, "Questions about the Meaning of Life," in *The Meaning of Life: A Reader*, 2nd edn, ed. E. D. Klemke (New York: Oxford University Press, 2000), 262.

the contributors, whether philosophers or theologians, share the sentiment that the question of life's meaning is one of preeminent importance, and one to which theists have something worthwhile, dare we say *vital*, to contribute.

Chapter precis

Our collection of essays begins with Joshua Seachris's claim that the classic formulation of the question—What is the meaning of life?— is best interpreted as the request for an ultimate meta-narrative or narrative-like explanation that narrates across those aspects and accompanying questions of life of greatest existential import to human beings, those that are part and parcel of the human condition. These questions concern how the universe came to be, how it will end, and the place of persons in it with their purposes and values. His goal in this essay is to explore the connections between that interpretation—the *narrative* interpretation—and Scripture's redemptive-historical narrative. He shows that the question in its classic form is naturally and plausibly understood to be the request for an ultimate ontological-normative framework expressed in a narrative or narrative-like explanation, and that the central narrative thread of Scripture—Scripture's *redemptive-historical narrative*—answers the question of life's meaning under its classical formulation.

Tim Mawson points out that not everyone has believed God's existence helps answer questions about life's meaning. Indeed, some philosophers have thought that life could only be meaningful in one or several significant senses if there is no God. For example, Sartre and Nagel seem to be of the opinion that if—perhaps *per impossibile* for Sartre at least—there were a God of the traditional classical theistic sort, then he would constrain our powers of self-creative autonomy in ways that would at least severely detract from the meaning of our lives, possibly even evacuate our lives of all meaning. By contrast, theists have thought that life could only be meaningful in one or several significant senses if there is a God of the sort Sartre and Nagel believe and hope does not exist. This line of thinking has more defenders, both historically and in the present day. Mawson argues that the best way of accommodating these two broad-based positions is to say that God, were he to exist, would detract from life's meaning in some senses and add to it in some others. Thus, from the point of view of hoping for meaning in life, we have both reasons to hope that God does not exist and reasons to hope that he does. His overall conclusion is that while there could be meaning in a Godless universe, there could be more and "deeper" sorts of meaning in a Godly one; Theism's being true is a mixed blessing, but it is, all-things-considered, still a blessing.

Stewart Goetz believes that the question "What is the meaning of life?" is sometimes a question about what, if anything, makes life worth living. He assumes this question is about what constitutes a person's happiness or well-being. The philosopher Derek Parfit believes that any plausible understanding of happiness must recognize that a large part of it is made up of experiences of pleasure. Goetz advocates the more expansive claim that happiness is made up of nothing but experiences of pleasure. He points out how hedonism about happiness helps answer certain objections about the desirability of immortality and discusses Robert Nozick's example of the experience machine, which many regard as the decisive refutation of the view that only experiences of pleasure make up happiness. Goetz concludes with some thoughts of C. S. Lewis about the hedonistic nature of happiness.

Trent Dougherty argues that it is reasonable to believe that life does have meaning in the sense of having a purpose that transcends anything that can be explained by the biological sciences from the fact that people so naturally believe that it does. In the spirit of C. S. Lewis, who argued for the existence of another world, perfect happiness, and God from desire that no earthly source can satisfy, Dougherty, using Bayes's Theorem, maintains that the fact that a belief that life has meaning comes so easily to people supports the truth of Theism over naturalism because this belief is more expected on the truth of the former than on the truth of the latter. A common kind of rebuttal to this type of argument is to "debunk" it by pointing out that people would believe there is a meaning of life even if there weren't. Hence, the fact that people believe in a meaning of life does not support Theism over naturalism. Dougherty considers this response to his argument and explains why he believes it is ineffective.

Nicholas Waghorn draws our attention to the idea that many people believe in a "perfection thesis," which is the idea that in order for their lives to have (ultimate) meaning it must be possible for them to attain a condition that is maximally valuable, a condition that cannot be improved upon. Because it seems unlikely that we can, through our own efforts, attain such a condition, and it appears (prima facie) much more likely that the God of classical Theism might be able to help us do so, the plausibility of the perfection thesis gives some weight to theistic answers to the question of life's meaning (although it does not establish them). But, says Waghorn, if people are able to exercise direct or indirect voluntary control over their desires, it may be that the demands of the perfection thesis can be made trivially easy to meet: individuals merely need to alter their desires so that they are maximally fulfilled by the condition in which their possessors currently find themselves—from their perspective, such a condition then cannot be improved upon. Waghorn offers some reasons to think that people cannot directly desire at will and suggests responses to reasons that have been advanced to think that they can. Finally, he argues that even if people can exercise voluntary control over their desires, it may nevertheless be harder to trivialize the demands of the perfection thesis than it first appears.

John Cottingham points out how it is often assumed the existence of the God of traditional Theism would make our human existence meaningful. However, there is an objection to this view that is analogous to the Euthyphro objection to God as the source of morality: either the purposes of a creator would be capricious and as such would not be enough to make our lives meaningful or they would correspond with human goals and activities that are independently intrinsically meaningful, in which case the appeal to God to make our existence meaningful would be redundant. After examining the implications of this dilemma, Cottingham concludes by asking what difference does eternity make. On the theistic picture, the ultimate meaningfulness of our actions comes from their taking their place, *sub specie aeternitatis*, as actions that eternally matter. Cottingham believes this amplifies the meaningfulness our actions already had on earth, and shields them from the backdrop of impermanence against which nothing in the long term matters very much.

Charles Taliaferro examines what Simon Blackburn terms the "immanent option" to life's meaning in which meaning is found in everyday goods to the exclusion of any transcendent notion of meaning or purpose that comes from a relationship with God. Blackburn proposes that we can find significance in the charm of a baby's smile, the movement of a lover, the performance of music, and so on, while suspending "big questions" surrounding God's existence and purpose for us. Taliaferro argues that truly loving the baby's smile raises questions about the fate of the baby itself. Deeply loving the baby leads one to hope that its life will not end but continue endlessly with the enjoyment of certain goods in relationship with God. Indeed, claims Taliaferro, it is hard to understand how continued enjoyment of these goods would not make for a more meaningful life. Who can rationally prefer the termination of enjoyment of what is good over its unending continuance?

Richard Swinburne also believes that an afterlife in relationship with God enhances life's meaning. He maintains that our lives are worthwhile insofar as we fulfill our obligations, cooperate with friends to end suffering and wrongdoing, need and are needed by those friends, and grow in knowledge and adoration of beauty and ultimacy. If there is a God, we have the opportunity to live a far more worthwhile life, in that we have enormously greater possibilities for pursuing these goals, as well as a far greater obligation to do so. We owe our lives and all that is good in them to God, and so we have obligations to worship God, the ultimate source of things, and to live God-pleasing lives. But we can also interact with him in helping each other to worship and live God-pleasing lives, and to grow in knowledge of the deepest truths. In doing these actions frequently, we get into the habit of doing them, and so should come to enjoy doing them. And God offers us the prospect, if on earth we make ourselves the kind of people who are suited for this, of growing (together with others) endlessly after death in knowledge about him, friendship with him, and adoration of him, and in helping him in his work of helping those still on earth. Because—if there is a God—that sort of life on earth and after death would be so much better than any other life could be, it is good to try to begin to live this life on earth, even if it seems to us by no means certain that there is a God. It is worth taking a risk to reach the best goals.

Paul K. Moser asserts that the philosophical debate about "the meaning of life" or, less ambitiously, "the meaning in life" includes a question about whether there is an overarching, all-inclusive purpose for human life. He adds that the debate does not concern whether everyone knowingly has such a purpose, because it is obvious that not everyone does. Instead, the debate concerns whether such a purpose is available to be known by humans and thereby to guide human lives. Moser's chapter explores this topic, contending that philosophers have overlooked an important option for resolving the matter: the affective Gethsemane option that directly involves a human being's will and affections relative to God's will and affections. In essence, meaning from God may be sensitive to a human's will and affections in a manner that makes the recognition of such meaning variable and elusive. In this regard, such meaning would fit with the elusiveness of God.

Terence Cuneo begins his chapter by describing an icon of St. Isaac the Syrian, which has hung on his office wall for nearly fifteen years. He notes how it includes not only an image of but also words attributed to St. Isaac himself. The words are these: "This life has been given to you for repentance. Do not waste it on vain pursuits." Cuneo finds this "dictum" very severe. Literally rendered, it tells us that the point of this life is to repent and that all else is vain pursuit. He adds that if one held that this life is simply a preparation and anticipation of the life to come, then what St. Isaac says might make sense, although it is not a very attractive position even by the standards of traditional Christianity. Might there, however, asks Cuneo, be a way to understand St. Isaac's dictum so that it sheds light on the meaningful life or that which this life is "for?" In the remaining part of his essay, Cuneo explores this question by taking a close look at the role that repentance plays in the tradition to which St. Isaac belonged, namely, Eastern Christianity. Specifically, he investigates the role of repentance in the liturgies of Eastern Christianity, paying close attention to the liturgical texts and actions performed in a liturgical context, gleaning from them various assumptions that the tradition makes about the role and purpose of repentance. Cuneo believes that this exploration helps us to arrive at an understanding of St. Isaac's dictum that throws light on the meaningful life.

Craig Bartholomew seeks to open a dialogue about the meaning of life between the biblical book of Ecclesiastes, as embodied in the struggle of Ecclesiastes's main character, Qohelet, and contemporary philosophy. Ecclesiastes is the narrative of the struggle of Qohelet to discover if life has any value "under the sun." Through the lens of an autonomous epistemology based on observation, reason, and experience alone, Qohelet explores area after area of life but keeps coming to the conclusion that all is enigmatic. Juxtaposed with his "enigma" conclusions are joy passages that reflect his Israelite upbringing and his positive experience of the world. The tension between "enigma" and "joy" evokes his crisis, and resolution finally comes at the end of the book where Qohelet ultimately finds his way back to belief in God as creator. Bartholomew relates Qohelet's "internal perspective" on the meaning of life to Thomas Nagel's well-known explanation of the absurdity of life in terms of our ability to examine our lives *sub specie aeternitatis* and Qohelet's affirmation of the everyday to Julian Baggini's investigation of what makes life worth living. Bartholomew also explores the question of evil, the challenge of sin, and the possibility of meaning without God, especially God as creator.

Tremper Longmann III, in our final chapter, also uses the book of Ecclesiastes to explore the question of the meaning of life. In the body of Ecclesiastes (Chapters 1:12–12:7), Qohelet speaks reflectively about his search for meaning in wisdom, pleasure, work, wealth, and status. His efforts fail because of three factors: (1) death, (2) injustice, and (3) an inability to discern the proper time. Thus, argues Longmann III, Qohelet advocates a *carpe diem* approach to life. A second wise man's words frame Qohelet's words (Chapters 1:1–11 and 12:8–14), and thus provides the authoritative voice of the book. This frame narrator evaluates Qohelet's perspective for his son (Chapter 12:12) and offers his own perspective on a meaningful life that is grounded in a proper relationship with God.

Part One

Clarifying the Question: Conceptual and Theistic Tools

1

The Meaning of Life and Scripture's Redemptive-Historical Narrative: Illuminating Convergences

Joshua W. Seachris

1. Introduction

The body of work within analytic philosophy on the topic of life's meaning continues to expand.[1] Nearly all of this development, however, is on the topic of meaning *in* life. Very little research directly addresses the meaning *of* life. As it turns out, the difference between "in" and "of" tracks interesting philosophical issues and is more than a trivial grammatical preference of one preposition over another.

The phrase "meaning of life" is part of the classic formulation of the question, "What is the meaning of life?" That question is accompanied by cosmic, desire-to-know (and often teleological and religiously oriented) connotations. In other work, I argue that such connotations track what I call the question's *cosmic-intelligibility* dimension. First and foremost, it is cosmic in scope and one in which the questioner is primarily concerned with the task of *making sense of*—intelligibility before praxis.[2] This dimension includes important questions that are part and parcel of the meaning of life (e.g., Why is there something rather than nothing? What is it all about? What is the point or purpose of it all? Why is there pain and suffering? How is it all going to end?).

Unfortunately, contemporary discussions have largely pushed such questions aside in favor of addressing another aspect of life's meaning—the

---

[1] Cf. note 1 in the Introduction.
[2] Intelligibility and praxis, though distinct, are not unrelated parts of the question, "What is the meaning of life?" When inquiring into life's meaning we desire to make sense of the world (or at least certain existentially relevant parts of it), and then to flourish within it— we want to pursue projects and have relationships that confer a distinct kind of positive normative status on our lives that has been labeled *meaningfulness*.

individualist-normative dimension, one that more directly tracks the realm of value, has a desire-to-live-well emphasis, and that is, as Thaddeus Metz notes in his recent book, primarily individualist in orientation.[3] The bulk of the contemporary discussion centers on trying to chart the normative territory of meaningful life (e.g., by considering questions like, What is meaningful life? What makes one's life valuable? In virtue of what is one's life worthy of great esteem? What makes one's life significant?). Discussions focused solely on the individualist-normative dimension are truncated though. A thick conception of life's meaning should make space for both dimensions.[4]

In contemporary discussions the cosmic-intelligibility dimension receives much less attention than the individualist-normative dimension. In fact, the form of the question most closely associated with concerns over cosmic intelligibility—What is the meaning of life?—is still met with criticism or simply neglected by contemporary analytic philosophers, who are nonetheless amenable to the question in its other, more normatively expressed forms. For example, Susan Wolf, who affirms something like the distinction I advocate above, notes that the question, when considered in its classic formulation, is fraught with all kinds of problems, conceptual and otherwise, and therefore not worthy of serious philosophical attention.[5] Echoing Wolf, James Klagge makes a similar claim, "'What is the meaning of life?' This question

---

[3] Thaddeus Metz, *Meaning in Life: An Analytic Study* (Oxford: Oxford University Press, 2013), 3.
[4] I introduce this distinction in my "General Introduction" to *Exploring the Meaning of Life: An Anthology and Guide*; "Meaning of Life: Contemporary Analytic Perspectives." *Internet Encyclopedia of Philosophy*; "The Meaning of Life as Narrative: A New Proposal for Interpreting Philosophy's 'Primary' Question." *Philo* 12 (Spring-Summer 2009): 5–23; and in most detail in a book manuscript in progress, tentatively titled, *What Is the Meaning of Life? De-Mystifying Our Ultimate Question*. One of the most prominent scholars in this developing field, Thaddeus Metz, affirms that the question exhibits both dimensions. See his "Introduction" in *Exploring the Meaning of Life: An Anthology and Guide*, 24; and his recent book, *Meaning in Life*, 3.
[5] Wolf states, "Many of you will be relieved to hear that I do not wish to revive the question of whether there is a meaning to life. I am inclined to accept the standard view that there is no plausible interpretation of that question that offers a positive answer in the absence of a fairly specific religious metaphysics." "The Meanings of Lives," in *Introduction to Philosophy: Classical and Contemporary Readings*, 5th edn, ed. John Perry, Michael Bratman, and John Martin Fischer (New York: Oxford University Press, 2010), 795. In another paper, Wolf makes a similar point, "... the question 'What makes lives meaningful?' is closely related to the question, 'What is the meaning of life?' Even if this latter question is not unintelligible, as the logical positivists thought, its obscurity and its scope are such as to make the risk of finding oneself talking pompous nonsense fairly great. And, one might think that what is not nonsense regarding this topic has already been said." "Meaningful Lives in a Meaningless World," *Quaestiones Infinitae* 14 (June 1997), 4.

sounds profound but has no answer. 'What kinds of lives are meaningful?' This sounds less profound, but it may at least have an answer . . ."[6]

Most of the other essays in this collection focus on normative aspects of the meaning of life question. Despite my misgivings above about a truncated dialectic focused almost exclusively on the normative, I am happy that my theistic colleagues direct their attention here. This is where many of the cutting-edge discussions are occurring, with more naturalists than theists participating. Such discussions can benefit from the addition of theistic interlocutors. But if I am correct in claiming that the question has another, equally important dimension centered on the quest for cosmic intelligibility, then fresh work is needed here too by theists, by those from nontheistic religious traditions, and by those who identify as naturalists.

By and large, my contribution here is Christian theistic in theological-philosophical orientation, though much of what I say in Section I presupposes no religious conceptual resources. My goal in this essay is to connect three topics: (1) the meaning of life, (2) the *narrative interpretation* of the question, "What is the meaning of life?,"[7] and (3) Scripture's redemptive-historical narrative (hereafter, R-H$_N$). I show that the question in its classic form, "What is the meaning of life?" is intelligible, is naturally and plausibly understood to be the request for an ultimate ontological-normative framework expressed in a narrative or narrative-like explanation,[8] and that the central narrative thread of Scripture directly answers the question of life's meaning under its classical formulation.

2. The meaning of life as narrative

In a separate work, I develop and defend the claim that the question in its classic form, "What is the meaning of life?" should be interpreted as the request for a narrative that narrates across those features of life of greatest existential import to human beings (I call this the *narrative interpretation*).[9]

---

[6] James C. Klagge, "From the Meaning of Life to a Meaningful Life," unpublished manuscript, 20.
[7] I initially developed this interpretation in "The Meaning of Life as Narrative: A New Proposal for Interpreting Philosophy's 'Primary' Question." I am currently developing and defending it in greater detail in *What is the Meaning of Life? De-Mystifying Our Ultimate Question*.
[8] In the remainder of the essay, I will drop the "narrative-like explanation" qualifier, though it should be assumed to implicitly accompany all such uses of "narrative."
[9] There are only hints of something in the neighborhood of this interpretation in the philosophical literature on the topic. See, for example, Garrett Thomson, *On the Meaning of Life* (London: Wadsworth, 2003), 132–133; John Cottingham, *On the Meaning of Life* (London: Routledge, 2003), 2, 9; John Wisdom, "The Meanings of the

On the narrative interpretation, when asking about the meaning of life we should view ourselves as requesting a narrative that helps us make sense of the universe and our lives within it (cosmic-intelligibility dimension) and that speaks to our desire to lead meaningful lives (individualist-normative dimension); in other words, a narrative that addresses existentially oriented epistemic and normative desires. It is the entire narrative itself that is the meaning of life, not an individual narrative element (e.g., the element that narrates purpose).

2.1 The narrative interpretation: An analogy

The question, "What is the meaning of life?" is analogous to the question asked in the following scenario. Consider the case of a father whose three young sons play in the basement while he finishes a book chapter in his study. During the middle of typing a sentence, he hears screaming and yelling: a scuffle is underway. He quickly heads to the playroom, there finding his sons pushing and yelling. Getting their attention, he raises his voice and asks, "What is the *meaning* of this?" Upon hearing their father's words, the two older sons immediately understand three things:

1. The meaning of their father's request.
2. That the way the father phrases his request, using the term "meaning," is entirely natural for the context in which it is spoken.
3. The sort of thing that would count as an appropriate answer.

It would be unlikely that his sons respond by asking, "But, daddy, what do you mean by that question?" Or, "Daddy, why did you use the word 'meaning?'" So what does the father mean when he asks, "What is the meaning of this?"

The short answer is that he desires an explanation as an interpretive framework (or background knowledge) through which to understand the state of affairs he observes—his children fighting. This explanation will likely include, among other elements, information about how and why the scuffle started. He needs access to such information in order to make sense of the data before him and then to take appropriate action. From these additional details, an explanation or narrative can be constructed, helping him to understand and respond to the scuffle, only a portion of which he has witnessed. Importantly,

---

Questions of Life," in *The Meaning of Life*, 3rd edn, ed. E. D. Klemke (New York: Oxford University Press, 2008), 259; and Julian Young, *The Death of God and the Meaning of Life* (London: Routledge, 2005), 1.

the fuller accurate narrative is the meaning the father seeks when asking, "What is the meaning of this?" Equally as important is the fact that the father is not only concerned about the *purpose* of his sons' fight. Though he wants to know something about his sons' intentions, the meaning he seeks is something broader than purpose alone. Meaning, though related, should not be equated with purpose, whether in this context or that of the meaning of life.

One might reasonably ask at this point, why refer to what the father requests as a narrative at all, and not just an explanation? This is an important question, one that I consider in greater detail elsewhere.[10] In this essay, I can offer only a brief response. Narrative is a fluid category, and it is therefore plausible to think of what the father requests and what the sons offer in terms of narrative or story.[11] Presumably, his sons will start by presenting the problem—who the characters are, under what circumstances their conflict began, and so on. They will likely recount a series of meaningfully related causes and effects leading up to the moment when their father found them. They may say something about their intentions and mental states in general, weaving teleological threads throughout their account. This is all very story-like, even if not a story in some paradigmatic sense like *The Brothers Karamazov* is a story. Whether or not one chooses to view the sons' explanation as a narrative or nonnarrative mode of discourse, importantly, the entire explanation is the meaning their father seeks, not simply one portion of it.[12] Equally as important, such meaning is wider than narration of purpose alone.

To ask the question "What is the meaning of life?" is to ask a question similar to the father who asked his sons, "What is the meaning of this [scuffle]?" Over the course of our existence, we encounter aspects of the world that have what I call an *existential charge* in virtue of their relationship to our interconnected yearnings to make sense of certain aspects of the world, our place within it, and

---

[10] Cf. footnote 7.
[11] Talk of "narrative" is widespread across academic disciplines, culture, and everyday life. We hear about the narrative of our solar system, of the modern Democratic Party, or of slavery in colonial America. Such uses often stretch the concept beyond its strict, paradigmatic use. For discussions of the nature of narrative and narrativity, see, for example, Brian Richardson, "Recent Concepts of Narrative and the Narratives of Narrative Theory," *Style* 34 (2000), 168–175; David Rudrum, "From Narrative Representation to Narrative Use: Towards the Limits of Definition," *Narrative* 13:2 (May 2005): 195–204; Marie-Laure Ryan, "Toward a Definition of Narrative," in *The Cambridge Companion to Narrative*, ed. David Herman (Cambridge: Cambridge University Press, 2007), 22–35; and Gregory Currie, *Narratives & Narrators: A Philosophy of Stories* (Oxford: Oxford University Press, 2010).
[12] To be more precise, it would be the story represented by the narrative. Obviously, the meaning would not include every semantic unit that his children used to answer his question down to the individual subjects, verbs, prepositions, and so on. Another way of putting it is that the same story could be narrated in a number of ways.

to live meaningful lives. These existentially charged aspects give rise to questions for which we seek an explanatory narrative framework in order to make sense out of them. In this sense, the existentially charged aspects of the universe that we encounter are akin to the portion of his sons' scuffle that the father witnessed. Like the father, we lack important parts of the narrative, at least for a season, and we desire to fill the existentially relevant informational gaps in our understanding of the universe we inhabit, and then to live accordingly.

2.2 Nuancing the narrative interpretation

If the meaning of life is a narrative, what kind of narrative is it? What makes it a meaning of life narrative, or, more to the point, what makes it *the meaning of life*? It will be a different narrative than, say, a narrative about westward expansion in the United States or the celestial history of the Milky Way galaxy. These narratives narrate aspects of the world that are not directly relevant to the meaning of life question. For any narrative to count as a meaning of life narrative, it must cross some relevant explanatory threshold by narrating across a cluster of existentially charged aspects of our world, those that are part and parcel of the human condition.

What are these aspects that possess an "existential charge?" I call them and accompanying questions around which a meaning of life narrative is constructed, EC_Q (existentially charged life aspects and accompanying questions). A narrative constructed around EC_Q is what I call a "candidate meaning of life narrative" ($CdML_N$). A $CdML_N$ constitutes an ultimate *metanarrative framework*, one that provides theoretical insight and practical guidance in the shadow of those existentially charged aspects and accompanying questions of life as captured by EC_Q. Meaning of life narratives, then, will be $CdML_N$'s. In order for a narrative to be a $CdML_N$ it needs to narrate across EC_Q (satisfy the formal condition). In order for a $CdML_N$ to be *the* meaning of life it must be true (satisfy the truth condition).

2.2.1 Meaning of life narratives: The formal condition

To count as a candidate meaning of life narrative, a narrative must first narrate the right stuff, and that stuff consists of a cluster of existentially charged aspects and accompanying questions common to human existence. Vatican II aptly highlighted these as part of the common human condition:

> What is man? What is the meaning and purpose of human life? What is upright behavior, and what is sinful? Where does suffering originate, and what end does it serve? How can genuine happiness be found?

What happens at death? What is judgment? What reward follows death? And finally, what is the ultimate mystery, beyond human explanation, which embraces our entire existence, from which we take our origin and towards which we tend?[13]

Vatican II's depiction of the kinds of questions that embody our existentially charged curiosities and longings in light of the human condition is repeatedly echoed in writings that are part of the meaning of life canon as it were.[14] Vatican II draws attention to the existentially charged aspects and accompanying questions of life in a way that captures the essence of what it is that we want to know when we ask, "What is the meaning of life?" We seek a narrative that narrates across this cluster of phenomena and accompanying questions, one that provides a relevant framework for understanding and living life in a rationally and existentially flourishing way.

With Vatican II and the rest of the meaning of life canon saliently lurking in the background, EC_Q consists of the following:

1. Existentially Charged Datum: something exists, we exist and I exist / Existentially Charged Question: Why does anything or we or I exist at all?
2. Existentially Charged Datum: our lives are partly ordered around goals / Existentially Charged Question: Does life have any purpose(s), and if so, what is its nature and source?
3. Existentially Charged Datum: we are often passionately engaged in life pursuits and projects that we deem valuable, significant and worthwhile / Existentially Charged Question: What grounds, if anything, the value, significance and worth of these pursuits and projects? A subjective state? Objective states of affairs? God?
4. Existentially Charged Datum: we experience pain and suffering, and are both victims and perpetrators of evil / Existentially Charged Questions: Why is there pain, suffering and evil? Does pain, suffering and evil render religious belief unreasonable?
5. Existentially Charged Datum: we experience death / Existentially Charged Questions: How does it all end? Is death final? Is there an eschatological remedy to the ills of this world?

---

[13] Austin Flannery, ed. *Vatican Council II: The Conciliar and Post Conciliar Documents* (Dublin: Dominican Publications, 1975), 738. Notice that Vatican II includes the question of life's meaning and purpose as a member within a larger set of questions common to the human condition. On the interpretation I propose, the question of life's meaning is the larger umbrella under which all the others are included.

[14] That canon ranges from the Old Testament book of Ecclesiastes to the writings of Dostoyevsky and Tolstoy to the existentialists like Camus and Sartre to contemporary analytic philosophers, among many others.

Points 1–5, more or less, constitute the cluster of considerations that track the meaning of life. Some more closely track the cosmic-intelligibility dimension, others the individualist-normative dimension, though all are interconnected in important and sometimes subtle ways. They are in need of narration. When we ask for the meaning of life, we should view ourselves as seeking the wider narrative framework that enables us to make sense of EC_Q and then live accordingly. A narrative that narrates EC_Q, a $CdML_N$, meets the formal condition on the meaning of life in virtue of narrating the right stuff, and can be defined thus:

> ($CdML_N$) = A candidate meaning of life narrative is one that narrates across some existentially relevant threshold of life aspects and accompanying questions largely captured by the category of EC_Q by adding an ultimate *meta*-narrative framework that helps us make sense of EC_Q and that provides practical guidance for leading a flourishing life.

There will, of course, be multiple narratives that meet the conditions of this definition. Additionally, there will be various degrees of overlap between elements in different $CdML_N$'s. For example, a $CdML_N$ with a deistic deity as a "character" will share narrative elements with a $CdML_N$ with a theistic deity. Or take naturalistic $CdML_N$'s that, while they might differ in the portion of the narrative that narrates whether there is objective value in the universe, share in the claim that there exists nothing apart from the natural world. The point here is that there will be multiple $CdML_N$'s. Admittedly, the category of narrative is a more natural fit for, say, Christian Theism than it is for naturalism. Naturalism, however, possesses the conceptual resources to offer a narrative-like explanation (given fluidity in the concept of narrative) that narrates across EC_Q, and therefore possesses a $CdML_N$. Regardless of debates about the fit or lack thereof between the category of narrative and certain ontologies, in order for a $CdML_N$ to be *the* meaning of life, it must satisfy a second condition—the truth condition.

2.2.2 Meaning of life narratives: The truth condition

The narrative interpretation presupposes that there can be only one meaning *of* life, though this does not preclude a rich variety in the ways meaningful life can be realized.[15] The meaning of life will be a narrative that has the

---

[15] The narrative interpretation has dual merits on this front. First, it takes seriously the use of the definite article in the classic formulation of the question (What is *the* meaning of life?). Second, it accounts for the near universal recognition that there is

right formal properties (narrates the right stuff) and narrative content that corresponds to reality. This should not be too controversial if we remember the case of the father. In order for the narrative the father sought to appropriately link to his request, it had to be about his children's scuffle (and not, for example, what they ate for breakfast), and it had to be true (they cannot be lying). If it fails to meet either of these conditions, it cannot be the meaning he sought.

A narrative that narrates across the relevant existentially charged aspects and accompanying questions of life, though deserving candidate meaning of life narrative status, will nonetheless fail to be the meaning of life if it is false, or at least if it fails to reach some nonarbitrarily determined truth-threshold. That is, the narrative needs to be true in the sense that, for example, someone might say, "The naturalistic story of the universe is true" or "The theistic story of the universe is true." Such claims are consistent with some of their constitutive elements being approximations of truth or even some of their (minor) constitutive elements being false. The entire narrative being true or false is accompanied by such a caveat.

When searching for the meaning of life we are in search of the true narrative that narrates across the cluster of issues related to our common human predicament, the crucial elements of which were captured by Vatican II and EC_Q. For a narrative to finally qualify as the meaning of life requires that it satisfy both formal and truth conditions. By combining these two requirements, I define the meaning of life as:

> (MofL) = the meaning of life is the true narrative that narrates across some existentially relevant threshold of life aspects and accompanying questions largely captured by the category of EC_Q by adding an ultimate (and true) *meta*-narrative framework that helps us make sense of EC_Q and that provides practical guidance for leading a flourishing life.

When we ask "What is the meaning of life?" we should view ourselves as asking for MofL. Though one might think that discovering MofL is unlikely given various other background beliefs and commitments, it is certainly nothing esoteric or exceedingly difficult to conceptualize. As it turns out there are a number of narratives embedded in religious traditions (and some in nonreligious traditions) and cultures that people know and live by, and which, on

> rich diversity in the way that meaningful life can be secured. It harmonizes what many think is an incompatibility between a feature of the classic formulation of the question and an undeniable inclusivity in the conditions for meaningful life. This perceived incompatibility is largely a function of people (many philosophers included) conflating two questions: What is the meaning of life? and What is meaningful life?

the narrative interpretation, qualify as CdML$_N$'s. In the next section, I consider one from my own religious tradition, the redemptive-historical narrative of the Christian Scriptures.

3. Scripture's redemptive-historical narrative as a candidate meaning of life narrative

Most theists in the Christian tradition will affirm that the canon of Scripture bears on the meaning of life in some way. What is much less clear, however, is precisely what one can point to in Scripture, and in so doing claim to have found the meaning of life. Depending upon how one interprets the question, "What is the meaning of life?" numerous answers emerge from Scripture and subsequent theological-philosophical reflection. For example, if one interprets the meaning of life question as asking, "What is the purpose of individual human lives?" the answer might be something like, "You shall love the Lord your God with all your heart, and with all your soul, and with all your mind ... You shall love your neighbor as yourself" (Matt. 22:37–39).[16] For those in the Reformed tradition it might be something like the answer to Question One of the Westminster Larger Catechism, "Man's chief and highest end is to glorify God, and fully to enjoy him forever," or it might simply be: experience perfect happiness.[17] Indeed, both Scripture and theological-ecclesial traditions are rich with theological information and liturgical practices that speak to the teleological-why(s) of our existence. Importantly, such purposes can be numerous, each part of a hierarchically structured, mutually reinforcing matrix of purposes in life, some coming from on high as it were, many others coming directly from our own desires and decisions. Similar claims can be made for any individualist-normative interpretation of the question along the lines of value, significance, and so on—Scripture and theological-ecclesial traditions have much to say about each.

One can carve and systematize Scripture so that it addresses life's meaning in this doctrinal, piecemeal fashion by connecting something it says to an

---

[16] All Scriptural citations are from the New Revised Standard Version.
[17] For a thoughtful contemporary defense of a theistic hedonist conception of purpose in life, see Stewart Goetz, *The Purpose of Life: A Theistic Perspective* (London: Continuum, 2012). Goetz develops a similar view in his essay in this volume. For Goetz, one can know the purpose of life apart from revealed theology, and that purpose is to experience perfect happiness, which is intrinsically good. What revealed theology does is narrate a story that provides an account of how we ought to pursue perfect happiness. According to Goetz, we know what ultimately makes life worth living and that we are created to experience it (perfect happiness) before we come to Scripture.

individualist-normative interpretation of the question,[18] but there is another, more organic way of looking at Scripture's relevance to life's meaning, a way that directly connects to the narrative interpretation. Scripture instantiates a redemptive-historical narrative (R-H_N) that, on the narrative interpretation, just is a candidate meaning of life narrative in virtue of narrating ultimate origins, purpose, value, significance, pain and suffering, futility, death, and ultimate ending. Within the candidate meaning of life narrative instantiated in Scripture, everything from the greatest and second greatest commandments, to the Genesis account of our origin and subsequent fall,[19] to the promises of the covenant, to the life, death, burial, and resurrection of Jesus of Nazareth, to the eschatological consummation of history, finds a natural home within R-H_N. R-H_N narrates across the cluster of existentially charged aspects and accompanying questions (EC_Q) that have long been recognized as deeply connected in some way with the meaning of life.

3.1 Scripture and narrative

Narrative is one among numerous scriptural genres including poetry, legal documentation, letters, parables, wisdom, prophecy, songs, prayers, moral instruction, doctrinal reflection, and so on. According to the Christian tradition, Scripture is a divine-inspired collection of books meaningfully woven together in theological and thematic unity for the purposes of revealing God, his redemptive plan, and most broadly His love, and for our full flourishing as human beings (cf. Deut. 6:3–5; Psalm 119; 1 Tim. 3:16–17).[20] Though one among many Scriptural genres, narrative functions centrally within the canon of Scripture in virtue of Scripture's narration of a "sprawling, capacious story" through which all of its other nonnarrative modes of discourse find their literary home.[21] Sidney Greidanus articulates nicely the priority that narrative takes:

> Of all the biblical genres of literature, narrative may be described as the central, foundational, and all-encompassing genre of the Bible. The

---

[18] One can undertake such a task by, for example, finding and organizing all the passages that speak to purpose (or significance, or value, and so on).

[19] Note that I am not taking a position on the proper *interpretation* of the Genesis account here. My claim is consistent with a number of interpretive strategies and conclusions about what that account actually communicates. This caveat applies to each of those areas that Scripture purportedly illumines.

[20] I gesture here at a relatively high view of the inspiration and authority of Scripture. The central claims of my essay, however, do not hang on such a view.

[21] Craig Bartholomew and Michael W. Goheen, "Story and Biblical Theology," in *Out of Egypt: Biblical Theology and Biblical Interpretation*, vol. 5, Scripture and Hermeneutics Series, ed. Craig Bartholomew, Mary Healy, Karl Moller, and Robin Parry (Grand Rapids, MI: Zondervan, 2004), 161.

prominence of the narrative genre in the Bible is related to the Bible's central message that God acts in *history*. No other genre can express that message as well as narrative.[22]

History has a *plot* if Christian Theism is true. Sartre and others are surely correct that if naturalism is true then any projection of emplotment on the world is just that, a fictitious projection.[23] On the contrary, if an ontology like the one presupposed by Theism is true, following Paul Fiddes, it is worth noting that such emplotment is no farce at all:

> emplotment of history has not been understood by Christians as a mere *projection* of a concord fiction [introducing plot, story, and the unification of an ending on the mere successiveness of history], but as the *discovery* of relations between events which have been plotted by the divine Logos into a scheme of promise and fulfillment, and which are sustained in their coherence by the presence of the Logos. History is regarded as God's story, and when the story has been revealed to us through the Bible, we can make sense of history.[24]

A central, though by no means sole, purpose of God's story is to help us make sense of history and the world in general. It is a story that illumines both the cosmic-intelligibility and individualist-normative dimensions of life's meaning.

Scripture, then, contains what some have called a grand *metanarrative*.[25] Metanarratives are ultimate theoretical-practical frameworks for understanding and leading flourishing lives in the world. Interestingly, Julian Young has argued that there is a striking correlation between the alleged diminution of supernatural or religious metanarratives and the rise of anxiety-laden searching for the meaning of life. He states, "For most of our Western history we have not talked about the meaning of life. This is because we used to be quite certain that we knew what it was."[26] He proceeds

---

[22] Sidney Greidanus, *The Modern Preacher and the Ancient Text* (Grand Rapids, MI: Eerdmans, 2000), 188.

[23] See, for example, Jean-Paul Sartre, *Nausea*. Trans. Lloyd Alexander (New York: New Directions, 1964); and Alan Dershowitz, "Life is Not a Dramatic Narrative," in *Law's Stories: Narrative and Rhetoric in the Law*, ed. Peter Brooks and Paul Gewirtz (New Haven: Yale University Press, 1998), 99–105.

[24] Paul S. Fiddes, *The Promised End: Eschatology in Theology and Literature* (Oxford: Blackwell, 2000), 9.

[25] In this context, I take the terms "metanarrative" "meaning of life narrative" "candidate meaning of life narrative" and "cosmic narrative" to be synonyms. I use them interchangeably in this essay.

[26] Young, *The Death of God and the Meaning of Life*, 1.

to note that the meaning of life was secured through what he calls a "true-world narrative:"

> Since journeys have a beginning, a middle and an end, a true-world account of the proper course of our lives is a kind of story, a narrative. And since true-world narratives (that, for example, of Christianity) are global rather than individual, since they narrate not just your life or mine, but rather all lives at all times and places, they are, as I shall call them, "grand" narratives.[27]

Young posits that such all-encompassing narratives lost traction in the modern world. With this perceived diminution of grand religious metanarratives in the West, people began to question the meaning of life more vigorously, primarily because deeply imbedded narrative elements in the residual cultural consciousness that in some way illumined the meaning of life had supposedly lost intellectual plausibility in a world where science was supplanting teleological-theological explanations with mechanistic-naturalistic ones.[28]

Regardless of whether one finds $R\text{-}H_N$ reasonable, Scripture clearly offers a candidate meaning of life narrative.[29] $R\text{-}H_N$ narrates the broad themes of creation-fall-redemption-consummation (CFRC). Even a cursory look at these themes reveals a narrative whose scope closely tracks the cluster of concerns and questions (EC_Q) around which candidate meaning of life narratives are built. In what follows, I briefly explore the points of connection between $R\text{-}H_N$ and EC_Q. I discuss only three of the first four (origins, purpose, pain and suffering) before devoting more sustained attention to the fifth: ending.[30]

---

[27] Ibid.
[28] Rollo May makes a similar point. Although he speaks of myth, the concept functions in much the same way as *metanarrative*. "A myth is a way of making sense in a senseless world. Myths are narrative patterns that give significance to our existence ... Myths are like the beams in a house ... they are the structure which holds the house together so people can live in it ... We in the twentieth century are in a [s]ituation of 'aching hearts' and 'repining.' Our myths no longer serve their function of making sense of existence, the citizens of our day are left without direction or purpose in life, and people are at a loss to control their anxiety and excessive guilt feeling." *The Cry for Myth* (New York: Norton, 1991), 15–16.
[29] Naturalism, despite a more tenuous fit with the concept of narrative in this context, also has a metanarrative or candidate meaning of life narrative, one complete with a naturalistic account of origins, of purpose (likely humanly created, though some objective elements may be present on objective naturalism), of what makes life valuable, of why pain and suffering are features of the universe, and of how it will all end, both for individuals and the universe in general.
[30] A nonnarrative version of something in the neighborhood of $R\text{-}H_N$ would be a creedal formulation of the Christian faith like the Apostles' Creed.

3.2 The redemptive-historical narrative: Ultimate causal origins

Bede Rundle has remarked that "The question, 'Why is there something rather than nothing?' has a strong claim to be philosophy's central, and most perplexing, question."[31] No doubt, this question often lurks in discussions over the meaning of life, largely because many think an answer to the *why* of existence will in some way illumine the *meaning* of existence. In this context, most do not ask merely an efficient causal-why question, but also, and perhaps more importantly, a final causal-why question. Many are suspicious that the ultimate answer to why there is something rather than absolutely nothing will involve intelligence and intentionality as part of the "brutest" fact of them all—that mind and intentionality are more ontologically fundamental than matter.

The opening chapter and verse of Scripture, where $R\text{-}H_N$ starts, unsurprisingly begins by addressing something important about origins, both cosmic and human, "In the beginning, God created the heavens and the earth" (Gen. 1:1a). The reason anything exists at all is because mind and intentionality are ontologically basic, precisely because God—an omnicompetent person with the property of aseity—is ontologically basic. All other existing substances and their properties in the universe (past, present, and future), including the space–time universe itself, have a derivative kind of existence. $R\text{-}H_N$ narrates, even if in minimalist fashion and while leaving out details about secondary process and mechanism, what any candidate meaning of life narrative must narrate, the question of ultimate origins.

3.3 The redemptive-historical narrative: Purpose

Related, we are driven to ask teleologically oriented questions about why we are here. These questions about purpose are more narrowly focused than the above question about why there is something rather than absolutely nothing. Such questions are certainly not requests for efficient-mechanistic causal information (or at least they are more than this), but requests for final-purposive causal information. They are not just questions about the entirety of existence (though they are often at least that); they are questions about human life and individual human lives. They span the cosmic-intelligibility/individualist-normative divide. Asking them reveals a desire to access the

---

[31] Bede Rundle, *Why There is Something Rather Than Nothing* (Oxford: Clarendon Press, 2006), vii. Himself not a theist, Rundle does not think that the fact that something exists warrants the conclusion that there must exist a personal being whose essence it is to exist. For another recent treatment of ultimate explanation from a theistic perspective, see Timothy O'Connor's *Theism and Ultimate Explanation: The Necessary Shape of Contingency* (Malden, MA: Wiley-Blackwell, 2008).

intentions "behind" the cosmos, intentions that perhaps encompass the reason for why *we* are here.

According to R-H$_N$, the purpose(s) around which humans are to order their lives are multilayered. At the most foundational level, R-H$_N$ reveals a triune God who creates out of a fecundity of love. We in turn are called to love God and to love others (cf. Matt. 22:37–39). We are called to glorify God (cf. 1 Cor. 10:31). We are called to worship God (cf. Ps. 95:6).[32] Our overarching purpose to love, glorify, and worship God was present in the garden, remained intact after the fall, continues today during the already-but-not-yet period of postlapsarian, pre-consummation redemptive history, and will remain our purpose at the consummation of "under the sun" history from "ages to ages" in the eschaton. Love expressed in worship and service, all to the glory of God, is the great *telos* of humankind.[33] Within this ultimate purpose, however, is vast spaciousness for other purposes, some of which are prescribed by God, but many of which we determine for ourselves. Vocation and re-creation are certainly included in this.[34] Candidate meaning of life narratives must address the issue of purpose. R-H$_N$ does so in a thick, multilayered way.

3.4 The redemptive-historical narrative: Evil, pain, and suffering

Pondering the sobering reality that our universe is one flooded with tears causes many to ask what the meaning of all of this could possibly be. R-H$_N$'s

---

[32] This love-glory-worship dynamic is found across Christian traditions in confessional and liturgical documents and practices. See, for example, the *Catechism of the Catholic Church*, the various documents comprising the Westminster Standards, and *The Divine Liturgy of St. John Chrysostom* to name a few.

[33] Pope Benedict XVI (Joseph Cardinal Ratzinger) nicely articulates such purpose in terms of covenant and worship: "… we can now define the intention of the account of creation as follows: creation exists to be a place for the covenant that God wants to make with man. The goal of creation is the covenant, the love story of God and man. The freedom and equality of men, which the Sabbath is meant to bring about, is not a merely anthropological or sociological vision; it can only be understood *theo*-logically. Only when man is in covenant with God does he become free. Only then are the equality and dignity of all men made manifest. If, then, everything is directed to the covenant, it is important to see that the covenant is a relationship: God's gift of himself to man, but also man's response to God. Man's response to the God who is good to him is love, and loving God means worshipping him. If creation is meant to be a space for the covenant, the place where God and man meet one another, then it must be thought of as a space for worship." *The Spirit of the Liturgy* (San Francisco: Ignatius Press, 2000), 26.

[34] Cf. the so-called Cultural Mandate (Gen. 1:28). I humbly urge naturalists who are quick to charge Theism with destroying human autonomy to take a more careful look at what R-H$_N$ (and Scripture overall) actually teach on the matter. The criticism that God is an egotistical tyrant and human beings are nothing more than his debased minions is made much too quickly by some naturalists.

treatment of the so-called problem of evil is at once honest and nuanced, though it also leaves questions unanswered. On this narrative, the problem is not dismissed, even if what it says—*and does not say*—surprises us. From the fall, to the plight of Job, to the probing reflections of Qohelet in Ecclesiastes, to the exile, to the crucifixion of Jesus of Nazareth, R-H$_N$ in no way minimizes the darker side of reality.

R-H$_N$ links the many aspects of the problem of evil to important meaning of life themes. The moral and relational breach upon which human death and subsequent misery is occasioned is also the occasion for the entire cosmos being subjected to a state of futility. The Hebrew word that powerfully captures this state is *hebel* (lit. "breath, breeze, vapor"), a word that possesses salient connotations of fleeting temporality, insubstantiality, vanity, meaninglessness, enigma, and futility in various contexts.[35] The royal sage-teacher in the body of the book of Ecclesiastes, Qohelet, begins his careful reflection on life "under the sun" with this striking pronouncement, "[*h^{a}bēl h^{a}bālîm*], says the Preacher [Teacher], [*h^{a}bēl h^{a}bālîm*]! All is *hebel*" (Ecc. 1:2). Saint Paul, in his Epistle to the church at Rome, extends this theme, "For the creation was subjected to futility, not willingly, but because of him who subjected it, in hope that the creation itself will be set free from its bondage to corruption ..." (Rom. 8:19–21a). Nothing in creation has been left unscathed by evil. And if *hebel* has the last word in the world's narrative, then life is, all things considered, futile and meaningless. But, for anyone who knows the story well, R-H$_N$ does not narrate evil, pain, and suffering in isolation from the hope-filled redemptive thread in the narrative. After all it is the *redemptive*-historical narrative. It is the narrative of a loving Heavenly Father. We are his beloved children, not orphans in this story.

3.5 The redemptive-historical narrative: Eschatology and narrative ending

This moves us naturally into the last element that any candidate meaning of life narrative must narrate, and one to which R-H$_N$ speaks directly—how it's all going to end. Discussions of the way life is going to end have occupied a prominent place in the meaning of life literature, especially in

---

[35] For helpful discussions of the meaning(s) of *hebel*, see, for example, Michael V. Fox, *A Time to Tear Down & A Time to Build Up: A Rereading of Ecclesiastes* (Grand Rapids, MI: William B. Eerdmans Publishing Company, 1999), 27–49 and Tremper Longman III, *The Book of Ecclesiastes*, The New International Commentary on the Old Testament (Grand Rapids, MI: William B. Eerdmans Publishing Company, 1998), 61–65. See also the essays by Longman and Bartholomew in this volume.

conjunction with worries that life may be irredeemably futile if the grave is the final word. In a previous work, I argued that there is a compelling reason for this close connection if the meaning of life is interpreted as a narrative.[36] The way a narrative ends is important. In virtue of being *the end*, it has great power to elicit a wide range of broadly normative human responses on emotional, aesthetic, and moral levels toward the narrative as a whole. This claim is important given the close connection between discussions of futility and life's meaning. Conclusions of such discussions, especially those of cosmic futility, are often connected with perspectives on how it is all going to end, human life and the universe as a whole. Furthermore, it has often been thought that naturalistic metanarrative endings threaten the entire narrative with cosmic futility and meaninglessness, whereas Christian theistic endings are generally thought to be less susceptible to such a threat.[37]

Why should one think that a narrative's ending has such retroactive power? Why can, for example, the *final* emotional state instantiated in a reader overshadow the cluster of varying emotional states instantiated in the reader throughout the narrative? What gives this final state evaluative salience out of which we then adopt a settled stance toward the narrative as a whole; why is the future privileged over the present? J. David Velleman notes:

> What's more, the emotion that resolves a narrative cadence tends to subsume the emotions that preceded it: the triumph felt at a happy ending is the triumph of ambitions realized and anxieties allayed; the grief felt at a tragic ending is the grief of hopes dashed or loves denied. *Hence the conclusory emotion in a narrative cadence embodies not just how the audience feels about the ending; it embodies how the audience feels, at the ending, about the whole story.* Having passed through emotional ups and downs of the story, as one event succeeded another,

---

[36] See my "Death, Futility, and the Proleptic Power of Narrative Ending," *Religious Studies* 47 (2011): 141–163.

[37] Optimistic naturalists, of course, dispute the claim that naturalistic endings destroy prospects for meaningful life. Part of this debate turns on what one thinks of "final outcome arguments," whereby evaluative emphasis is placed on the final outcome of something. Temporal prioritizing in the meaning of life context might not be arbitrary as many naturalists claim though. This section provides at least one plausible reason for thinking that not all prioritizing of the future over the present and past is misguided. Theistic endings are not immune, however, from criticism on this front. Quite apart from metaphysical worries about the possibility of postmortem existence, one thinks of normative worries as voiced, for example, in Bernard Williams's famous essay "The Makropulos Case: Reflections on the Tedium of Immortality" in *Problems of the Self* (Cambridge: Cambridge University Press, 1973), 82–100. There is a growing body of literature on this topic, of which Williams's piece is a seminal contribution.

the audience comes to rest in a stable attitude about the series of events in its entirety. [emphasis added][38]

This is no small point. The ending marks the last word, after which nothing else can be said, either by way of remedying problems or destroying felicities that have arisen within the narrative.

If the last word is that hope is finally and irreversibly dashed, then despair and grief will be indelible at the end; if the last word is that deep longings have been satisfied, then joy will be indelible at the end. Perhaps more importantly, one cannot backtrack into a narrative, for example, where the grief felt at a tragic ending is the final word, and expect that one's emotional stance toward any specific event within the narrative or the narrative as a whole will not now be affected, in some sense, by the ending of the narrative. The ending relevantly frames the entire story. This framing falls broadly within the normative sphere, and includes a salient emotional component. The evaluative priority attached to narrative ending resides in its being the last word, one accompanied by the finality and indelibility of a settled normative stance toward the entire narrative. As Christiaan Moster notes:

> The ending is a necessary part of the story, notwithstanding its open-endedness; it is not a dispensable part. It affects proleptically every part of the story; no part can be considered apart from it ... Regardless of how unexpected or incongruent the end of a story is, it is decisive for the story's meaning.[39]

The end (*telos*) toward which a narrative advances and the actual end of the narrative (closure—vis-à-vis some contextualized "problem"—not an absolute *terminus*) are important components of a candidate meaning of life narrative. Unsurprisingly, R-H_N is deeply preoccupied with these issues. Is postlapsarian history moving from misery to felicity, from rebellion to redemption, from death to life? Not only do we wonder if there is more and long for more in this world saliently characterized by *hebel*, even the creation itself is said to anticipate deliverance from the death, decay, and futility that characterize life "under the sun." Importantly, R-H_N balances Qohelet's concerns about futility with hope, hope grounded in God's redemptive economy. God's wider redemptive work is a robust project by which remedy is being brought to the entire cosmos, someday to culminate in a new heavens and new earth where evil, pain, and suffering will be eradicated forever.

---

[38] J. David Velleman, "Narrative Explanation," *Philosophical Review* 112 (January 2003), 19.

[39] Christiaan Mostert, "Theodicy and Eschatology," in *Theodicy and Eschatology*, ed. Bruce Barber and David Neville (Adelaide, Australia: ATF Press, 2005), 106.

The focal point of this wider redemption is the person and work of Jesus of Nazareth. In him, the futility inherent within fallen creation is remedied in a multifaceted way. In the person of Christ, traditional Christian theology understands that the second person of the Trinity, the Son, took upon himself human flesh in the incarnation event to dwell with his people (lit. "tabernacled," which is a semantic-theological point of profound redemptive-historical significance). God himself enters into this world characterized by *hebel* to provide the ultimate remedy.[40] Jesus identifies with the plight of humanity. He enters the world's narrative. He reveals the Father and what true relationship with God looks like. He serves others in love. He lives a perfect life. He suffers and dies by means of the Roman crucifixion. Jesus is then physically resurrected on the third day, his resurrection's significance being deep and multilayered. Christ's resurrection is referred to in Scripture as the firstfruits (cf. 1 Cor. 15:20), as a sign and guarantee of, among other coming realities, the final salvation and resurrection of his people, the transformation of a creation that groans in futility, and the eventual definitive triumph of truth, goodness, and beauty over evil.

Depending on one's theological views and exegesis of key passages, the crucified Jesus was a substitutionary atonement, a propitiation for God's righteous wrath, a *Christus Victor* over the destructive powers at work within our fallen world, and the divine guarantee that God cares about the world and desires a felicitous ending to this narrative more than we do.[41] In R-H_N, Jesus' resurrection functions not only as the metaphysical blueprint for our own, but also as an event which transforms the desires for postmortem existence and a blessed ending from mere wishful thinking into robust hope, as hope, in contrast to wishful thinking, is rational to the extent that it is legitimately grounded (cf. 1 Cor. 15:1–58).

On R-H_N, death does not usher in the final and irreversible extinction of the human person. Conscious, eventual re-embodied, existence continues for humans after initial biological demise. The grave is not the end on R-H_N.

---

[40] This Christian theistic claim is also a central and powerful element in a Christian theodicy or defense. It may not provide an answer to *why* God allowed evil to occur in the first place or allows any particular instance of evil, but it does show that God gets his hands dirty so to speak. He identifies with the plight of sufferers by suffering himself in the person of Jesus. Charges of capriciousness, carelessness, and lack of love against God are rendered less credible by this and by the incarnation in general.

[41] Christ's atonement is an event multifaceted in meaning and scope. No one theory, considered in isolation, likely does justice to its full import. There has been much speculation, historically, about how best to view the nature of the atonement. With respect to views stressing the substitutionary and propitiary nature of Christ's death, some contemporary biblical scholars and theologians (and philosophers) see such views as morally problematic. I cannot comment on this here, though I am aware of the debate.

Death is only penultimate; it is only one, albeit deeply salient and often painful portion of a larger narrative where the ending of "life under the sun" to borrow from Ecclesiastes is a kind of closure that then ushers in an ending *that itself never ends*.[42]

God's wider redemptive economy encompasses personal, corporate, and cosmic dimensions whereby indefectible *shalom* comes to infuse the ending that never ends. Redemption, as robustly construed on Christian Theism, is not about spiritual escape from this world or from the necessarily limited conditions of corporeal existence. Rather, it is about peace, justice, reconciliation, restoration, the reign of God's glorious kingdom, and the defeat of darkness being brought to all aspects of the cosmos to the glory of God. This final blessed state, anchored in and resulting from Jesus' resurrection, is, as the prophet Isaiah depicts, something of a return to the Garden of Eden, where deep harmony between humanity, creation, and God comes to full fruition, and where sin in all its manifestations, disease, and death are abolished forever (cf. Isa. 11:1–9). Here, there will be no children dying, criminals pillaging, rapists violating, tornadoes destroying, or tearful mourners in despair.

This true Sabbath rest and ultimate *shalom*, prefigured in the creational narrative itself, will have arrived, as God "descends" to be with his people forever:

> Then I saw a new heaven and a new earth, for the first heaven and the first earth had passed away, and the sea was no more ... And I heard a loud voice from the throne saying, "Behold, the dwelling place of God is with man. He will dwell with them, and they will be his people, and God himself will be with them as their God. He will dwell with them, and they will be his people, and God himself will be with them as their God. He will wipe away every tear from their eyes, and death shall be no more, neither shall there be mourning, nor crying, nor pain anymore, for the former things have passed away." (Rev. 21:1–4)

Pain, suffering, and death speak neither loudest nor last in $R\text{-}H_N$. Life and love speak more powerfully and indelibly. The significance and scope of redemption do not, however, magically erase from personal and cosmic histories all traces of darkness. Evil really occurred, continues to occur, and will always occupy a pre-consummation place in the narrative. But it will be

---

[42] See my "Death, Futility, and the Proleptic Power of Narrative Ending," 147–150 for a discussion of one way to avoid the apparent contradiction of positing an ending that itself never ends.

eclipsed and somehow—we know not how (cf. 1 Cor. 2:9; 13:12a)—its narrative salience will be reoriented from the perspective of the end. Perhaps this coming repositioning of evil in the cosmic narrative is akin to the Japanese art of *kintsukuroi*, a method for repairing broken ceramics with a special lacquer mixed with gold, silver, or platinum. This technique seeks to "redeem" the broken ceramic by refashioning (even highlighting) rather than disguising the breaks. The process often results in something more beautiful than the original. Perhaps the dark narrative elements of this world can be similarly redeemed as our personal narratives and the cosmic narrative continue past their "under the sun" endings into the eschaton when everything sad will come untrue.[43]

Discussions of death, futility, and the way it is all going to end are part and parcel of discussions of life's meaning. Viewing the meaning of life as a narrative provides a compelling way of locating death and ending within broader meaning of life territory. If the meaning of life just is a narrative, it is clear why we are concerned with the way it is all going to end. Any candidate meaning of life narrative must have something to say about this. R-H_N speaks directly to this and the rest of the concerns and questions encapsulated in EC_Q, thus meeting the formal condition that any putative meaning of life narrative must meet in order to be a candidate meaning of life narrative; namely, it narrates the right stuff. Whether it meets the truth condition is a question for another time.

4. Postscript: The redemptive-historical narrative as the meaning of life

The narrative interpretation of the question, "What is the meaning of life?" takes seriously both the cosmic-intelligibility and individualist-normative dimensions of life's meaning. Life's meaning, on this interpretation, just is the true narrative that sufficiently addresses the cluster of issues (EC_Q) encompassing both dimensions. R-H_N, the narrative thread throughout Scripture that recounts God's redemptive action in human and cosmic history, is a candidate meaning of life narrative. What if it is more? I conclude by noting a couple of important points that follow from this hypothetical.

First, the meaning of life is not some individual narrative element or doctrine within R-H_N like, for example, to love God or to serve God or to worship

---

[43] This is an allusion to Samwise Gamgee's question to Gandalf after being rescued from Mt. Doom in J. R. R. Tolkien's *The Return of the King: Being the Third Part of the Lord of the Rings* (Boston: Houghton Mifflin Company, 1965), 230.

God or to experience deep joy. While meaningful life on Christian Theism certainly includes such life orientations and psychological states, meaningful life and the meaning of life, while related, are not the same in my view. The meaning of life is the entire redemptive-historical narrative of Scripture, not just a single element of that narrative.[44] En route to narrating the meaning of life, however, $R\text{-}H_N$ also addresses the individualist-normative dimension by offering practical guidance for leading a meaningful, flourishing life.

Second, contrary to widespread but perhaps waning views, the meaning of life is neither nonsensical nor something esoteric nor accessible only to those with some special gnosis. This is because, on the narrative interpretation, the meaning of life just is $R\text{-}H_N$, a narrative whose ultimate "author" is a God who lovingly condescends to the limitations—cognitive and otherwise—of his creatures. One will know the meaning of life to the extent that she knows $R\text{-}H_N$, and one will lead a meaningful life to the extent that she appropriates the relevant normative elements of $R\text{-}H_N$, ultimately by following Jesus in loving God and neighbor through the power of the Holy Spirit. Thankfully, one need not be a philosopher or theologian in order to do either of these things.[45]

---

[44] Similarly, the meaning the father sought in the above analogy is not an individual narrative element but the entire narrative. See Section 2.1 "The narrative interpretation: An analogy."

[45] I thank Stewart Goetz for his helpful comments.

Part Two

Meaningfulness and God

2

What God Could (and Couldn't) Do to Make Life Meaningful

Timothy Mawson

Some philosophers have thought that life could only be meaningful if there is no God. Sartre, for example, seems to have been of the opinion that if—*per impossibile* for Sartre—there were a God of the traditional classical theistic sort, he would constrain our powers of self-creative autonomy in ways that would evacuate our lives of all meaning. I wish to outline Sartre's view in the hope of rendering a (more modest) variant of it plausible.

In his lecture "L'existentialism est un humanism," Sartre contrasts the way in which a paperknife gets its meaning, *viz.* from the purpose had by its creator in creating it, with the way in which we humans may give our own lives meaning, by choosing for ourselves which purposes to adopt; we only have this freedom, he suggests, because we live in a Godless universe. The following is a famous passage from that work in which he outlines the view:

> If one considers ... for example ... a paper-knife ... one sees that it has been made by an artisan who had a conception of it ... Thus the paper-knife is ... an article ... which ... serves a definite purpose.... Let us say ... that its essence ... precedes its existence.... When we think of God as the creator, we are thinking of him ... as a supernal artisan.... God makes man according to a ... conception, ... as the artisan manufactures a paper-knife ... [The] essence of man precedes ... existence ... [On the other hand,] if God does not exist there is at least one being whose existence comes before its essence ... That being is man ... Man is ... that which he makes of himself.... [He] is [thus] of a greater dignity [than a paperknife] ... If ... it is true that existence is prior to essence, man is responsible for what he is. Thus, ... [atheistic] existentialism ... puts every man in possession of himself as he is, and

places the entire responsibility for his existence squarely upon his own shoulders.[1]

It seems to me that in this passage—and elsewhere in his writings—Sartre hits upon an important sense in which a person's life may have more or less dignity, by which I shall be taking it he is most charitably interpreted as meaning be more or less meaningful,[2] according to the degree of self-creative autonomy he or she enjoys and Sartre makes a true point about it, *viz.* that, in this sense of meaningfulness even if no other, God—were he to exist—would detract from the meaningfulness of our lives. As a prelude to defending a variant of Sartre's view, I should concede a little bit of ground: he rather overstates his case in two ways. First, Sartre overstates his case by suggesting that our lives can only be meaningful *at all* if we live in a Godless universe. Sartre assumes that, were God to exist, we would be reduced to the status of paperknives (or—my own preferred analogy—to the status of junior widget-affixers). This might be true if one adds to bare Theism a "meticulous providence" view of God's plans for his creatures; on such a view, at its extreme, God has a plan for every aspect of our lives and a preferred option for every choice that faces us, however small; his purpose for us is that we have no area in which we may exercise self-creative autonomy whatsoever. All of our essence precedes our existence, as Sartre might have put it. But

---

[1] I believe I have preserved sufficient of the original text to convey accurately Sartre's meaning, but I confess the pruning is severe. (Sartre, I'm sad to report, does not seem to have chosen to value concision when he was constructing an essence for himself. One might incline to excuse him for this somewhat by considering the fact that this was originally a lecture the text of which he did not intend to be published, were it not for the fact that *Being and Nothingness*, which he did write for publication, displays the tendency to an even greater extent.) The translation I am using may be found in Jean-Paul Sartre, *Existentialism and Humanism*, trans. Philip Mairet (Brooklyn, NY: Haskell House Publishers, 1977).

[2] The reason for thinking this most charitable is that it is not plausible that it is our dignity per se that is threatened by other-imposed purposes. Sartre, like Baier after him, seems to me to mischaracterize the threat, which they nevertheless correctly identify. Consider the case of Anne Frank. Anne Frank's life has great meaning, even though we have every reason to believe that large parts of it and its overall trajectory did not serve the purposes that she had. Her life serves a purpose that is of value (the purpose of the Anne Frank Foundation—interestingly then a purpose that was only assigned to her life after it had ceased), a purpose that is larger and more significant in terms of positively evaluable consequence than any purpose her diaries reveal her to have had during her lifetime. This example serves for me to illustrate the fact that giving someone's life a purpose that they did not choose, even when it is one which the evidence suggests they would not have chosen (in her case, the evidence is provided by her diaries and the ambitions and girlish hopes for herself that she outlined there), does not necessarily detract from their dignity; indeed, it seems to me that Anne Frank obtains dignity through the purpose-giving activities of the Anne Frank Foundation. It also seems to gain a meaning, but—and this is the point at which I would agree with Sartre—it does not gain any Sartrean meaning.

there is obviously scope for adding to bare Theism an understanding of God's providential plan for us which is "looser" than this and indeed such a looser understanding is commonplace; God's very purpose for us is in part that there be areas in which we may exercise the sort of self-creative autonomy that Sartre sees as essential for meaningfulness. Most theists hold that, in his terms, the essence that precedes our existence is in part one whereby our existence precedes some of our essence. The extent of the "looseness" within God's purposes for us is of course precisely the extent to which the theist may hope to mitigate the problem Sartre diagnoses without challenging its fundamental logic. Indeed, a peculiar sort of deism, whereby God, though causally responsible for initiating the universe, did so on a whim and has never had any purposes whatsoever for any of his creatures, would evade Sartre's problem entirely.[3] Second, Sartre overstates his case by suggesting

---

[3] I say "entirely," but it may be objected that we would still be governed by natural laws and thus, even on such a peculiar deism, at least some of our essence would precede our existence. However, that natural laws precede our choices is surely something that any plausible atheism would concede and yet the passage quoted makes it clear that the atheist Sartre thinks that purely natural constraints *do not* detract at all from our powers of self-creative autonomy. The fact that, say, I'm not free to fashion for myself the essence of someone who can fly to the moon simply by flapping his hands does not to any extent detract from my life's meaningfulness in the Sartrean sense. The problematic thing about God in this context, to Sartre's mind, is the *purposive* constraints that any God more like the theistic God than the peculiar deistic God inevitably imposes on us, not the natural constraints that any of these Gods *qua* creators of the natural world would inevitably impose on us. Personally, I would be in agreement with Sartre that there is a relevant distinction here, though I would get to this agreement via points on which we would disagree. The way I see it, natural constraints demarcate an area of possible action for us, whatever it is we're physically capable of doing in the situations we find ourselves in; moral constraints demarcate a subset of this area (and usually a proper subset) as what we're morally permitted to do; finally, if there's a God who has purposes for us, these purposes demarcate a subset (and sometimes at least a proper one) of what we would have been morally permitted to do absent his purposes. And thus it does not seem wrong to me to say that the theistic God's purposes for us constrain our powers of self-creative autonomy in a qualitatively distinct way from the natural laws that he has laid down for us, and a way in which it would not have been constrained had we lived in a Godless universe or a universe created by the peculiar deistic God.

As Seachris has pointed out to me, there are also threats to Sartrean meaning in certain Godless universes (i.e., to say possible worlds in which Theism is false); *viz.* ones where something other than God nevertheless has the authority to lay down a purpose for one. This doesn't help Theism avoid the Sartrean thesis that I am seeking to articulate, of course, but it does show that some nontheistic views would be subject to a similar worry. Seachris also points out that certain natural facts will spread Sartrean meaningfulness around unevenly (e.g., one born to overpowering and controlling parents will have less of it than one born to less directive parents). There are important issues here, ones which merit further discussion, but for now I wish to encourage us to think that we may say, "So, be it"; let us then "divide through" by these natural facts and we'll see that in two otherwise similar worlds, one in which Theism is true (a Godly world) and one in which it is not (a Godless world), there's less Sartrean meaning in the Godly one than in the Godless.

that there are no other senses of meaningfulness which we may reasonably care about (if only by omitting to mention the possibility of other senses) and which God, were he to exist, might help us in achieving rather than limit our chance of achieving. I have elsewhere argued for a version of the "pluralism" thesis about life's meaning—roughly that there are a number of different and legitimate meanings of "meaning" (and indeed "life") in the question of life's meaning.[4] If there are other senses, then perhaps some of the sorts of meaning that they capture are more important than Sartre's and thus perhaps, in helping us achieve meaning in these senses, God overall brings more to the party than he takes away. That indeed would be my view and we'll return to it later. But, for the moment, I wish to make the point that these two concessions—though cogent—should not be taken to detract from Sartre's achievement in hitting upon a sense of meaningfulness in human lives from which God detracts or—as Sartre would have preferred it—would detract were he to exist. God's existence, should he exist, is not unqualifiedly good news from the point of view of our lives being meaningful even if it is on balance good news. His existence is, one might say, a mixed blessing. This is the modified Sartrean thesis that I wish to defend in this chapter.

Let us ground ourselves in a mundane situation to see this Sartrean sense of meaningfulness in operation. Doing so will do two things—first, it will render in more vivid colors and thus make clearer the sort of meaningfulness that Sartre is talking about and, second, it will render it plausible that we value this sort of meaningfulness.[5]

Imagine, then, that a friend of yours works at a car factory and that, one day, he says to you this:

> I'm resigning from my position as Junior Widget-Affixer, as it is a meaningless position, meaningless in the sense that I'm given no

---

[4] T. J. Mawson, "Sources of Dissatisfaction with Answers to the Question of the Meaning of Life," *European Journal for Philosophy of Religion* 2.2 (2010): 19–41.

[5] I need to do the latter as a separate exercise to the former because another part of my view—offstage rather in this piece—is that not all meaning-adding activities are value-adding activities. One can make a human life more meaningful, it seems to me, in a perfectly legitimate sense of "meaningful," by making it more significant, but significance can be achieved in dis-valuable ways as well as valuable ones. Hitler, Stalin, Pol Pot, and so forth had more meaningful lives in this sense (though not in others) than the average, but they had overall worse lives because they achieved meaningfulness in the sense of significance in ways which were so terrible. It does not seem to me as it does to some that meaningfulness in a life is always per se a good-making feature; it seems to me that it depends on the type of meaningfulness one has in mind and sometimes—as with significance—on how that type is achieved. So, I shall spend some time arguing not just that Sartre has a legitimate sense of meaningfulness in mind in his discussion, but also that it's a sort of meaningfulness the having of which in a life is always per se a good-making feature.

responsibility for designing any significant aspect of my role; all those details are laid down by Management.

You would understand fully what your friend was saying to you and indeed think that, if the situation was more or less as he had described it, he was right in his analysis; his job really is meaningless in the Sartrean sense. The plans of others have limited his scope for self-creative autonomy to vanishing point, at least in the workplace. You might of course wish to argue your friend out of his decision to resign. You might say, for example, "But think of what the job means for your family—it means a roof over their heads and meals on the table." However, in bringing this consideration or similar considerations forward you would, it seems to me, have to be doing one of two things, neither of which would fundamentally undermine Sartre's case.

One thing you could be doing is using Sartre's sense of meaning, but disagreeing with your friend that the job really is meaningless *simpliciter* in that sense. It might be that your friend's taking and staying in the job of junior widget-affixer, while meaningless in its own terms, is a manifestation of a role over which he *has* taken responsibility in designing significant aspects, the role of provider for his family; and thus, when described in these terms, it can be said to be meaningful. If so, then from a larger perspective to which your friend may switch without self-deceit, the job may be seen as meaningful even though it remains, from a narrower perspective to which he may also switch back without self-deceit, meaningless. It could be then that what you are doing with your comments is simply encouraging your friend to switch to considering this wider context. Of course your reasoning, if it is as sketched here, is in principle defeasible. If the fact is that your friend conceives of himself as needing to be the provider for his family only because he does not feel able—much though he wishes he were able—to go against the gender-stereotyping in his society, then the wider context in which he *qua* worker finds himself would not be any more of an expression of his self-creative autonomy than the narrower context.

Another thing you could be doing is using a different sense of meaning to the Sartrean sense which your friend had employed—meaning as valuable causal consequence, perhaps. I do not here wish to defend at length the view that meaningfulness may also be construed as valuable causal consequence, but I must do something to defend it and to show that it does not reduce to meaningfulness in Sartre's sense to make my argument at this point. A couple of examples by way of illustration will do something to defend it.

Consider then the following two situations. First, a woman puts a small donation into a charity box on her way to work and quickly forgets about it; the box is subsequently lost along with all the monies in it; her act is naturally called "meaningless." Second, a similar woman puts a small donation into a charity box and similarly forgets all about it, but this donation is not lost and is in fact just sufficient to enable the charity to which it goes to finish building a well that then supplies clean water to a village that previously had none; many lives are thereby saved; her act is naturally called "meaningful."

So "meaningfulness" in one sense can be a matter of valuable causal consequence. And meaningfulness in a life in that sense can, it seems to me, be present to extents that are not perfectly correlated with meaningfulness in a life in Sartre's sense. We can thus see that this is a different sort of meaningfulness; we can do this by adding details into the thought experiment concerning your friend, such that this sort of meaningfulness too becomes either determinately absent from or determinately present in that case as we imagine it, and by seeing as we do so that we do nothing to affect the degree of Sartrean meaninglessness present.

First then, let us suppose that you happen to know this about the factory in which your friend works: after your friend has affixed widgets to the things that pass him on the conveyor belt, these things pass into another room where an equally depressed junior widget-remover takes them off. Were you to know that, you would know that there was an added sort of meaninglessness (absence of valuable causal consequence) to your friend's role, added that is to the sense of meaninglessness that Sartre has in mind—lack of self-creative autonomy. Second, you happen to know this about the factory: the widgets your friend is attaching are actually crucial parts of the cars to which he attaches them, cars which go out into the wider world and are used as small ambulances, being instrumental in saving many lives. That fact, were it to obtain, would seem to add this sort of meaningfulness to his activities, but it would not thereby affect the meaninglessness of his role in Sartre's sense.

So, if you are using a sense of meaning that equates meaningfulness with valuable causal consequence, it seems to me that you might well be speaking truly when—using your sense—you say that the job is meaningful and yet your friend be speaking truly when he—using Sartre's sense—says that it is not: you are simply speaking past one another. Of course the fact that in the situation we are imagining you think it cogent to make your claim suggests the possibility that you suppose that yours is a sort of meaningfulness which outweighs, or perhaps even "trumps" (is somehow lexically prior to), the Sartrean meaninglessness of your friend's job. But even so, you should not think that your friend's job having meaning in your sense makes it any less meaningless in Sartre's sense. In encouraging your friend to stay in his job in this fashion (in contrast to the first) you are not in any sense challenging the accuracy of his analysis of its meaninglessness in the sense of meaninglessness that he is using, just challenging its completeness as an analysis of its meaningfulness in all senses, by drawing on another sense of meaningfulness. Of course, as a defender of the pluralist thesis, I think that this sort of talking-past one another is quite often the correct diagnosis of disputes concerning life's meaning, but it is worth noting that, even if it is, the disputes can still be substantial as they, on correct diagnosis, can turn out to be disputes about which sort of meaning is more important or, as it is usually put, "deeper." Be that as it may, it seems to me that we have seen no reason to think that there's not a determinate sense of "meaning" that Sartre has hit upon—self-creative autonomy—and that it is absent from your friend's current job in the car factory, assuming it is as he has described it to you. And I think, further, that we are in a position to see that it is a sense of meaning which we value in life. To see that we value it, let us suppose your friend continues as follows:

> By the way, I've been offered the position of Executive Vice-President on the senior management team at the company; were I to accept, I'd be in charge of long-term strategic planning and "blue skies" thinking. The pay and other conditions—pension and so forth—would be as with my old job as Junior Widget-Affixer.

In that case you would surely unqualifiedly encourage your friend to resign from the first job and take up the second. This new job would mean the same in the sense of "meaning" you were using—roof over family, meals on table—and, in addition, mean more in Sartre's sense. But that you'd encourage him to make this move, rather than be neutral with respect to him doing so or staying in his current job, suggests that you *do* value meaningfulness in Sartre's sense of meaningfulness, even if not much (if, say, you'd have happily seen it trumped by meaning in the "valuable causal consequence" sense). So, one's life's having meaning in the determinate sense of meaning that Sartre has hit upon is, one thinks, its having something valuable. Of course one thought experiment and our imagined reactions to it are hardly proof of such claims, but they are, I think, indicative. We do value meaningfulness in this Sartrean sense; we do value, as he puts it, existence preceding essence.

Sartre presumed that we live in a Godless universe. This presumption appears to have been buried so deep in his psyche that he never felt the need to support it with anything but the briefest (and flimsiest) of arguments. We may disagree with him in this presumption and we may (probably do) have argument on our side when we do so. But, even if we do, I contend that we should admit that the fact that we don't live in a Godless universe means that our lives are not as meaningful in the sense that Sartre has well marked out, not as meaningful in this sense as they would have been if, *per impossibile* then, Sartre had been right in his atheism. (I assume throughout that the issue of God's existence is one of a metaphysical necessity.) As already conceded, if there is a God, then our positions mightn't yet be akin to that of paperknives, or even junior widget-affixers; they might be more akin to those of executive vice-presidents and thus we still have at least some—to some tastes, more than enough—meaning in Sartre's sense of meaning. And, as already conceded, it may be that the sorts of meaningfulness that God helps us achieve outweigh the loss in the Sartrean meaningfulness that, even with the loosest sort of purpose for us (short of the peculiar deism I mentioned), he cannot but force us to incur. The point is simply that we cannot have *as much* meaning in Sartre's sense as if Sartre had been right in his atheism and that that, in itself, is bad for us. We won't be "self-employed," as it were, free to style ourselves as president, chairman of the board, chief executive officer, and anything else that might catch our fancy. At the most fundamental level—like it or not, *realize* it or not—we will be "working" for someone else in the sense that there will be a God who has at least some purposes for us that are not as they are as a result of our choosing them for ourselves, but rather are as they are as a result of his choosing them for us. At least some of our essence will precede our existence.

The issue of whether "bootstrapping" meaning in Sartre's fashion is really possible needs further investigation before we can rest content with this conclusion. Some believe that Sartre's account of meaning is logically incoherent.[6] As my discussion of his view will already have suggested, this seems to me too hasty; it seems to me that if Sartre is wrong, he is wrong of necessity, but the sort of necessity in virtue of which he is wrong is a metaphysical one, not a logical one. If Sartre is wrong, he is wrong for metaphysical reasons (there just is a God and he is the metaphysical ground of all value), not logical ones (that his view does not make sense, that there is no logically possible world in which it is true). Nevertheless, it will be instructive to spend a moment or two looking at how an argument against Sartre's logic might best be made and how it might best be met, for looking at this will enable us to state the modified Sartrean thesis more fully and more powerfully.

The most plausible line to take against Sartre's logic is—it seems to me—not to deny that he has hit upon a sense of meaningfulness and that in general individuals' lives can be more or less meaningful in this way in proportion to the amount of responsibility they have for deciding on certain of their contents—in proportion to the extent to which, as one might put it, their existence precedes their essence. Rather, it is to insist that, in the limiting case, where essence did not precede existence to any extent whatsoever, this

---

[6] John Cottingham, for example, has pressed this point against me in discussion.

general relationship would break down. In other words, the most plausible attack on Sartre's view would be to allow that one may generate meaning in the sense that Sartre discusses, but insist that this is only so in cases where there is some wider context of meaningfulness already in place. And, if God is necessary for this wider context, then it's not the case that we could only fully have the sort of meaning in a Godless universe; on the contrary, we could only have any of it in a Godly one.

The example of the factory worker, at least as presented so far, does not do anything to undermine this challenge to the modified Sartrean thesis, as, were the friend one is imagining to move to the projected position on the senior management team, there would still be, above any of his individual meaning-generating choices, an overarching structure of meaningfulness into which those choices needed to fit. He would still be on the senior management team of a car factory, in charge of—presumably then with some responsibility to other members of the board and/or the shareholders for— long-term strategic planning. His role wouldn't leave him free to choose to sack all the workers and leave the factory the largest piece of "ready-made" art ever created or to decide not to think about anything that might happen more than five minutes in advance of whatever board meeting he was on his way to attend. One might argue that if we try to think-away this sort of background altogether—think-away those parts of his essence which would still precede his existence in this new job—no possibility of meaning-creating choices of the sort Sartre has identified would survive. On one occasion, Kant entertained the whimsy that a bird might reflect on the nature of the air through which it moved in flight and decide that it would fly even faster were it to find itself in a complete vacuum, but we of course can see that such a thought would be mistaken—an understandable mistake perhaps (especially for the bird-brained), but a mistake nonetheless.

In this vein, let us imagine you meeting your friend from the car factory again after several years. This time, he says to you this:

> Since we last spoke, I've been promoted to the top of the firm—"God," as I like to style myself now. Now I'm not responsible to anyone, no shareholders, nobody at all. If I like, I could turn the company from car production to the production of something else entirely, or to the production of nothing at all. I could spend my days just twiddling my thumbs if I chose and to no-one, other than myself, would I be responsible for such a choice; I am able, if you like, to re-write my job description in any fashion I wish, as and when it appeals to me, and thus I am always maximally deserving of the "Employee of the Month" badge, which I thus regularly award to myself. Do you know what? I find

this position just as meaningless as I did my original position as "Junior Widget-Affixer."

It must be conceded that the last sentence of this would not come as a complete surprise given what had gone before. And this might be taken to provide some support for the anti-Sartrean argument I am trying to articulate. But I think we do better to interpret what is going on in this imaginary situation not as your friend finally failing to be able to secure meaningfulness for himself in Sartre's sense as he reaches the top of the ladder, but as the friend losing meaningfulness in another sense of meaningfulness while still having increased meaningfulness in Sartre's sense. The "God" job really is more meaningful in Sartre's sense of meaning than the job as part of the senior management team, which in turn really is more meaningful in this sense than the job as junior widget-affixer. However, your friend's positions in the company as he has moved through to the "God" job, while becoming more meaningful in Sartre's sense with each move, have, at least at the end of this process, become less meaningful in at least one other—perfectly legitimate, but different—sense and thus, when he now considers the overall meaningfulness of his current position in the "God" case, he inclines to describe it as "just as meaningless" as his original position. A good contender for this sense of meaningfulness is fulfilling known purpose in some appropriate larger scheme of things. Again, as I have argued for it elsewhere, I don't wish to defend at length the claim that this is a legitimate sense of meaningfulness; I just offer it up in the hope that it will be obvious that it is. Once your friend finds himself in the "God" job, he no longer has any of this meaningfulness left and he is decrying this loss in what he is now saying to you.

The correct conclusion seems to be then that Sartre's is a sense of meaningfulness which it is logically possible for a human life to hold fully. Whether or not it is metaphysically possible for our lives to be or to be made fully meaningful in this sense depends, obviously, on metaphysics—if Classical Theism is true, then they certainly are not and cannot be made so. (Though God's life would of course then be fully meaningful in Sartre's sense.[7]) If there is no God of the classical theistic sort, then perhaps this logical possibility is a metaphysical possibility for us. But perhaps it is not, even then. (Some other issue in metaphysics may prevent it.) In any case, the type of impossibility in which generating meaning in Sartre's sense of meaning by one's choices

---

[7] Seachris points out to me in discussion that it would perhaps be better to put this "as fully as is logically possible," as there may be some of the so-called paradoxes of the divine attributes—perhaps especially those concerning the "tension" between omnipotence and necessary perfect goodness—which could be argued to "constrain" even God in this respect. Perhaps, but in any case there is no higher authority with purposes for God.

would be impossible were it not the case that one's essence already preceded one's existence to at least some extent is, I would suggest, if it exists at all, a metaphysical impossibility, not a logical one. Sartre's position at this point is a logically coherent one.[8] In some logically possible worlds, some of us do fully have meaningfulness in Sartre's sense, though of course these logically possible worlds are not metaphysically possible if God exists. To make that point is just to state one part of the modified Sartrean thesis that I am arguing for, *viz.* that God makes it logically impossible for us to have fully meaningful lives in the Sartrean sense of meaningful. Given that if Theism is true, God's there of metaphysical necessity, it follows that it's metaphysically impossible for any of us to have fully meaningful lives in the Sartrean sense and that is, in itself, bad for us.

Even though arguments against the logical possibility of ultimately "bootstrapping" meaning for oneself in the Sartrean way do not work, such arguments do reveal again the truth of the pluralistic understanding of life's meaning that, as I said earlier, I have argued for on independent grounds elsewhere: Sartre's is a perfectly legitimate sense of meaning, but there are other, equally legitimate, senses—fulfilling known purpose in some appropriate larger scheme of things, for example. Possibly these arguments even reveal that we care more about our lives being meaningful in one or more of these other senses of meaningful than we do about them being meaningful in Sartre's sense, or at least that we do so once our lives are past some, perhaps vague, threshold of meaningfulness in Sartre's sense. We might think the arguments do this if we imagine that we would encourage the friend, if the opportunity arose (and surely he could make it arise), to resign from the "God" job and go back to the job on the senior management team. We might even find ourselves thinking that God, if he does exist, leads a *less* overall meaningful life than us even while having meaningfulness in Sartre's sense to the maximum extent possible, for God's life has no purpose in an appropriate larger scheme of things, there being no appropriate larger scheme of things into which he fits. If we give the sort of meaningfulness that Sartre talks about a lexical priority to other sorts, we'll resist this thought. But if we give the "fulfilling-a-known-purpose-in-some-appropriate-larger-scheme-of-things" sort of meaningfulness lexical priority, we'll be unable to resist it.

In any case, it has emerged that God, if he exists and is not either maximally meticulous or the peculiar deistic God that I mentioned in passing

---

[8] I say "at this point." I would concede that this is only so because certain values retain their value across all logically possible worlds, which additional thesis Sartre himself would have denied; so be it, Sartre was shackled to the corpse of moral antirealism; we need not be. With it being the case that in every logically possible world Sartrean meaningfulness is in itself valuable, Sartre's position at this point is a logically coherent one.

earlier, has had—of logical necessity—to strike a balance in what he has given us between two sorts of meaningfulness—meaningfulness as self-creative autonomy and meaningfulness as purpose in some appropriate larger scheme of things. The more he gives us the former, the less he can give us the latter. This is because there is an inverse relationship between these two sorts of meaningfulness. Those, if any, who do achieve a life of full meaningfulness in the Sartrean sense—perhaps some of us do so if atheism is true (Sartre himself perhaps?); God alone does so, if atheism is false—cannot have any meaning in the sense of purpose in an appropriate larger scheme of things. A life fully meaningful in Sartre's sense is one that cannot have a purpose in some appropriate larger scheme of things, as there cannot be an appropriate larger scheme of things for such a life. And a life that has a purpose in a larger scheme of things cannot be fully meaningful in Sartre's sense. If there is a unique way in which the balance between these two sorts of meaningfulness is best struck for all of us, God in his perfection will of course have selected that. If there is not, other possibilities open themselves.

After considering a final objection to the modified Sartrean thesis I'm defending, we'll explore the issue of whether there is plausibly a unique place to strike the balance best for all of us and (spoiler alert) what follows from there not being one. But for the moment I just wish to underscore the simpler point that is the conclusion so far: if we assume for ease of exposition a single right spot to strike it, in striking the balance there (in not being either a maximally meticulous God, on the one hand, or the peculiar deistic God, on the other), then—whatever the overall goodness of his striking the balance there—God has done as Sartre insisted he would have to do, made our lives less meaningful in the Sartrean sense than he would have done had he struck the balance a bit closer to the peculiar deistic end of the spectrum. Of course again I must stress that to have struck the balance a bit closer to the peculiar deistic end of the spectrum might have been to have made our lives overall less meaningful. But that is not the point. The point is that however overall less meaningful it would have made our lives, it would have made them more meaningful in the Sartrean sense, a sense of meaningfulness which in and of itself we rightly value. If you complain to the doctor that the medicine he is giving you tastes terribly bitter and the doctor explains to you how making it even the tiniest bit sweeter would have had inevitable side-effects such that it would have been, all-things-considered, worse for you, then you should indeed stop complaining, but what you were complaining about—it's being terribly bitter—was in and of itself a bad feature of the medicine (even though, in having it, the medicine was overall better for you than it would have been had you not had it).

I now wish to consider a way in which one might seek to block this conclusion. It might appear that we can "reclaim" this loss of meaningfulness in Sartre's sense simply by appropriating to ourselves God's purposes for us. If your friend had found himself inescapably in the role of junior widget-affixer, shouldn't he just have reconciled himself to that? Very plausibly, yes. Wouldn't his doing so have made this role more meaningful for him? Very plausibly, yes again. Wouldn't its making the role more meaningful for him be its reclaiming the meaningfulness in Sartre's sense that he had been in danger of losing? I shall argue not; it would simply be his gaining in meaningfulness in the sense of felt satisfaction at fulfilling a known purpose in an appropriate larger scheme of things. Similarly, it seems to me, appropriating for oneself God's purposes for one is not reclaiming in any sense the Sartrean meaninglessness engendered by God's having these purposes for one.

We may, if we come to believe in God and learn of his purposes for us, appropriate these purposes for ourselves and thus, post facto, they become purposes of our own choosing; indeed, reacting in this way would seem the only rational thing to do in the light of such revelations. But (a) this will not in fact happen for all of us, at least *antemortem* (some, after all, remain atheists) and it will not happen perfectly for any of us *antemortem*; and, more importantly, (b) even if we did perfectly appropriate these purposes to ourselves (as, on Theism, we will do *postmortem*[9]), this would not make it the case that the purposes were as they were because we had chosen them; rather, it would be us choosing them because we recognised them to be inescapably as they were. And this second point is sufficient to defend the modified Sartrean thesis against the line of attack that I have in mind, *viz.* that we may simply reclaim meaningfulness in Sartre's sense by appropriating to ourselves God's purposes for us. Seneca may have said, "The wise man escapes necessity by willing that which necessity will force upon him"; it's certainly the sort of half-truth that pervades Stoicism. But it is a *half*-truth: you don't really escape necessity this way; you are just, perhaps, enabled to fool yourself into thinking that you have escaped it. Similarly, the sort of meaningfulness that a purpose gets for a person solely in virtue of its being most fundamentally a purpose of his or her own choosing is not added to by a person choosing to appropriate to himself or herself the preexisting purpose for him or her that is had by someone else even if the wise thing to do is to appropriate it to himself or herself; even if it is ultimately inescapably what he or she will do because his or her nature is such as to necessitate it; and even if, by appropriating it to himself or herself, he or she gains another sort of meaningfulness, as he or she may well do (and would do in this case), *viz.* a certain sort of

---

[9] Or at least those of us destined for Heaven will do.

satisfaction. It is helpful in this context to draw-in the notion of alienation, for I think we can use it to help those of us who are theists understand why it is that the claim that on Theism we are, in one sense if not others, alienated is one truth which will inevitably be hard for us to believe, or—better—hard for us to feel.

In the case of your imagined friend, the junior widget-affixer, one may think that the meaninglessness of his job was generated by his being, as Marx might have put it, alienated from the product of his labor. One thing Marxists are keen on pressing is that one must not interpret the notion of alienation as it is deployed in such claims merely as a psychological state of dissatisfaction. The alienation of your friend is, at least in part, his having no responsibility for designing the objects that pass him by on the production line and having no responsibility for deciding on even the smallest details of how he contributes to them or how they go on to be used. If he took the job on the senior management team, at least some of this lack of responsibility would disappear; thus the greater meaningfulness of the second position in Sartre's sense: less of his essence would precede his existence, one might say; he would become less alienated. Conversely, if your friend was simply hypnotized so that he (falsely) believed of himself that he had designed the objects that passed him by and decided the smallest details of how he contributed to them and how they went on to be used or if he simply took a pill so that he became entirely satisfied with the facts as they were, while, in either case, his appreciation of his level of alienation might decrease, possibly even vanish entirely, in neither case would his true level of alienation be affected. Being a theist is analogous to having taken the latter route, which is, I hazard, why those of us who are theists find the Sartrean/Marxist claim that Theism alienates us so prima facie implausible; we certainly don't *feel* alienated by our Theism. Indeed, the more we take ourselves to have succeeded in appropriating to ourselves God's purposes for us, the more satisfied—at one with the universe, our fellow man, the supernatural order, and everything else of value—we feel. But of course if the Sartrean/Marxist claim is true, feelings won't be a good guide here.

Marx famously characterized religion as the "Opium of the Masses" and it seems to me that as a theist one should concede that the analogy is at least somewhat apposite.[10] If Theism is true, belief in it offers an opiate to this sort of alienation. While it's being true makes the sort of appropriation to oneself

---

[10] In doing so, I'm assuming that utilizing opium carries in itself no ineradicable negative connotations; opiating oneself against pain would be, were there no side effects, to make one's life better. Similarly, the theist that I am thinking of will insist that opiating oneself against the sort of Sartrean/Marxist alienation that we undergo if Theism is true is to make one's life better.

of the purposes of God the only rational response and the only response consonant with our deepest and most fundamental desires, this appropriation does nothing to remove our alienation from these purposes in the Sartrean/Marxist sense. They're still fundamentally as they are because of God's will, not ours. But we can make a virtue out of a necessity here. I'm reminded of perhaps the most famous saying attributed to someone who certainly wasn't a Marxist. Henry Ford reportedly said, "Any customer can have a car painted any color that he wants so long as it is black." As a customer, on hearing this, the most rational thing for you to do might well be to reconcile yourself to having your car painted black. But even supposing complete success in this—you perfectly appropriate to yourself Ford's choice of color—your car is black not because you choose that it be black, but rather because Ford chose that it be black. The choice of color was most fundamentally his, not yours; you are still in this way alienated from it however good you feel about it. This would remain so even if Ford genetically-engineered prospective customers so that their most natural and deepest desire was for black even before they discovered that this was the only color cars came in. So, it's not that one can object to the conclusion that if God exists our lives must have less meaning in Sartre's sense by pointing out that we can simply appropriate to ourselves God's purposes for us and thereby reclaim meaning in Sartre's sense. It's not simply that we cannot point this out because in fact none of us do (*antemortem* at least) perfectly appropriate to ourselves God's purposes for us, but rather and more fundamentally because, even if we did, that would be at best us perfectly "opiating" ourselves to the alienation that we nevertheless continued to undergo.

The situation here is assuredly made more complex by the fact that appropriating to ourselves God's purposes for us isn't *simply* to opiate ourselves to this alienation; it is also to add to the meaningfulness in our lives. Indeed it is the felt satisfaction at this adding that is doing the opiating. The point to stress though is similar to one made before—appropriating to ourselves God's purposes for us adds to the meaningfulness of our lives in a different sense of meaningfulness from the way that these purposes being as they are because God chose them, rather than because we chose them, detracts from the meaningfulness of our lives. It adds by adding to the meaningfulness of our lives both in the sense of fulfilling a known purpose in some appropriate larger scheme of things and (usually) in the sense of felt satisfaction at fulfilling a known purpose in some appropriate larger scheme of things.

Let us suppose, for example, that God has a special purpose for me and this special purpose is that I do my best to contribute to philosophical understanding of the meaning of life. If so, it seems plausible to say that my life is being made more meaningful in some sense of meaningful by my writing this piece than it would have been had I been doing something else, even had that something else been writing a piece on some other area of philosophical significance that equally interests me. As it is though, I'm writing this piece and thus aligning myself with the purpose that God has for me. It seems to me that this alignment is best construed as contributing to the meaningfulness of my life in some sense of meaningfulness even if I don't know it is happening. That is meaningfulness in the sense of fulfilling some purpose in an appropriate larger scheme of things. Be that as it may, it is very plausible to suggest that the fact that God has this purpose for me can contribute all the more to the meaningfulness of my life if I do realize it (then it'll bring meaningfulness in the sense of knowingly fulfilling a purpose in an appropriate larger scheme) and if I appropriate the purpose to myself, making the alignment part of the description under which I will myself to continue on in the activity of writing this piece (then it'll bring meaningfulness in the sense of a peculiar sort of felt satisfaction at knowingly fulfilling a purpose in an appropriate larger scheme). This felt satisfaction may indeed—I am suggesting—be described as "opiating" one against one's persisting alienation in the Sartrean/Marxist sense, though "opiating" would need to be stripped of any pejorative overtones, but so be it. If a worker finds himself in a particular job in the factory as a result of some prudent decision by the managing director, then his being there, rather than anywhere else, has a meaning-giving purpose, but it will only fully have meaning *for* him—the particular worker—if he realizes this and willingly assents to it. His subsequent known alignment with this purpose will quite probably bring felt satisfaction, one which could be described as an opiate, but it need not make him oblivious to the fact that the purposes for himself which he has now fully appropriated to himself are as they are because the managing director chose them, rather than because he chose them, and thus reflections of this sort need not make us, if we are "opiated" theists, oblivious to the fact that the modified Sartrean thesis about our continuing alienation is true.

So, again we see God's "dilemma": if God is meticulous enough in his providential purposing for me so that his purpose for me is that I write on this topic rather than any other, then that adds to my life's meaning and I can in principle add still further by appropriating to myself that purpose; if he reveals that this is his purpose for me, for example, then I can will myself to continue on writing on this topic rather than any other because of this and thus gain the sort of meaning that comes from my knowing of this aspect of what I am doing that it is fulfilling a purpose in an appropriate larger scheme of things. No doubt I shall gain in addition an extra sort of satisfaction thereby with the activity; and perhaps increased motivation to persevere with it; and perhaps other goods too. All to the good. But then my scope for self-creative autonomy will have been reduced relative to what it would have been had God simply had for me the purpose that I write on any philosophical topic that interests me. More of my essence will precede my existence. If, by contrast then, God is not so meticulous, his purpose for me being merely that I write on any topic in philosophy that interests me, then the particular nature of the topic on which I am writing is meaningless in the sense where to be meaningful something must fulfill a purpose in an appropriate larger scheme of things—any philosophical topic in which I was interested would have done as well. So, I cannot, by willing myself to continue on writing on this topic rather than some other, gain the sort of meaning that comes from my knowing of this aspect of what I am doing that it is fulfilling a purpose in an appropriate larger scheme of things. And thus that peculiar sort of satisfaction will be denied me on this point. Less of my essence will precede my existence. Unless we go for either the maximally meticulous view or the peculiar deistic view of God's purposes for us, we are construing one of God's purposes for us as being that we get to choose for ourselves what purposes to have within certain parameters; in Sartre's terms, we are saying that we do indeed have an essence that precedes our existence, but a part of this essence is that over some areas our existence precedes our essence. We are only disagreeing among ourselves over where God has struck the balance.

This looseness in God's providential plan for us only makes sense, I think, given a certain sort of pluralism about "the" good life, but such a pluralism is very plausible on independent grounds.[11] I want to conclude by arguing that, given it, God's existence adds more to the meaningfulness of some people's lives than it does to others. A number of lines of argument support this conclusion. The first is a pretty straightforward one.

Some people devote their lives to philosophy; others to music; others to promoting education; yet others to ministering to the sick; and yet others to scientific discovery. And of course most of us split our time and energies between a number of such goods. According to a plausible pluralism about

---

[11] Note, this sort of pluralism is different from the sort of pluralism already mentioned, which is solely about the legitimate meanings of "meaning" (and "life") in the question of life's meaning. The view I have in mind when I speak of pluralism about "the" good life is the view that usually goes by the name "value pluralism" and is usually sourced to Isaiah Berlin (though he himself cites predecessors). It is summed up nicely at the start of W. A. Galston, *Liberal Pluralism: The Implications of Value Pluralism for Political Theory* (Cambridge: Cambridge University Press, 2002): 5–6. However, in one of his clauses, Galston defines pluralism by its commitment to the view that there is no one chief good. The sort of pluralism I have in mind, while satisfying the other criteria Galston outlines, is compatible with thinking that there is one chief good. So, the beatific vision might be the ultimate and chief good, but there still be, at a subordinate level, the sort of plurality of goods that pluralism as he defines it commits one to thinking holds all the way up.

"the" good life, each of these ways of living is potentially a good way of living and, in many cases even if not all, not capable of being ranked relative to the others. As will have become apparent, it seems to me that on Theism we should think of God as having in general left it to us which of the sets of values internal to these activities we choose as our "area(s) of specialization," as it were, as long as we maintain a minimum standard in various "areas of competence," if you like—that is a morality. As some of these ways of living as they particularize themselves in individuals are more meaningful in a godly universe than in a godless one and some are more in a godless one than a godly one, so—straightforwardly—God's existence will make some people's lives more meaningful than it will make other people's. So, for example, two values internal to the discipline of philosophy are following one's reason wherever it leads and reaching important truth. That being so, theistic philosophers of religion who are in other respects like atheistic philosophers of religion are leading more meaningful lives than their atheistic peers if they live in a godly universe; they are leading less meaningful lives if they live in a godless one. Meaning-wise, God's existence then, even if overall a blessing for all, is a blessing that falls unevenly on philosophers of religion per se.[12] There are other lines of argument that lead to the same conclusion.

It seems to me that there are a number of different ways in which God could have permissibly struck the balance between the two sorts of meaningfulness on which we have been focusing. One way to justify this claim would be to point out that these two sorts of meaningfulness, while related conceptually to one another such that you can only have one to the extent that you lack the other, seem to be in an important sense incommensurable and from this alone it might seem to follow that there would have been a number of ways of striking a balance between them that would not be incompatible with God's perfect goodness. That being so, he may have struck it differently for different people or for one and the same person at different times. Then the extent to which, meaning-wise, God's existence is a blessing will vary between these different people or vary for the same person over time or at least not be determinately *in*variant. In addition, in that another sort of meaningfulness is generated by the extent to which this balance is struck as one would oneself have chosen to strike it, this generates the possibility for either a consonance or dissonance between this last sort of meaningfulness and the choices that God has made for one, again making his existence

---

[12] This is perhaps unsurprising; it's close to trivial that if Theism is true, then that in itself makes arguing for atheism a less philosophical activity than arguing against it; if atheism is true, then that in itself makes arguing for Theism a less philosophical activity than arguing against it.

more or less of a blessing, meaning-wise, for different people or for one and the same person at different times. And then finally, there is a certain type of "interference" in our life-plans which God, it seems to me, is probably obliged to engage in and which will spread meaningfulness around unevenly. Let me say a bit more about that.

The sort of pluralism about "the" good life that I sketched previously applies generally, but, in the case of particular people, God, in his perfect goodness, may find himself required to interfere and make certain sorts of lives that would otherwise have been permissible, indeed good, bad for the people who had hitherto been leading them. There is thus potential for a certain type of bad luck—"meaning luck," one may call it (to parallel the more familiar "moral luck")—to fall on those people with whose lives he does have to interfere for these moral reasons, bad luck in that it makes God's existence less of a blessing, meaning-wise, for them than it is for others who are in relevant respects otherwise like them. This is so because God is plausibly required by his perfect moral goodness to strike the balance in different places for different people or the same person at different times so as to achieve his overall purposes for us collectively.

For example, suppose that it was particularly important in the Divine economy that one of two brothers, Jonah and Jonas (the latter of which you've never heard of, for good reason), go and preach to Nineveh, but that either brother would have fulfilled the purpose equally well. God, in his perfect goodness, had to choose one and let us say that it was as the text would suggest: he chose Jonah. That was in a sense bad news for Jonah—he had to work while his brother was free to go on holiday to a place they'd often talked about as "the perfect getaway location," Tarshish. Jonah—who may well have quite-permissibly committed himself to a vision of the good life involving holidaying in Tarshish—found that, of a sudden, more of his essence was being made prior to his existence, as Sartre would have put it. That wasn't where he'd have struck the balance. That God chose Jonah to be the Prophet threatened Jonah's enjoyment of another sort of meaningfulness as well. One legitimate sense of the term "meaningful" seems to me to be such that in that sense a life or period within a life is meaningful just to the extent that in his or her most reflective moments the person living it feels content with it. Jonah had less of this meaningfulness while he was three days in the belly of the big fish than his brother, Jonas, who was simultaneously spending those three days sitting on a beach with his jug of sangria. It's just hard to feel content with anything when you're in a belly of a fish; it's just easy to feel content with anything when you're on a beach with a jug of sangria. But in another sense God's choice was bad news for Jonas; he didn't get to be a Prophet; to use his next few months to fulfill a known purpose in some appropriate larger scheme of things; to gain ultimate satisfaction from that. (Not that it's obvious from the text that Jonah gained satisfaction from his ultimately fulfilling a purpose in an appropriate larger scheme of things either, but I like to think that he did, eventually.) Jonas just spent these months drinking sangria on a beach and has since been forgotten about entirely, while Jonah's name lives forever. So, each has lost out, in various senses, by God's making the decision that he has—striking the balance in two different places for the two different brothers. And, in other senses, each has gained by his doing so. It is implausible to maintain that these differences cancel out and leave the brothers equally blessed, meaning-wise. If we *do* suppose that, as it stands, God's existence is an equal blessing, net, to both brothers, we can see how it could easily have been an unequal one by varying contingent features of their circumstances in our imagination. For example, we may posit that in fact Jonas found his sangria a little bit too sweet for his liking and thus found that he couldn't, while drinking it, feel quite as satisfied as originally posited with his life when considered as a whole. Contingent features like this seem unlikely to be as finely balanced as they'd need to be across the whole of humanity at any one time and over time to mean that God's existence contributes evenly to the meaningfulness of all. And, if that's so, it's an extra reason to suppose that God's existence is, as I am putting it, more of a blessing for some than for others.

By way of summing up: as we have observed, at least as a junior widget-affixer, the factory bell rings and one can go home; engage in leisure pursuits of one's choice; and so on. Junior widget-affixer may be a meaningless job in Sartre's sense, but it is only a job; a junior widget-affixer has, we may suppose, a life outside work. As we have seen, it is indeed from this that there emerges scope for argument to the effect that even in Sartre's sense of meaningfulness, there may be a wider context in which what is meaningless in a narrower context becomes meaningful. The junior widget-affixer is assuredly alienated from the product of his labor *qua* worker, but he is perhaps not *qua* provider for his family. Be that as it may, the most inescapable product of one's labor, alienation from which is thus alienation of the most inescapable sort, is one's life itself; one has no life outside one's life. So, if one has the same sort of relationship to one's life as a whole as in the thought experiment one's friend has toward his role as junior widget-affixer, there is no respite for the alienation one is under, unless that one is free to redesign that aspect so that it better accommodates one's wishes. On Theism (in contrast to the peculiar sort of deism that has been mentioned now and again), there just are limits to the extent to which one can redesign one's purposes, limits imposed on us by our creator's purposes for us; and so we just are alienated in this sense to at least some extent. We have conceded that there is perhaps still respite for the feeling of alienation; as well as "disreputable" opiates (one might, for example, get drunk or in other ways dull one's sensibility to the relevant facts), there is the more "reputable" opiate of a theistic religion, reputable in that it need not dim one's awareness of the Sartrean/Marxist alienation one continues to undergo and it adds meaningfulness of different sorts to counterbalance this alienation, plausibly more than counterbalance it. The possibility that one might become reconciled to one's "job"—the plan for one's life that God has—is not then, as we have seen, incompatible with the modified Sartrean thesis I have been advancing: alienation is not dissipated by one's appropriating to oneself the purposes that God has for one even if appropriating to oneself God's purpose for one does add to the meaningfulness of one's life in perfectly legitimate (if different from Sartre's) senses of meaningfulness; it adds to it in the sense of allowing one to see aspects of one's life as fulfilling a part in some appropriate larger scheme of things and it adds to it in the sense of allowing one, if one appropriates those purposes to oneself, to find a certain sort of satisfaction from fulfilling those purposes. But the extent to which one can gain meaningfulness in these senses is the extent to which one does not have meaningfulness in Sartre's sense. So God's existence is a mixed blessing, even if it is on balance a blessing for all of us, and God's existence is more of a blessing for some of us than it is for others.

The arguments I've advanced latterly for God's existence adding to the meaningfulness of our existence unevenly over the population and over time for some individuals have assumed certain controversial things about value and God's perfect goodness. One may thus resist this aspect of my conclusion in a number of ways. One might, for example, insist on a sort of "theodical individualism," whereby God's perfect goodness won't allow any individual to suffer a loss of meaningfulness in any sense of meaningfulness that isn't ultimately strictly necessary for that individual to gain equal or greater meaningfulness in just that same sense; but that principle seems obviously absurd to me. An alternative, and more plausible, principle would have it that God's perfect goodness requires him to be a net meaning-maximizer for every individual; there are no "victims of the system" when it comes to meaningfulness. But that too seems on reflection implausible; meaningfulness—even "net," "overall," or "deep" meaningfulness—isn't the only good nor, intuition suggests, is it always the most important one. I therefore don't think it is plausible to think that God would be obliged to prioritize meaningfulness over other goods even were he a value-maximizer for each of us considered individually. And then, finally, I don't think theodical individualism itself is very plausible.

So, in conclusion, even if God is a net contributor to the meaningfulness of all our lives—everyone's life is made, on balance, more meaningful by his existence than it would have been had, *per impossibile*, it been the same and yet he not have existed—God cannot help but detract in one sense from the meaningfulness of all our lives (the modified Sartrean thesis) and he cannot help but contribute more to the meaningfulness of some of our lives than he does to others. As I have been putting it, his existence, even if overall a blessing for all of us, is a mixed blessing for all of us and one that's mixed differently for some of us. Of course we are not left entirely impotent bystanders to all this. We have it in our hands to make ourselves into the sort of people to the meaning of whose lives God can contribute as much as metaphysical necessity allows and we may reasonably hope and pray to avoid bad "meaning luck," as reasonably as we hope and pray to avoid other sorts of bad luck. If there is a God, he wishes that we do just this for ourselves; he knows our hopes; and he hears and answers our prayers. So, in this respect as in many others, the meaning of our lives is dependent on the choices we make.

Hedonistic Happiness and Life's Meaning

Stewart Goetz

1. Introduction

As is the case with just about any topic in philosophy, the meaning of life is a subject about which there is much disagreement. Philosophers cannot even agree about how long the issue has been a matter for consideration. Iddo Landau has entitled one of his recent papers "Why Has the Question of the Meaning of Life Arisen in the Last Two and a Half Centuries?"[1] Yet, according to Susan Wolf, while the question "What is the meaning of life?" was once taken to be a paradigm of philosophical inquiry, it no longer is. She writes that "[i]n philosophy classrooms and academic journals ... the question has nearly disappeared, and when the question is brought up by a naïve student ... or a prospective donor to the cause of a liberal arts education, it is apt to be greeted with uncomfortable embarrassment."[2] So Wolf believes hardly anyone is discussing what Landau thinks philosophers are addressing for the first time in the long history of the discipline.

I am inclined to think that Wolf's position on the historicity of the question is closer to the truth, at least within the domain of analytic philosophy. However, Wolf herself is one of many in analytic circles who in the last thirty or forty years have begun to address once again the meaning of life. And I believe this is for the good. Like her, I am convinced that when people query about life's meaning they are asking something important and intelligible. In her words,

> when people do ask about the meaning of life, they are evidently expressing some concern or other, and it would be disingenuous to

---

[1] Iddo Landau, "Why Has the Question of the Meaning of Life Arisen in the Last Two and A Half Centuries?" *Philosophy Today* 41 (1997): 263–269.
[2] Susan Wolf, "The Meaning of Lives," *Exploring the Meaning of Life: An Anthology and Guide*, ed. Joshua Seachris (Malden, MA: Wiley-Blackwell, 2013), 304.

insist that the rest of us haven't the faintest idea what that is ... Rather than dismiss a question with which many people have been passionately occupied as pure and simple nonsense, it seems more appropriate to try to interpret it and reformulate it in a way that can be more clearly and unambiguously understood. Though there may be many things going on when people ask, "What is the meaning of life?", the most central among them seems to be a search to find a purpose or a point to human existence.[3]

According to Wolf, when people ask about the meaning of life they are most concerned about the idea of a purpose *of* life (to distinguish it from the purposes *in* life for which people perform actions), which is typically concerned with the question of God's existence and the creation of a human person for a purpose.[4] However, the question "What is the meaning *of* life?" can also plausibly be understood to raise other concerns. One that I want to focus on in this chapter, in part because I believe an answer to it provides the most plausible answer to the question about the purpose of life, can be expressed in terms of the following question: "What, if anything, makes life worth living?" I am going to assume that this is a question about what constitutes our well-being or happiness (for my purposes, these are the same) and defend a hedonistic response to it. Derek Parfit has written that "[o]n any plausible theory [of our well-being], hedonism covers at least a large part of the truth ... "[5] In an expansive Parfitian spirit, I think it is plausible to hold that hedonism covers the whole truth about the matter. Like Thaddeus Metz, "I identify [pleasure] with happiness ... "[6] Pleasure is fit to compose the entirety of happiness because it is an experience that is intrinsically good (it is good in and of itself/ it does not derive its goodness from a relationship to anything else).

For the duration of this chapter, I will occasionally refer to the hedonistic view of happiness that I am going to defend as "hedonism," while fully realizing that in the strict sense "hedonism" is the thesis that pleasure, and

---

[3] Ibid., 304–305.
[4] Wolf also writes that she is "inclined to accept the standard view that there is no plausible interpretation of [the purpose of life] question that offers a positive answer in the absence of a fairly specific religious metaphysics." Ibid., 305. And in another paper, she says the following: "[T]he question 'What makes lives meaningful?' is closely related to the question, 'What is the meaning of life?' Even if this latter question is not unintelligible, as the logical positivists thought, its obscurity and its scope are such as to make the risk of finding oneself talking pompous nonsense fairly great." Susan Wolf, "Meaningful Lives in a Meaningless World," *Quaestiones Infinitae* 14 (June 1997): 4. I will conclude this chapter with some brief talk about "religious metaphysics." Hopefully, it is not pompous nonsense. Thanks to Joshua Seachris for pointing me to this additional paper by Wolf.
[5] Derek Parfit, *On What Matters*, Vol. I (Oxford: Oxford University Press, 2011), 40.
[6] Metz, *Meaning in Life*, 78.

pleasure alone, is intrinsically good. One can be a hedonist about happiness without being a hedonist in the strict sense. My goal in this chapter is to defend hedonism against various criticisms. I begin in the next section by briefly explaining how the naturalist ontology of contemporary philosophy is to some degree, if not wholly, anti-hedonist in spirit. Given this ontological framework, it is no mystery why hedonism is opposed by many present-day philosophers. From ontology, I turn in Section 3 to how the idea of hedonistic happiness helps to provide answers to certain objections that the naturalists Julian Baggini and Bernard Williams raise against the concept of immortality (eternal life). But while hedonism helps to provide the resources for a satisfactory conception of immortality, it has been widely rejected on the basis of Robert Nozick's thought experiment about an experience machine. Drawing extensively from an important paper by Matthew Silverstein, I argue that Nozick has failed to make his case against hedonism. In Section 4, I look briefly at three other arguments against a hedonistic understanding of happiness. I conclude that like all of the preceding arguments, they fail in their objective. As a result, hedonism emerges unscathed. Finally, I turn in Section 5 to the topic of how one can integrate hedonism into a theistic account of the purpose of life and Christianity by briefly considering the thought of C. S. Lewis. Lewis believed that pleasure is what makes life worth living and that God created us for the purpose that we experience that pleasure. Hence, he believed the answers to the questions "What, if anything, makes life worth living?" and "What is the purpose of life?" are deeply related.

2. Pleasure and naturalism

Among contemporary professional philosophers, the idea that our wellbeing is wholly constituted by experiences of pleasure is generally unpopular. Nevertheless, as Nicholas White points out, though unpopular, a hedonistic understanding of happiness is "so attractive ... that virtually every philosopher who's not a hedonist has felt obliged to explain why not."[7] It is hard not to believe that at least part of the explanation for the contemporary rejection of hedonism about happiness is the popularity of the philosophical doctrine known as naturalism. The term "naturalism" is not easy to define, even though Barry Stroud points out that "'Naturalism' [is] ... rather like [the term] 'World Peace.' Almost everyone swears allegiance to it," though "once you start specifying concretely exactly what it involves ... it becomes increasingly difficult to reach and to sustain a consistent and

---

[7] Nicholas White, *A Brief History of Happiness* (Oxford: Blackwell, 2006), 54.

exclusive 'naturalism.'"[8] According to Parfit, metaphysical naturalists (for my purposes, naturalists) are those who maintain that all properties and facts must be of the types that the natural sciences can investigate. Thus, he says that irreducible reasons (purposes) to act, because they are normative, are incompatible with naturalism.[9] Many naturalists are well known for holding that when the final explanatory story is told it will exclude ultimate and irreducible teleological explanation of any event in the physical world.[10] This exclusionary spirit of naturalism is often extended to other aspects of our psychological lives. For example, though he is not concerned with naturalism per se, the following comments of Jaegwon Kim about the status of consciousness in contemporary philosophy help provide a broader perspective on what certain kinds of naturalism exclude:

> For most of us, there is no need to belabor the centrality of consciousness to our conception of ourselves as creatures with minds. But I want to point to the ambivalent, almost paradoxical, attitude that philosophers [e.g., naturalists] have displayed toward consciousness ... [C]onsciousness had been virtually banished from the philosophical and scientific scene for much of the last century, and consciousness-bashing still goes on in some quarters, with some reputable philosophers arguing that phenomenal consciousness, or "qualia," is a fiction of bad philosophy. And there are philosophers ... who, while they recognize phenomenal consciousness as something real do not believe that a complete science of human behavior, including cognitive psychology and neuroscience, has a place for consciousness in an explanatory/predictive theory of cognition and behavior ...
>
> Contrast this lowly status of consciousness in science and metaphysics with its lofty standing in moral philosophy and value theory. When philosophers discuss the nature of the intrinsic good, or what is worthy of our desire and volition for its own sake, the most prominently mentioned candidates are things like pleasure, absence of pain, enjoyment, and happiness ... To most of us, a fulfilling life, a life worth living, is one that is rich and full in qualitative consciousness. We would regard life as impoverished and not fully satisfying if it never included experiences

---

[8] Barry Stroud, "The Charm of Naturalism," in *Naturalism in Question*, eds. Mario De Caro and David Macarthur (Cambridge, MA: Harvard University Press, 2004), 22.
[9] Parfit, *On What Matters*, Vol. I, 109.
[10] For example, see David Armstrong, "Naturalism, Materialism, and First Philosophy," *Philosophia* 8 (1978): 261–276; David Papineau, *Philosophical Naturalism* (Oxford: Blackwell, 1993); and Alex Rosenberg, *An Atheist's Guide to Reality: Enjoying Life without Illusions* (New York: W. W. Norton & Company, 2011).

of things like the smell of the sea in a cool morning breeze, the lambent play of sunlight on brilliant autumn foliage, the fragrance of a field of lavender in bloom, and the vibrant, layered soundscape projected by a string quartet ... It is an ironic fact that the felt qualities of conscious experience, perhaps the only things that ultimately matter to us, are often relegated in the rest of philosophy to the status of "secondary qualities," in the shadowy zone between the real and the unreal, or even jettisoned outright as artifacts of confused minds.[11]

Just about any introductory course in the philosophy of mind will include material on the problem of *qualia*: how can something like an experience of pain be reduced to, or given an exhaustive functionalist analysis in terms of,[12] what is nonpsychological and/or nonmental in nature? While the focus of the discussion about *qualia* has largely been on pain, the experience of pleasure (and, thereby, hedonistic happiness) poses essentially the same issues. Hence, Kim believes *qualia* of any kind are the bug-a-boo for any naturalistic exclusionary metaphysic (henceforth, naturalism). I agree, but I think it is important to understand that experiences of pleasure (and pain) pose problems for naturalism not only because they are irreducibly psychological in nature (*qualia* genuinely exist) but also because their reality provides the content for irreducible teleological explanations of a good bit of our bodily behavior. In other words, not infrequently I intend to perform some action *A* for the purpose that I experience pleasure (or avoid pain). But because such explanations are ultimately excluded by naturalism, pleasures (and pains) are explanatorily impotent.

So if we really do have irreducible experiences of pleasure, naturalism must be false. I have argued in other places that there are good reasons to maintain that naturalism is false.[13] In what follows, I am going to assume naturalism's falsity and proceed to examine certain issues surrounding hedonism, including alleged problems for its truth.

---

[11] Jaegwon Kim, *Physicalism, or Something Near Enough* (Princeton, NJ: Princeton University Press, 2005), 10–12.

[12] According to functionalism, a *quale* like pain can be fully analyzed in relational terms such as cause and effect. Thus, a pain is the kind of event that has certain causes (e.g., a punch in the mouth) and produces certain effects (e.g., grimaces, curses). The problem with functionalism is that it leaves out the intrinsic nature of pain, which is what pain feels like. And, obviously, a functionalist analysis of pleasure will leave out the intrinsic nature of pleasure, which is what pleasure feels like.

[13] Stewart Goetz and Charles Taliaferro, *Naturalism* (Grand Rapids, MI: William B. Eerdmans, 2008); and "Making Things Happen: Soul in Action," in *The Soul Hypothesis: Investigations into the Existence of the Soul*, eds. Mark Baker and Stewart Goetz (New York: Continuum, 2011), 99–117.

3. Hedonic happiness and its critics

I begin with theistic hedonism, which is the view that God creates human persons for the purpose that they experience nothing but pleasure, where this purpose is realizable in an individual's unending afterlife (immortality). Some have maintained that the concept of immortality itself is problematic. For example, Julian Baggini formulates this supposed problem as follows:

> [a]n eternal life might turn out to be the most meaningless of all. What would be the point of doing anything today if you could just as easily do it tomorrow? As Albert Camus put it in *The Plague*, "The order of the world is shaped by death." The very fact that one day life will end is what propels us to act at all ... Life must be finite to have meaning, and if finite life can have meaning, then this life can have meaning ... [L]ife's meaning has to be found in the living of life itself, and the promise of eventual death is necessary to make any action worthwhile at all.[14]

Elsewhere, Baggini adds that "[m]oments of pleasure are precious *because* they pass, because we cannot make them last any longer than they do."[15]

I believe hedonism provides the conceptual framework that solves the alleged problem that is posed by Baggini. It is precisely because pleasure is intrinsically good that there is no need for death to make action both possible and worthwhile and to provide life with that which makes it worth living. When it comes to pleasure, its goodness is attractive and provides the reason for our pursuit of it. One desires not to delay the experiences of pleasure precisely because of their intrinsic goodness. There is no need for impending death to motivate one to act to experience them. Moreover, it is because of their intrinsic goodness that moments of pleasure are precious and would be so even if they never passed. Indeed, it is because experiencing pleasure is intrinsically good that one desires that it never end and last forever, which implies that one desires that one never die but live forever.

Like Baggini, Bernard Williams has serious questions about the intelligibility of the idea of immortality.[16] In summarizing and discussing Williams's

---

[14] Julian Baggini, *What's It All About? Philosophy and the Meaning of Life* (Oxford: Oxford University Press, 2004), 54–55.
[15] Ibid., 133.
[16] Bernard Williams, "The Makropulos Case: Reflections on the Tedium of Immortality," in *Problems of the Self*, ed. Bernard Williams (Cambridge: Cambridge University Press, 1973), 82–100.

essay in what follows, I draw heavily from John Martin Fischer's paper "Why Immortality Is Not So Bad."[17]

Williams sets forth two necessary conditions of immortality and its desirability: (1) that the future person be the same as (numerically identical with) the individual concerned, and (2) that the future life of that individual be attractive to him in the sense that his future goals, projects, values, and interests must be suitably related to his present goals, projects, values, and interests. If they are not suitably related, then there is a risk that he will now find it difficult to regard those future goals, projects, values, and interests as sufficiently interesting to support a present desire that he have them as his own in the future.

If we assume we are capable of surviving from this life into the next (e.g., if we assume that we are souls that can survive death), condition (1) is fulfilled. What about condition (2)? Can it be fulfilled? Williams thinks not. With regard to condition (2), Williams poses a dilemma: Either an individual's fundamental desires, interests, purposes, and projects remain the same over time, or they do not. If they do remain the same, then, given that their number is finite, they will eventually be satisfied or fulfilled and boredom will ensue. If they do not remain the same (they change too much), then the individual's future desires, interests, purposes, and projects will not be similar enough to his present desires, interests, purposes, and projects to make him now desire to survive to be the subject of what is so different. The person will simply prefer to go out of existence.

What about the first alternative? Fischer points out that there is a distinction between self-exhausting and repeatable pleasures. A self-exhausting pleasure is one that is associated with an activity, the performance of which terminates any further need to do it again. An example Fischer provides is of an activity that you desire to do just once to prove to yourself that you can do it:

> Imagine ... that you are somewhat afraid of heights, and you have been working hard to overcome this phobia. You form the goal of climbing Mt Whitney just to show yourself that you have overcome the fear—just to show yourself that you can control your life and overcome obstacles. Upon climbing the mountain, you may in fact be very pleased and proud. Indeed, you may be deeply satisfied. But also you may have absolutely no desire to climb Mt Whitney (or any other mountain) again. You have

---

[17] John Martin Fischer, "Why Immortality Is Not So Bad," *International Journal of Philosophical Studies* 2 (1994): 257–270.

accomplished your goal, but there is no impetus toward repeating the relevant activity or the pleasure that issues from it.[18]

But as Fischer also notes, there is another kind of pleasure. There is repeatable pleasure:

> Here an individual may well find the pleasure highly fulfilling and completely satisfying at the moment and yet wish to have more (i.e., to *repeat* the pleasure) at some point in the future (not necessarily immediately). Certain salient sensual pleasures leap immediately to mind: the pleasures of sex, of eating fine meals and drinking fine wines, of listening to beautiful music, of seeing great art, and so forth ... Given the appropriate distribution of such pleasures, it seems that an endless life that included some (but perhaps not only) repeatable pleasures would *not* necessarily be boring or unattractive.[19]

Fischer goes on to point out that religious persons can experience not only repeatable pleasures of the sort just mentioned but also repeatable pleasures that come with the repeatable activities of worship of and thanks to God. Thanking God for the repeatable (and unrepeatable) pleasures that he has granted is itself a source of additional pleasure.

Consider, now, the second alternative, which is that an individual's future goals, projects, values, and interests must be similar enough to his present goals, projects, values, and interests so that they will now be attractive to him. If they are not presently attractive, then he will now fail to find them sufficiently interesting and will not desire to have them as his own in the future. Without such an interest, nonexistence will seem preferable to immortality. In response to this horn of the dilemma, Fischer writes that

> it seems that an individual could value such an [unending] existence if he or she felt that the change in character would result from *certain sorts of sequences* ... Surely in our ordinary, finite lives we envisage certain changes in our values and preferences over time. For example, one may currently value excitement and challenge; thus, one might wish to live in an urban area with many career and avocational opportunities (but with lousy weather and a high crime rate). Still, one might envisage a time in the future when one will be older and will prefer warm weather, serenity and security ... Thus, there are quite ordinary cases

---

[18] Ibid., 262–263.
[19] Ibid., 263–264.

in our finite lives in which we envisage changes in our characters—our values and preferences—and which are not so unattractive as to render death preferable. Why, then, could not the same be true of immortal existence?[20]

What Fischer says is surely correct, but it is important to note that Christian religious persons (and, I will assume, at least some Jews and Muslims) typically expect a significant positive *change or discontinuity* concerning moral character in the heavenly afterlife that will not render unending existence unattractive. Indeed, if such a change did not occur (if immoral activity were not completely eliminated), something would be amiss and perfect happiness would be impossible. However, the main point is this: If it is true, as I am assuming, that what each of us most fundamentally desires is to experience pleasure, then so long as this desire persists, it is not necessary to have a stability of nonmoral interests and purposes whose satisfaction is a source of pleasure. Indeed, the pleasure that satisfies this most fundamental desire might come from what are in terms of the present radically different and even unimaginable interests and purposes. Moreover, contrary to what Williams says, this potential difference between present and future interests and purposes does not pose a problem for desiring the survival of death. This is because, at bottom, what is necessary to make postmortem existence attractive is that one's life be perfectly happy, not that there be continuity between present and future nonmoral interests and purposes.

It is doubtful, then, that Baggini or Williams provides a convincing reason to think that the idea of a perfect hedonistic happiness is unintelligible because of issues arising out of the idea of immortality. However, Robert Nozick has concerns about the concept of hedonistic happiness that are related to immortality and regarded by many as decisive for a rejection of hedonism. Nozick asks us to consider a thought experiment in which there is an experience machine that is capable of providing anyone who connects to it with desired experiences, potentially for eternity. According to hedonism, the desired experience is pleasure.[21] Before connecting, one can program the machine to simulate what one would consider an ideal life consisting of activities that provide only experiences of pleasure. In principle, it makes no difference what the activities are: they could be writing a great novel, playing football, having sex, eating a favorite food, and even reading philosophy.

---

[20] Ibid., 267–268.
[21] Daniel Haybron says that "most philosophers have rejected hedonism and other mental state accounts [of well-being], mainly because of experience machine-type worries." *The Pursuit of Unhappiness: The Elusive Psychology of Well-Being* (New York: Oxford University Press, 2008), 34.

Once connected, one is not actually doing these things. One believes one is, but the belief is false. But no matter: one is experiencing pleasure and that is what is important.

Nozick asks whether we would connect to the machine. He believes we would not, and for three reasons. First, we care about or desire that we genuinely do things. We care about being agents, as opposed to patients. Once connected to the experience machine, one is nothing but a patient. Second, we care about or desire to be persons of a certain kind. This idea is strongly connected with the first reason for connecting to the machine: the actions we care about make us certain kinds of people. Third, we care about or desire to be in contact with a deeper reality than that which is man-made. What we supposedly learn from consideration of the experience machine is that we rightly believe our well-being or happiness consists, at least in part if not in whole, of things other than experiences of pleasure. And this is allegedly made clear by the fact that, when presented with a possible scenario where we experience nothing but pleasure, we seem to desire things other than, and more than, pleasure.

When I consider the experience machine, I respond with "I will connect!" The only hesitation I have arises out of a fear that the machine might malfunction and leave me in a very unhappy condition. Nevertheless, I recognize that many others are reluctant to connect. Thus, if Nozick's argument is mistaken, it should be possible to offer an explanation of why their hesitation to connect to the experience machine does not count against a hedonistic understanding of happiness. In an interesting paper, Matthew Silverstein seeks to provide just such an explanation.[22] He begins by conceding that Nozick's appeal to what we desire as the basis for rejecting hedonism about happiness establishes that we desire more than machine-produced happiness. But what must be established in addition to this is that some strong link exists between what we desire and what makes for our well-being, where this well-being is not pleasure.

So how might this link be established? For starters, Silverstein suggests one might believe the experience machine supports the idea that it is the actual satisfaction or fulfillment of desires that constitutes our happiness (this is a straightforward desire-satisfaction understanding of happiness). But, says Silverstein, the fulfillment of a desire not uncommonly does not make one happier (improve one's well-being). For example, I well remember talking with a friend's spouse many years ago and listening to how she had worked for twenty some years to fulfill her desire to be a partner in a law

---

[22] Matthew Silverstein, "In Defense of Happiness: A Response to the Experience Machine," *Social Theory and Practice* 26 (2000): 279–300.

firm. She related to me how, when she finally satisfied that desire, she was so disappointed. Her family life suffered, relationships at work suffered, and in the end she gave up the partnership and sought a different line of work in law. I'm fairly confident that most of us can tell a similar story about how we had a desire only to discover upon its satisfaction that our happiness suffered.

But maybe there is a way other than fulfillment to connect desire with well-being. Silverstein suggests one might take the connection between desire and happiness to be evidential in nature: what we desire provides us with evidence for what will make us happy. Because one is interested in human well-being, one will need to focus here on desires that are nearly universal to all humans. (Silverstein implicitly excludes desires for food and drink, presumably because the jeopardizing of the fulfillment of these is not typically cited as a concern by those who say they would not connect to the experience machine.) The problem now, says Silverstein, is that our near-universal desires do not provide thoroughly reliable evidence as to what constitutes our well-being. He suggests that we consider wealth. In our culture, wealth often contributes to happiness (yet, if the truth be told, it also often contributes to unhappiness). Yet, there are people around the globe who have well-being without wealth. They might even desire wealth, but because of their situations might not be able to have it. Nevertheless, their well-being does not suffer. Presumably, the same problem will arise for other things for which there are near-universal desires, e.g., music, education, etc.

To further illustrate the inadequacy of the supposed evidential connection between what is nearly universally desired and happiness, Silverstein suggests we consider a thought experiment in which people almost universally desire to smoke for its own sake (which means that people do not smoke for the pleasure that comes from doing so). When the American Cancer Society (or its international equivalent) presents a cure for smoking, all who smoke refuse. On the face of it, we have a near-universal desire whose existence does not present evidence for what constitutes our happiness. Silverstein emphasizes that we cannot object to this example by insisting that it depicts an impossible scenario, namely, one in which there is no ultimate connection between desire satisfaction and pleasure. This objection would amount to a concession of the truth of hedonism.

In the end, if desires do not necessarily establish an evidential connection between what is desired and our well-being and the satisfaction of desires does not always constitute happiness, then the fact that we desire things other than pleasure does not show that there is more to our well-being than hedonic happiness. Perhaps someone can state a connection between desire and well-being that undermines hedonism about happiness and avoids the kinds of problems to which Silverstein draws our attention. However, at this point I will move on and summarize Silverstein's account of how the reluctance expressed by so many not to connect to the experience machine can be reconciled with a hedonist account of happiness.

Silverstein begins by pointing out how the reluctance to connect to the machine can, at least in part, be plausibly explained by concerns about values other than well-being that are confused with it. Here, it is helpful to recall Nozick's first reason for not connecting to the experience machine, which is that we desire to act/do something. But not just any desire to act will suffice to capture Nozick's point. For example, a desire to roll a rock up a hill over and over again without end (the example is inspired by the myth of Sisyphus) or a desire to pick and count blades of grass forever are nonstarters. Therefore, Nozick, with his second explanation for why we would not connect to the experience machine, maintains that we have a desire to be persons of a certain kind. Most plausibly, he has in mind that we desire to be persons with moral character and are reluctant to connect to the experience machine because we are concerned about a loss of moral value. The idea here is that by connecting to the machine one abandons relationships with relatives, friends, political causes, etc., and with one's absence from the lives of these others, one cannot fulfill one's moral obligations to them. Silverstein notes that this is a genuine loss of value, but it is not a loss of the value of one's own happiness. (I will leave aside in what way fulfilling one's moral obligations helps others, though it seems most plausible to think it helps them with their happiness, which would bring us full circle to the issue of what constitutes their happiness.)

At this juncture, the opponent of hedonism might suggest that the example of the experience machine be tweaked so that one is convinced that no one will be worse off when one connects. Perhaps this is because everyone else will also be connected to the machine so that there will be no loss of moral value when one connects because there will be no need to help others. Even with this modification of the experience machine and the guarantee that there is no confusion between moral value and well-being, many individuals will probably still desire not to connect to the machine. Might there, then, be other values that can also be confused with well-being and are relevant for explaining why one does not desire to connect to the machine? What about aesthetic value—the machine is aesthetically displeasing and it is the confusion of this value with well-being that leads certain persons to desire not to connect? After all, the experience machine is just that, a machine, and connecting to it disconnects one from the aesthetics of what is natural. So desiring not to connect to the machine might be based on confusion about aesthetic and prudential value.

Silverstein believes it is plausible to hold that confusions of the kind just mentioned do occur and provide explanations for why some people desire not to connect to the experience machine. Nevertheless, he also thinks it is plausible to hold that they do not explain all cases of reluctance to connect to the machine. Can hedonists about well-being come up with other plausible explanations for why people do not want to connect to the experience machine that are consistent with the truth of hedonism?

Silverstein thinks they can, and in a way that is not only thoroughly consistent with hedonism but also makes clear that we desire certain things only because they lead to hedonic happiness. To this end, he believes we need to keep clear the distinction between those things that are instrumental to hedonistic well-being and that well-being itself. Perhaps the close link between the two leads people to come to desire for their own sake things that reliably lead to pleasure. "Our desires," says Silverstein, "have a tendency to outstrip their [hedonistic]-happiness-based origins; and ironically, it is the fact that certain events are accompanied by experiences of happiness [pleasure] that ultimately propels us to desire things other than happiness."[23] The idea here is as follows: because one derives pleasure from a certain kind of activity, one can come to desire the activity for itself. And when one realizes that performing the activity is impossible when connected to the experience machine, one concludes that it is better not to connect to the machine. A realization that a desire for pleasure has given rise to a desire for the activity itself that produces the pleasure sometimes occurs when one no longer derives pleasure from doing the activity. Up until that time, one simply cannot imagine life without the activity, but when one tires of the activity one realizes that it was really the pleasure from the activity and not the activity itself that one ultimately desired. Athletes sometimes "lose a love for the game." What is going on here is they no longer get pleasure from the game that gave them so much for such a long period of time.

The fact that we can transfer our desire for pleasure to the activity that gives rise to the pleasure and overlook the relationship between them helps bring to light yet one other issue that supports the view that a desire not to connect to the experience machine does not indicate a rejection of a hedonistic conception of well-being. The hedonist John Stuart Mill wrote in his autobiography that "I now thought that this end [happiness] was only to be attained by not making it the direct end. Those only are happy (I thought) who have their minds fixed on some object other than their own happiness ... Aiming thus at something else, they find happiness by the way."[24]

---

[23] Ibid., 294.
[24] John Stuart Mill, *The Autobiography of John Stuart Mill* (New York: Signet Classics, 1964), 112.

What Mill was referring to was what Henry Sidgwick described as the "fundamental paradox of Hedonism, that the impulse towards pleasure, if too predominant, defeats its own aim."[25] Because we understand that a pursuit of happiness often ends up making the experience of that happiness ever more elusive, we end up desiring and pursuing such things as friendship, authenticity (being a certain kind of person), etc., for their own sake and forgetting that these things ultimately become desired only because of their close instrumental connection with pleasure and the self-defeating nature of a direct pursuit of happiness itself. Hence, when one is reluctant to connect to the experience machine because it will, say, cut one off from one's friends, what one overlooks or forgets is that friendship is not really desired as a component of one's well-being but ultimately only because of its instrumental value in relationship to that well-being.

Finally, what about Nozick's third explanation for our desire not to connect to the experience machine, which is that we want to be connected to deeper reality? Julia Annas echoes Nozick's point when she writes that "[p]leasure is too trivial an item in life to be the most important thing in it, or the goal round which life is organized."[26] Two points are relevant in response.

First, we can explain our attachment to reality in the same way that we explained our attachment to friendship: because a connection to reality is for the most part instrumental to pleasure, an offer that includes being cut off from it, whether by the actions of others (e.g., their deception and lies) or by our own choices (e.g., recreational drugs), is rejected.

Second, there is the implication in Nozick's remark that experiences of pleasure are not "deeper" reality. Here, I think we should hearken back to Kim's comments. We live in a philosophical age that is largely naturalistic in character and, therefore, devalues consciousness at the altar of science and materialistic metaphysics. If there is anything that screams out against this contemporary view it is experiences of pleasure (and pain). And if there are levels of reality, there is no good reason to deny pleasure a place at the foundation. It surely seems to belong there. Perhaps this explains why contemporary philosophers like Thomas Nagel and Galen Strawson are taking a serious look at a view like panpsychism,[27] which holds that the fundamental constituents of reality have both psychological and nonpsychological properties.

---

[25] Henry Sidgwick, *The Methods of Ethics*, 7th ed. (New York: Dover Publications), 48.
[26] Julia Annas, *Intelligent Virtue* (Oxford: Oxford University Press, 2011), 132.
[27] Thomas Nagel, *Mortal Questions* (Cambridge: Cambridge University Press, 1979), 181–195; and Galen Strawson, "Realistic Monism: Why Physicalism Entails Panpsychism," in *Consciousness and Its Place in Nature: Does Physicalism Entail Panpsychism?*, ed. Anthony Freeman (Charlottesville, VA: Imprint Academic, 2006), 3–31.

4. Additional challenges to hedonic happiness

In this section, I consider three additional arguments against hedonism. The first comes from Julia Annas, who criticizes hedonism by calling attention to the kind of life we would want our children to lead:

> Suppose I ... want my child to lead a happy life. I will want my child to enjoy her activities and have feelings of pleasure. But could this be what makes her life a happy one? This strikes two wrong notes. I will scarcely think that my wish has been granted if my child lives a life enjoying activities which are ... addictive. And even if an activity is a serious one, something has gone wrong if the person's life is made a happy one not by the activity but by the feeling of enjoyment she gets from it. Any parent would be disconcerted to find that their child had grown up to regard her life as happy because of the enjoyment she got from, say, helping others, but would unhesitatingly drop helping others the minute she ceased to enjoy it.[28]

Of course, no reasonable parent wants his or her child getting pleasure (being happy) from addictive activities. But the problem here is not with the hedonistic concept of happiness but with the likely long-term bad effects of the addictive behavior, which typically will include much pain and suffering for the addict. Addiction purchases short-term happiness at the likely expense of long-term unhappiness. One would find it harder to discourage addictive behavior as a source of happiness, if there were no long-term bad effects that resulted from it.

Would any parent be disconcerted to learn that his or her child had grown up believing that the happiness the child experienced consisted of the pleasure he or she got from helping others? It is hard to understand why this would be a justified reaction. Would a parent be bothered if the child dropped helping others the minute it ceased getting pleasure from doing so? Probably, but again the issue in such a case would not be whether or not the happiness consisted of the experiences of pleasure. Because of the fact that others are being helped through the child's activity, a parent would likely recommend patience and hope that the helping of others once again became pleasurable. If it did not and the parent was a naturalist who believed that one's existence ended permanently at the grave, he or she might reasonably advise the child to cease and desist from the activity. This is not because the

---

[28] Annas, *Intelligent Virtue*, 132–133.

child no longer has a reason to help others. Rather, it is because an argument would be needed to explain to the child why it should sacrifice its happiness for the sake of the happiness of others, where the happiness of the others consisted of their experiences of pleasure. In a naturalistic world, it is not immediately obvious why one should sacrifice one's own happiness for the happiness of others. But this is a large topic and because of constraints of space I must leave it here.

The second argument against hedonism is an epistemic objection to the idea that a person could knowingly experience nothing but pleasure. J. L. Mackie raises this issue in his classic paper "Evil and Omnipotence," which is about the argument from evil against the existence of God. Mackie claims that pleasures and pains are respectively first-order goods and evils and that the free will defense of God's existence fails because God could have created persons such that they always freely choose the good and, thereby, never cause pain.[29] My concern here is not with the reasonableness of Mackie's response to the free will defense but rather with the idea that sentient persons in a world created by an omnibenevolent, omnipotent, and omniscient God would experience nothing but pleasure. Mackie is aware that some will claim that a world of rational beings experiencing nothing but pleasure is metaphysically impossible because good and evil are logical opposites, the existence of one without the other being impossible.

Mackie is convinced that there is no metaphysical problem with persons experiencing nothing but pleasure because good and evil are not logical opposites. But might there be an epistemic problem? If perfect happiness consists of nothing but experiences of pleasure, could a person recognize that he or she is perfectly happy? Here, Mackie hesitates:

> I suggest that it is not really impossible that that everything should be, say, red, [but] that the truth is merely that if everything were red we should not notice redness, and so we should have no word "red"; we observe and give names to qualities only if they have real opposites. If so, the principle that a term must have an opposite would belong only to our language or to our thought, and would not be an ontological principle, and, correspondingly, the rule that good cannot exist without evil would not state a logical necessity.[30]

Mackie is suggesting that if God were to create a world and it was important that its rational inhabitants know that they are happy, then, if they could

---

[29] J. L. Mackie, "Evil and Omnipotence," in *The Problem of Evil*, ed. Marilyn McCord Adams and Robert Merrihew Adams (Oxford: Oxford University Press, 1990), 33.
[30] Ibid., 29–30.

only know of their happiness in contrast with some evil in the world, God would have to allow for a dash of pain here and there, but no more than would be required to make this knowledge possible. But need Mackie concede this epistemological point? Might inhabitants of a world who experience nothing but pleasure know that they are experiencing pleasure and nothing but pleasure? To help us think about this puzzling topic, consider the following discussion of John Williams in his book *Hating Perfection*. According to Williams, we are subtle creatures in the sense that we are able to make comparisons that are always relative. Consider justice. In Williams's view, we could not recognize it without injustice. And the badness of injustice is relative to the situation. It is not an absolute notion. Thus, while sweatshops in Asia are very bad relative to labor standards in most parts of the United States and Europe, they would be judged pretty good if the comparative framework were the labor conditions in Auschwitz. And take the common cold.

> I normally do not feel sorry for myself when I catch cold. I consider the symptoms minor. But if the world had few diseases and almost no discomfort from disease, then, other factors being equal, I would view the "common cold" as a major calamity, and feel sorry that I must suffer its horrible, relentless symptoms. My friends might send me flowers when I catch cold.[31]

However, Williams believes there is one exception to the rule: pain. Because of its intrinsic nature, one knows that one would be better off not experiencing it. And one would know this, even if pain were the only thing that one was experiencing. So one's judgment about its badness is not relative to the situation in which one finds oneself and the comparisons that one can make. As Williams sees it, one could go to hell (conceived of as an eternal existence in which one experiences nothing but pain) and know that one was in hell. Hence, if one were asked if one wanted to connect to an experience machine that provided nothing but unending experiences of pain like those which come with having one's tooth drilled, one would deny the invitation without a second thought.

But, says Williams, things are different with pleasure. One cannot go to heaven because were one to experience nothing but pleasure one would not know that one was in heaven because one would have nothing with which to compare the experiences of pleasure. There is nothing intrinsic about the goodness of pleasure. Hence, there could be no rational grounds for

---

[31] John F. Williams, *Hating Perfection: A Subtle Search for the Best Possible World*, rev. ed. (Amherst, NY: Humanity Books, 2013), 167.

connecting to the experience machine that provided nothing but unending experiences of pleasure that come from one's favorite activity because one would not know that one was experiencing pleasure.

I am not sure how to respond to Williams's argument except to say that I do not find it convincing. If an experience machine that provides an experience of hell of which one is aware as being hellish is a coherent possibility, which it seems to be, I fail to see why Nozick's thought experiment about an experience machine that provides the experience of heaven of which one is aware as being heavenly is not also coherent. Hence, I am inclined to think hedonistic happiness emerges unscathed from this epistemic objection.

I will close by considering one other argument against the idea of perfect happiness as the unending experience of nothing but pleasure. According to Owen Flanagan,

> Happiness is said to have worth in and of itself. Suppose this is true. Would it follow that a life with many happy times in it was worth living? Not necessarily. Properties of parts do not confer the property on the whole. My parts are small, I am large. Happy times, even many of them, might not constitute a worthwhile life. But I am skeptical in any case that a life's meaning could be intrinsic.[32]

So, if happy times are times of experiencing pleasure, Flanagan believes a life of experiencing nothing but pleasure might not be a worthwhile life. His reason for saying this is that the properties of the parts do not confer the property on the whole. At least not necessarily. But a hedonistic conception of happiness need not be grounded on a universal affirmation of the principle that the property of the whole is conferred by the property of the parts. All that need be affirmed is that sometimes the property of the whole is conferred by its parts, and sometimes it is not. It all depends upon what the property is. And in the case of pleasure, a life of nothing but pleasure makes for an overall happy life.

5. C. S. Lewis and hedonic happiness

According to Silverstein, "[h]edonism is an intuitive theory."[33] Thaddeus Metz, who identifies pleasure with happiness, acknowledges that "people who are sane … would invariably want eternal bliss."[34] Elsewhere, I have

---

[32] Owen Flanagan, "What Makes Life Worth Living?" in *The Meaning of Life*, 2nd edn, ed. E. D. Klemke (New York: Oxford University Press, 2000), 199.
[33] Silverstein, "In Defense of Happiness," 290.
[34] Metz, *Meaning in Life*, 127.

defended at length the hedonist view of happiness and argued that it is plausible to think God creates human persons for the purpose that they be perfectly happy.[35] The Christian theist C. S. Lewis believed God is also a hedonist about happiness.[36] He rejected naturalism[37] and maintained that "The characteristic of ... Pleasures is that they are unmistakably real, and therefore, as far as they go, give the man who feels them a touchstone of reality."[38] Therefore, it is no surprise to learn that God, who is at the foundation of all reality, is "a hedonist at heart ... He makes no secret of it ... "[39] Concerning pleasure, Lewis wrote that "the smell of Deity ... hangs about it."[40] Lewis believed that God created each one of us for the purpose that we experience a perfect happiness that consists of nothing but experiences of pleasure. Thus in his book *The Great Divorce* Lewis has one of the ghosts state and ask "I wish I'd never been born ... What are we born for?" In response, another spirit answers, "For infinite happiness."[41] In personal correspondence, Lewis wrote that "God not only understands but *shares* the desire ... for complete and ecstatic happiness. He made me for no other purpose than to enjoy it."[42] But while we are made for the purpose of enjoying perfect happiness, many believe it is a bad thing to yearn for it. Lewis strenuously protested against these persons:

> If there lurks in most modern minds the notion that to desire our own good and earnestly to hope for the enjoyment of it is a bad thing, I submit that this notion ... is no part of the Christian faith. Indeed, if we consider the unblushing promises of reward and the staggering nature of the rewards promised in the Gospels, it would seem that Our Lord finds our desires not too strong, but too weak. We are half-hearted creatures, fooling about with drink and sex and ambition when infinite joy is offered us, like an ignorant child who wants to go on making mud

---

[35] Stewart Goetz, *The Purpose of Life: A Theistic Perspective* (New York: Continuum, 2012).
[36] Stewart Goetz, *A Philosophical Walking Tour with C. S. Lewis: Why It Did Not Include Rome* (New York: Bloomsbury 2015).
[37] C. S. Lewis, *Miracles* (New York: Harper Collins, 2001).
[38] C. S. Lewis, *The Screwtape Letters* (New York: Macmillan, 1961), 58.
[39] Ibid., 101.
[40] C. S. Lewis, *Letters to Malcolm: Chiefly on Prayer* (New York: Harcourt, 1992), 89, 90.
[41] C. S. Lewis, *The Great Divorce* (New York: Harper San Francisco, 2001), 61.
[42] C. S. Lewis, *The Collected Letters of C. S. Lewis: Volume II; Books, Broadcasts, and the War, 1931–1949*, ed. Walter Hooper (New York: HarperSan Francisco, 2004), 123. Julian Baggini writes "the truth [is] that unrelenting happiness is not a natural or even healthy condition for human beings." *What's It All About?*, 104. I'm confident that Lewis would simply laugh at this "truth." Unrelenting happiness is not healthy? Given that Lewis believed the experience of perfect happiness is the purpose for which we are created, he would have responded to Baggini that anything less than the experience of it is unnatural.

pies in a slum because he cannot imagine what is meant by the offer of a holiday at the sea.[43]

Not only is the desire for perfect happiness not bad, but also Lewis believed that the desire for it is itself evidence for the existence of the afterlife:

> [W]e remain conscious of a desire which no natural happiness will satisfy. But is there any reason to suppose that reality offers any satisfaction to it? "Nor does being hungry prove that we have bread." But I think it may be urged that this misses the point. A man's physical hunger does not prove that man will get any bread; he may die of starvation on a raft in the Atlantic. But surely a man's hunger does prove that he comes of a race which repairs its body by eating and inhabits a world where eatable substances exist. In the same way, though I do not believe (I wish I did) that my desire for Paradise proves that I shall enjoy it, I think it a pretty good indication that such a thing exists and that some men will.[44]
>
> If I find in myself a desire which no experience in this world can satisfy, the most probable explanation is that I was made for another world. If none of my earthly pleasures satisfy it, that does not prove that the universe is a fraud. Probably earthly pleasures were never meant to satisfy it, but only to arouse it, to suggest the real thing.[45]

Our ultimate purpose for which we are created is, then, that we be perfectly happy. This implies that being moral is not what life is ultimately about. Indeed, happiness will endure, while morality will pass away:

> All right, Christianity will do you good—a great deal more good than you ever wanted or expected. And the first bit of good it will do you is to hammer into your head ... the fact that what you have hitherto called "good"—all that about "leading a decent life" and "being kind"— isn't quite the magnificent and all-important affair you supposed. It will teach you that in fact you can't be "good" (not for twenty-four hours) on your own moral efforts. And then it will teach you that even if you were, you still wouldn't have achieved the purpose for which you were created. Mere *morality* is not the end of life. You were made for something quite different from that ... The people who keep on asking if they can't lead a decent life without Christ, don't know what life is about; if they did

---

[43] C. S. Lewis, *The Weight of Glory and Other Essays* (New York: Harper Collins, 2001), 26.
[44] Ibid., 32–33.
[45] C. S. Lewis, *Mere Christianity* (New York: Harper San Francisco, 2001), 136–137.

they would know that a "decent life" is mere machinery compared with the thing we men are really made for. Morality is indispensible: but the Divine Life, which gives itself to us and which calls us to be gods, intends for us something in which morality will be swallowed up.⁴⁶

[The moral realm] exists to be transcended ... [It is a] schoolmaster, as St. Paul says, to bring us to Christ. We must expect no more of it than of a schoolmaster; we must allow it no less. I must say my prayers to-day whether I feel devout or not; but that is only as I must learn my grammar if I am ever to read the poets.

But the school-days, please God, are numbered. There is no morality in Heaven. The angels never knew (from within) the meaning of the word *ought*, and the blessed dead have long since gladly forgotten it.⁴⁷

And while Lewis believed that we have libertarian free will, it is doubtful that he would have seen it as a kind of good that in contemporary terminology is worth wanting. It too, like morality, will ultimately be swallowed up by the perfected state of ecstatic happiness. At least free will as it is involved in morality will not survive:

You may ask, do I then think that moral value will have no place in the state of perfection? Well it sounds a dreadful thing to say, but I'm almost inclined to answer No. It [the state of perfection] is never presented in Scripture in terms of service is it?—always in terms of suggesting fruition—a supper, a marriage, a drink. "I will give him the morning star." May not that be one of the divine jokes—to see people like Marcus Aurelius and [Matthew] Arnold & [John Stuart] Mill at last submitting to the fact that they can give up being *good** and start *receiving* good instead.

*I don't mean, of course, "can begin being bad", but that when the *beata necessitas non peccandi* [the blessed necessity of not sinning] is attained, the will—the perilous bridge by [which] we get home—will cease to be the important thing or to exist, as we now know it, at all. The sword will be beaten into a ploughshare. The supreme volition of self-surrender is thus a *good suicide* of will: we will thus once, in order to will no more.⁴⁸

If neither morality nor the free will it presupposes is going to exist in our end state, why do they exist in the first place? Lewis believed the need for freedom of choice arises because of the great good of perfect happiness for which we

---

⁴⁶ C. S. Lewis, *God in the Dock* (Grand Rapids, MI: Eerdmans, 1970), 112.
⁴⁷ Lewis, *Letters to Malcolm*, 115.
⁴⁸ Lewis, *The Collected Letters of C. S. Lewis: Volume II*, 463–464.

are created. To receive that good, we must choose to surrender ourselves in the sense that we must choose to abandon our pursuit of pleasure on our terms. In other words, not only might it be self-defeating to pursue pleasure/happiness directly as Mill and Sidgwick believed, but also it is immoral to choose to reserve the right to pursue it in whatever way one deems appropriate. Thus, Lewis held that morality is essentially a choice between claiming the prerogative to pursue pleasure however one desires and surrendering that claim.

> "[A] crucifixion of the natural self is the passport to everlasting life."[49]
>
> "This is the ultimate law—the seed dies to live, the bread must be cast upon the waters, he that loses his soul will save it."[50]
>
> "God designed the human machine to run on Himself ... That is why it is just no good asking God to make us happy in our own way without bothering about religion."[51]
>
> "[T]he proper good of a creature is to surrender itself to its Creator ... When it does so, it is good and happy."[52]
>
> The moment you have a self at all, there is a possibility of putting yourself first—wanting to be the centre—wanting to be God, in fact ... What Satan put into the heads of our remote ancestors was the idea that they could "be like gods"—be their own masters—invent some sort of happiness for themselves outside God, apart from God. And out of that hopeless attempt has come nearly all that we call human history—money, poverty, ambition, war, prostitution, classes, empires, slavery—the long terrible story of man trying to find something other than God which will make him happy.[53]

Elsewhere, Lewis wrote that a Christian is "one [who] believes that men are going to live forever, [and] that they were created by God and so built that they can find their true and lasting happiness only by being united to God ...."[54] And he believed that being united to God was like being at home: "As Dr Johnson said, 'To be happy at home is the end of all human endeavour.' (1st to be happy, to prepare for being happy in our real Home hereafter: 2nd, in the meantime, to be happy in our houses.)."[55,56]

---

[49] Lewis, *The Weight of Glory*, 172.
[50] C. S. Lewis, *The Problem of Pain* (New York: Harper Collins, 2001), 154.
[51] Lewis, *Mere Christianity*, 50.
[52] Lewis, *The Problem of Pain*, 88.
[53] Lewis, *Mere Christianity*, 49.
[54] Lewis, *God in the Dock*, 109.
[55] C. S. Lewis, *The Collected Letters of C. S. Lewis: Volume III; Narnia, Cambridge, and Joy 1950-1963*, ed. Walter Hooper (New York: Harper San Francisco, 2007), 580.
[56] Thanks to Joshua Seachris for his helpful suggestions.

4

Belief That Life Has Meaning Confirms That Life Has Meaning: A Bayesian Approach

Trent Dougherty

1. Introduction

The purpose of this essay is to set forth in as clear and simple terms as I can the basics of a broadly Bayesian argument for the existence of God (a God who bears the primary metaphysical descriptive features of the Abrahamic God) from a key fact concerning the meaning of life: people so naturally believe life *does* have meaning. The conclusion I will draw is that this fact significantly favors Theism over naturalism. Because this has not been done before, I am merely laying the foundations (broadly, not deeply), so much will remain in merely suggestive form. Some might think I should have considered other data, and they are welcome to publish their own arguments, but I hope, in what follows, to at least illustrate one sensible method for laying out the case for a broad Theism of the sort that underlies Christian Theism from belief that life has meaning. And I think what I do here for data concerning the meaning of life is part of an important research project in extending Bayesian apologetics (I make no apology for that term) from the traditional data concerning the existence, origin, and nature of life on earth to other aspects of human life. There are ever so many features of the world and our lives that are relevant to the case for and against Theism (I would love to see a similar essay written on the theme of the professions: how the existence and practice of law and medicine bear on the issue). I strongly suspect that our brains are keeping track of this anyway, that our reflective credence in Theism is far too low, and that our instinctive credence, typically much higher, is in fact more accurate. But as I say, my main goal in this essay is to lay the foundations for further work by giving an overview of how certain data concerning the meaning of life feature in a Bayesian assessment of the data.

Bayesians come in many stripes, and I'll discuss my methods briefly before setting forth the argument. I wish to cast no aspersions on other versions of Bayesianism by my choice to focus on Bayes factors, and I think my arguments will come out about the same using any of a sizable family of Bayesian methods. The argument is very simple in many ways; this is the beauty of the Bayesian method. If the method is correct, then many issues that seem complex on the surface can be made quite simple (in their structure) and therefore much simpler to evaluate (it cannot of course solve all issues concerning the content, but if we have the structure right, we have won half the battle). My position is that once the primary data are plugged into the appropriate Bayesian filter, it is clear that they support Theism over naturalism. Thus the argument itself will take up very little space (especially since care will be taken to make the method and concepts sufficiently clear). The bulk of the essay will then be in answer to an obviously tempting objection which I will spend some time setting out. But this is how it goes sometimes in philosophy: a very simple argument is given a more complex objection, and one has to circle round that objection to contextualize it in a way that shows it doesn't have the purported import. And so it is in this essay.

Again, there may be ever so many other objections and much more to be said about the ones I do treat. But I only have space here to indicate the general tenor of my reply (though I do think I end up saying most of what will need to be said). The objection is a kind of so-called debunking argument and so the discussion will parallel—in a way I hope is a bit more philosophically transparent—discussions of other debunking arguments. I ask the reader to be careful, however, to guard against assuming that what they have read elsewhere about debunking arguments applies so easily here.

This essay has five parts. First come sections of prolegomena on the method I will apply and the concepts I will employ. Spending time on these will make the argument very easy to present. Next, therefore, the argument will be presented. The final two sections will consist in a statement of the objection and a regrettably lengthy reply. (Alas, nonsense is simpler to state than to clear away.) Here is the outline of this essay:

- Methodology
- Terminology
  - "Meaning"
  - "Theism"
  - "Naturalism"
- The argument from natural belief in meaning
- Objection: belief in meaning in life comes *too* easily

- Reply: the debunking argument is bunk
  - Regimenting the EDA (Evolutionary Debunking Argument): a generic EDA
  - If only they HAAD a better idea: a particular EDA
  - Structural problems for debunkers
- Conclusion

2. Methodology

Many readers will be familiar with Bayes' Theorem (BT), which looks like this in its most common form, where "P(E)" is the "prior probability" of the evidence (some paradoxes lay that way, but they needn't detain us), "Pr(H)" is the prior probability of H (roughly its probability coming into the present line of evidential consideration), and "Pr(H|E)" is "posterior probability" of H, that is, the probability of H taking into account only E in light of your prior information.

$$\Pr(H \mid E) = \frac{\Pr(H \mid E) \times \Pr(H)}{\Pr(H)}$$

What BT is able to do is to tell you the total probability of some hypothesis, H, on a given body of evidence, E. We can also read off of it certain key relations. The probability of H on E varies in direct proportion to the prior probability of H and the "reverse probability" (often called the "likelihood" term) and varies in inverse proportion to the prior probability of E.

Often, what we are really interested in isn't the total probability of a hypothesis (which is hard to figure anyway[1]), but rather which of a pair of alternative hypotheses some given evidence favors. Then, we often use the odds form of BT:

$$\frac{\Pr(H1 \mid E)}{\Pr(H2 \mid E)} = \frac{\Pr(E \mid H1) \times \Pr(H1)}{\Pr(E \mid H2) \times \Pr(H2)}$$

This gives us a ratio of total posterior probabilities between two competing hypotheses. Put in this order of numerator and denominator, if the ratio is "top heavy" then H1 "wins," and if it is "bottom heavy," then H2 "wins." And success is measured by the degree of "lopsidedness" of the ratio. The bigger the proportion is in either direction, the better that is for the hypothesis

---

[1] Though I think Swinburne does it excellently in *The Resurrection of God Incarnate* (Oxford: Clarendon Press, 2003).

on the big side. Pr(E|H1) is the degree to which H1 "predicts" (leads us to expect) E. Likewise for Pr(E|H2). BT tells us that predictive power and simplicity (as I think of the "pure" priors) are the two factors that determine the probability of a hypothesis.

The first term on the right-hand side of the equation is called the "likelihood ratio" and the second term is the ratio of the prior probabilities. Now, there's a lot of controversy about prior probabilities. I've had my say on that,[2] and here I will simply set those controversies aside by focusing on the first term and measuring the weight of evidence in terms of "Bayes factors." Bayes factors are used to assess hypotheses in genetics, ecology, sociology, psychology, and elsewhere.[3] Some confirmation theorists think that the Bayes factors are the only thing that really matters anyway, including many medical researchers. I'm of a different school. I think that the prior probabilities are important. Furthermore, I think consideration of prior probabilities favors Theism very, very much. However, I will set such controversies aside and focus just on the question of which of two relevant hypotheses, broad Theism, T, and naturalism, N (where we understand that roughly as the view that "Nature is all there is or was or ever will be"; more on that later). So in this case, we drop out the final term and look only at the likelihood ratio. Our question here is which hypothesis—Theism or naturalism—is better supported and to what degree—by the prevalence of human belief in meaning in life.[4]

3. Terminology

In this section, I will say a few things about how I will understand three key terms. I will not give definitions, as definitions are almost impossible to get

---

[2] Trent Dougherty and Paul Draper, "The Explanatory Argument from Evil," in *The Blackwell Companion to the Problem of Evil*, ed. J. P. McBrayer and D. Howard-Snyder, (Oxford: Wiley-Blackwell, 2013), 67–82.

[3] http://www.stat.cmu.edu/~kass/papers/bayesfactors.pdf

[4] Some theists—so-called skeptical theists—question whether we can sensibly assign conditional probabilities to such events on Theism (See Michael Bergman, "Skeptical Theism and the Problem of Evil," in *Oxford Handbook to Philosophical Theology*, eds. Thomas Flint and Michael Rea (Oxford: Oxford University Press, 2009), 374–399). I criticize skeptical Theism in a number of places. See Dougherty, "Epistemological Considerations Concerning Skeptical Theism," *Faith and Philosophy* 25:2 (2008): 172–176; Dougherty, "Further Epistemological Considerations Concerning Skeptical Theism," *Faith and Philosophy* 28:3 (2011), 332–340; Dougherty, "Skeptical Theism, Phenomenal Conservatism, and Probability," in *Skeptical Theism: New Essays*, eds. Dougherty and Justin McBrayer (Oxford: Oxford University Press, 2014); and Dougherty and Draper, "The Explanatory Argument from Evil," 67–82. Most atheists, certainly all who advance an argument from evil, are committed to the falsity of skeptical Theism. So I side with such atheists against the skeptical theists.

right. We get along perfectly well without definitions in ordinary life. But we want more precision here than in everyday life (though not a false sense of precision), so I will say some things to try to delimit the scope of what I have in mind. My position is that no remaining vagueness can cause trouble for my argument, and that if the argument works, it works on any reasonable disambiguation of the terms involved.

3.1 "Meaning"

What would it be for one's life to have a meaning? Perhaps there are multiple notions that can sensibly be said to answer to our ordinary discourse about the "meaning of life." But I shall only treat a robust notion that I have always taken to be the essence of such talk. By a life's having a "meaning" I shall understand that life's having a purpose that transcends anything which can be explained by the biological sciences, even in principle, and that is not in the end bound for the scrap heap. That is, one that will go on everlastingly to some good end or other. This is not for one moment to deny that some form of broadly evolutionary process—whether more on the neo-Darwinian side or one involving more saltation—is the proximate cause of all (or at least very nearly all) our biological features (with relevant relations to properties which are emergent from, dependent upon, or realized in biological systems and processes). Biologically evolved living organisms can have purposes either by the biological process *itself* having a purpose or by its *products* having purpose (and if the latter, then, ipso facto, the former).

A thing can have a purpose, in the sense I have in mind, only if it arose from a plan in the right kind of way and has the right kind of destiny. A life has a meaning if it has the right whence and wherefore. Thus, the present notion of a life's having meaning excludes some popular weaker notion of a life's having meaning (great as those things might be as part of a truly meaningful life) as the principle sense of the term. So, for example, people are said to find more meaning in life when they have children than when they do not. I take it the relevant features being attributed to the parents are properties like "satisfaction" and "fulfillment." Parents might be more likely to feel like their efforts in life "amount to something." This is, generally speaking, as it should be, and I don't want to take anything away from it. However, a life in which it *just so happened*, by sheer chance, that child rearing was fulfilling but that was destined for annihilation in the end would still count, on the present notion, as a meaningless life. The folk question "Does life have meaning?" or "What is the meaning of life?" I take to be ambiguous between the strong and weak senses of meaning. Probably the former wording aims somewhat more at the stronger sense and the latter at the weaker.

The "plan" for one's life that follows from life's having meaning in this sense might be very detailed and validate the popular phrase "everything happens for a reason," or it might include no more than that the individual was a part of a larger plan such that no individual part of their life has any particular plan.[5] So someone counts as believing life has a meaning, roughly, when they believe that their life has some kind of purpose in the minimal sense that their life is the result of agency rather than chance.[6]

3.2 "Theism"

By "theism" I shall understand the view that there is a being capable of knowing[7] and acting and exercising these capacities in a way limited by logic alone. The unlimited capacity to know I will call "omniscience," and the unlimited ability to act I will call "omnipotence." I assume that only weakness of mind could keep a being from being motivated to bring about good states of affairs and only weakness of will could keep a being from acting on this motivation. Thus, I take it that an omnipotent and omniscient being is also, ipso facto, omnibenevolent: it is internally motivated to bring about good states of affairs in proportion to their goodness and always acts to promote goodness.[8]

This derived property of omnibenevolence generates the predictive power of Theism. To the extent that a state of affairs is good, to that extent it is unsurprising[9] given Theism. There are ever so many kinds of good states of

---

[5] See Peter van Inwagen, "The Place of Chance in a world sustained by God," in *God, Knowledge, and Mystery: Essays in Philosophical Theology*, ed. Peter van Inwagen (Ithaca, NY: Cornell University Press, 1995) for a rather minimalist account.

[6] People's beliefs are messy. They are messy in lots of ways. Three ways are that they are vague, they change a lot over time, and people don't always explicitly believe what their beliefs entail. Thus my primary datum is infected with some vagueness as well. At the center of the target is belief that one's life is the result of some kind of cosmic plan. This clearly entails the existence of supernatural agents. To one side of the bulls-eye is belief that life has a purpose without the believer realizing this entailment. To the right of the target is full-blown belief that a particular divine being, such as the Abrahamic God, has created one with a purpose. My position is that confirmation theory can handle somewhat vague data quite easily. But since the latter two theses logically entail the first, I am happy to select that as my official datum if forced to do so. Thanks to the editors for pressing me to clarify this.

[7] Whether the right cognitive capacity actually involves knowledge is unimportant. What's important to me is the ability of this being to have a credence for every proposition that exactly matches its objective probability (and, indeed to know the conditional probability of any given proposition relative to any other). I speak in the old fashioned way for ease of exposition.

[8] This does not necessarily imply any maximizing motive, for the standard reasons that promote satisficing.

[9] At the level of generality we are working with, the distinction between the unsurprising and the probable can safely be ignored. It is unsurprising that a professor drinks coffee.

affairs. Some of them are incompatible (and some may be incommensurable), so sometimes an arbitrary choice will have to be made. But, in general, Theism predicts good states of affairs: it is not morally neutral. This is why the existence of bad states of affairs for which there is no known greater good to justify them would be a problem for Theism. And the existence of unjustified bad states of affairs would refute Theism.

People disagree about what is good and what is bad. Given this understanding of Theism, a person should assign a low probability to a state of affairs given Theism only when *they* think that state of affairs is intrinsically bad.

3.3 "Naturalism"

By "naturalism" I shall understand roughly the opposite of Theism. As Plantinga tends to put it, it is approximately the view that, "There's no God or any such person like God." It entails that there are no supernatural powers responsible for the origin or destiny of the universe. It entails that there are no supernatural powers interested in promoting good and avoiding evil. Naturalism is morally neutral, in that it is a form of "hypothesis of indifference," that is, the universe is indifferent to our suffering or joy and all moral properties. It thus makes no predictions concerning a state of affairs based on its value.

4. The argument from natural belief in meaning

It has long been part of theology that we are programmed for religious belief. Solomon says, "You have placed eternity in our hearts," and Augustine says, "Our hearts are restless until we rest in thee." Hugh of St. Victor discussed the "*occulis contemplationes.*" Even Calvin believed in a "*sensus divinitatis.*" A natural interpretation is that God manipulated the process in such a way that we ended up with a natural predilection for belief in him, or at least in the supernatural, to aid us in coming to believe in him without forcing us or drawing too specific conclusions for us. In line with this tradition, I want to suggest that the following datum significantly confirms Theism.

> Belief that life has meaning comes very naturally to humans.

I doubt that it will be doubted that this is a datum. In fact, many naturalists will think it comes *too* easily, but we will treat that objection below. Of

There are ever so many kinds of coffees. We may not be able to predict which exact one she drinks, but it will remain unsurprising that she drinks coffee. The choice between coffees will often be, despite what aficionados claim, arbitrary.

course, "very naturally" is vague, but the greater the proportion, the stronger the evidence, so that can be adjusted on a sliding scale accordingly as one finds the empirical evidence. That most of the world's inhabitants have subscribed to some kind of pretty serious religion is evidence that the belief that life has meaning is very widespread across times and cultures. Some religions don't clearly include doctrines that entail that life has an ultimate meaning. I take most forms of Buddhism to *not* include (and probably exclude) doctrines that imply life has a purpose in the robust sense I have in mind, for, doctrinally anyway, Buddhism is atheistic or at least makes no use of the idea of a creator who could make the world for a purpose. I can't make any sense (at all) out of the notion of an impersonal force giving life purpose. But even Buddhism, which might be a borderline case, is such that most of its actual adherents hold to belief in a personal God (how they square that with the documents of Buddhism I don't know, but I am assured by people in the know that this is common knowledge). And lots of people who are in that doleful category "spiritual but not religious" also believe that "everything happens for a reason." So there are also lots of people on the outskirts of the primary datum that can serve as partial witnesses to the datum.

Two recent books that discuss the empirical evidence for the ease with which humans attribute the relevant kind of cosmic agency are Justin Barrett's *Why Would Anyone Believe in God?* and more recently, *Born Believers*, and C. Stephen Evans's *Natural Signs and Knowledge of God*.[10] There are many details that must be glossed over here, but in the end it seems sufficiently clear that belief that life has an origin and destiny in some kind of cosmic plan is quite widespread, perhaps very widespread (perhaps near universal).

Here is the relevant question for our purposes: is this fact more to be expected assuming naturalism is true or assuming Theism is true? Well, there are all kinds of reasons why a supernatural being would want to "rig" the system to promote belief in life having a purpose. If there is a God of anything like the sort Christian Theism posits, then we could sensibly expect God to want people to believe life has a meaning because he would want them to believe *truly* and would want them to seek out the particulars of life's meaning and to live accordingly. It would be somewhat surprising if there were a God who gave life meaning and most people didn't believe life had meaning (under normal circumstances: materialist ideology of the Communist state is not a normal circumstance). It would be at least somewhat surprising if God

---

[10] Justin Barrett, *Why Would Anyone Believe in God?* (New York: AltaMira Press, 2004); *Born Believers* (New York: Free Press, 2012); C. Stephen Evans, *Natural Signs and Knowledge of God: A New Look at Theistic Arguments* (Oxford: Oxford University Press, 2012).

didn't embed belief in cosmic purpose in our psychology. Let's represent this by saying that Pr(D1|T) = 0.6.

Now what about naturalism? There is here no particular reason at all to expect fairly widespread belief in cosmic purpose. I will deal below with just so stories from the so-called cognitive science of religion, but there is nothing in naturalism that leads us to expect that this kind of belief will be favored in any way. Whatever evolutionary role it plays, if it plays any at all, which is dubious, might have been played by any of a score of other behaviors. It would be a kind of fluke if this kind of widespread belief in a purposeful universe and the supernatural agent required for it were to arise without any kind of nudge. It would be something on the order of shocking that it should occur. That would give it a probability of 1/1000 at most and perhaps much, much lower, like 10^{-6} or 10^{-9}. A "lottery" with odds of 10^{-4} would only pay about $5000 on a $1 ticket, which isn't very impressive. A respectably impressive lottery will have odds of winning at least as low as 10^{-7}. I am inclined to think the odds are not this high, so perhaps we should use a middling figure like the unimpressive lottery. Then we get the following Bayes factor

$$\frac{\Pr(D1 \mid T)}{\Pr(D1 \mid N)} = \frac{0.6}{10^{-4}} = 6000$$

Now according to the standardly accepted scale of evidential weight, this counts as "off the charts." It is *massive* confirmation. Yet the figures are conservative. I've stated the reasons for the values, and I stand by them. However, suppose I'm just way off. Suppose D1 is only *half* as to be expected on T as I have said, and, suppose further, it is *twice* as likely on N as I have said. That still delivers a Bayes factor of 1500 for T over N, still totally off the charts. In order to get the Bayes factor down onto the high end of the charts we have to say that my initial figures were off by *an order of magnitude* in both directions. That is, that D1 is a *tenth* as likely as I estimated on T—that, somehow, it is justified to be nearly certain that God wouldn't do this—and that it is *ten times* more likely on N than I estimated. I simply see no way of escaping that D1 favors T over N very, very strongly.

5. Objection: Belief in meaning in life comes *too* easily

I claimed in the positive phase of this essay that the fact that belief that our lives have ultimate meaning comes so naturally to us counts significantly in favor of Theism over naturalism. Part of this belief, as I have defined my terms, includes belief—implicit or explicit—in some kind of deity or higher power. The content is left quite vague, for the data are vague. Billions of people believe that life derives meaning from the plan of the Abrahamic God, but perhaps nearly as many have a much more vague picture of how their lives fit into an overarching and earth-transcending plan by some higher power. The relationship between belief in meaning and belief in a higher power has some slippage and there are varying degrees of explicitness and detail in people's minds connecting transcendence with the transcendent, and at times below I will use the phrase "the meaning stance" to refer to the general phenomenon under discussion.

The kind of objection I wish to treat is one that is likely to arise pretty spontaneously in many readers' minds. In every forum in which I have ever presented the ideas at the core of this essay, the first objection that has come up has been some kind of evolutionary debunking argument. The idea, at a first approximation, is that the meaning stance is fully explicable as the product of naturalistic evolution. I'll begin with an informal characterization of this objection in the form of an "evolutionary debunking argument," broadly construed.[11] We'll see that it is not at all clear there is anything to this kind of objection. Indeed, it is not even clear that it is of the right *form* to count as an objection to my argument. Nevertheless, because of the ubiquity of this response, I feel it needs to be thoroughly vetted. Therefore, I'll give a somewhat more formal characterization of the objection. This will reveal more pointedly the failure of an EDA-based rebuttal to my argument. Below, I'll raise doubts about there being any hope for any forthcoming EDA-based or EDA-type objection to my argument. As I indicted above, the slogan for this objection is that the belief that life has meaning (which usually comes as a result of believing it to have been the result of some transcendent agent) comes easily all right, all *too* easily. Following, I give an informal presentation of the evolutionary debunking argument reply to my argument.

The debunking reply to the kinds of argument I've put forth is, in a way, very natural. However, the "naturalness" is of a defective sort: it is all too common. The regularity with which such "explaining away" arguments are used—and, unfortunately, accepted—gives them an air of credibility. This is especially so since they have a lofty (in a way) intellectual heritage starting at least with Freud. They are closely related to the "you only believe that because ..." arguments, which C. S. Lewis called "bulverism."[12]

They also have some plausibility, as Lewis illustrates in the early chapters of *Miracles*, because in the strong cases—when the origin of the belief, process,

---

[11] Standard examples of such an argument are S. Street, "A Darwinian Dilemma for Realist Theories of Value," *Philosophical Studies* 127 (2006): 109–166; Richard Joyce, *The Evolution of Morality* (Cambridge, MA: MIT Press, 2006).

[12] See C. S. Lewis, *Undeceptions: Essays on Theology and Ethics* (London: Bles, 1971), 225. For a more recent treatment, see Roger White, "You Just Believe That Because ...," *Philosophical Perspectives* 24 (2010): 573–615.

or disposition is stated, assumed, established, or stipulated to be solely, mostly, or largely the product of a process not aimed at truth-tracking—they work effectively at establishing that the belief or behavior doesn't track truth (a behavior tracks truth when, essentially, the proposition that makes intelligible the behavior is likely to be true).

As Lewis points out, debunking arguments almost always go both ways. None of us wants to be judged by a higher power. We all wish we could, in the end, not have to give an account of our actions in this life. So atheism is definitely a belief that would be an instance of wishful thinking. It is a kind of Oedipus complex writ large: wanting to kill off Father God in order to ravish Mother Nature, whether as part of the capitalist-industrial complex or as a squishy kind of vague nature adoration. This kind of back-and-forth is going nowhere. So for the debunking argument to defeat the Bayesian argument, we'll have to regiment it into a stronger format.

A better (i.e., stronger, I'm not claiming it's more accurate, only more charitable) interpretation of debunking arguments than "you only believe that because" is the "you'd believe that anyway" argument. That is, the debunker says, "Even if there were no meaning in life or no evidence for meaning in life, you'd still believe it." This does avoid one kind of ad hominem fallacy, but it still has the Bulveristic vice of addressing the *person* rather than the *argument* and so remains a version of the ad hominem fallacy, even if of a less egregious variety. I've made no claims about why anyone believes anything. I've made claims about certain evidence confirming a certain hypothesis. So this version of debunking is a dead end here. But there is a version worthy of consideration in the neighborhood: You'd have that same *evidence* even if it were misleading. In this case, the data are the observations that describe the meaning stance. In the next section, we will look at two precisifications of this argument—one general and one specific—in a bit of detail to see clearly where they go wrong.

6. Reply: The debunking argument is bunk

This section targets two specific forms of the objection vaguely described in the previous section. Both versions are found to be complete failures.

6.1 Regimenting the EDA: A generic EDA

A prime example of a debunking argument (which must ultimately be an evolutionary argument whether understood strictly or broadly) is related to Marx's statement that "religion is the opiate of the people." If we take the idea to be that people need religion as a crutch to survive and approach it from a naturalistic evolutionary standpoint, then we get something like the following. The basic assumption is that the process of natural selection is not aimed at truth. It is aimed at getting the right body parts in the right place at the right time to ensure propagation of the genome. So our first premise will be this.

1. Natural selection pressures are not aimed at truth.

Given that natural selection is not aimed at truth, it would be quite an astounding coincidence if anything it produced tracked the truth. Another basic assumption is that no such astounding coincidence has occurred. This cannot, of course, be ruled out with complete certainty, but it is a very reasonable assumption. So that gives us the second premise of the argument.

2. If natural selection pressures are not aimed at truth, then any noetic system which is the result of natural selection pressures will be unlikely to reliably track truth (objective features of mind-independent reality).

From these two premises we get the following lemma:

3. Any noetic system that is the result of natural selection pressures will be unlikely to reliably track truth (objective features of mind-independent reality).

The naturalist naturally assumes that every feature we have that isn't by pure chance is the result of natural selection (which has an environmental nonchance factor). From this it follows that the mental system which produces religious belief is the result of natural selection. That gives us the final premise.

4. The noetic system that produces the tendency to take the meaning stance is the result of natural selection pressures.

Putting all these premises together, we get this debunking argument against religious belief.

Evolutionary Debunking Argument against the Meaning Stance

1. Natural selection pressures are not aimed at truth.
2. If natural selection pressures are not aimed at truth, then any noetic system which is the result of natural selection pressures will be unlikely to reliably track truth (objective features of mind-independent reality).
3. Any noetic system which is the result of natural selection pressures will be unlikely to reliably track truth (objective features of mind-independent reality). From 1 and 2
4. The noetic system that produces the tendency to adopt the meaning stance is the result of natural selection pressures.

5. The noetic system that produces the tendency to adopt the meaning stance is unlikely to reliably track truth (objective features of mind-independent reality). From 3 and 4
6. If the noetic system that produces the tendency to take the meaning stance is unlikely to reliably track truth, then the behaviors which constitute that stance are unlikely to track truth (where that means, to be a bit more precise, it is not the case that observation of those behaviors raises the probability of the propositions that make intelligible those behaviors—in the sense of "completing" them—much above .5).
7. Therefore, the behaviors which constitute that stance are unlikely to track truth. From 5 and 6

This regimented argument appears much better than the off-the-cuff version, but it is of no value against the theist.

First, premise 4 has a strong and weak interpretation. The strong interpretation would prove too much, and land its advocate in complete skepticism. That is, if we take "our noetic system" in the broadest sense as "our minds" then it applies to the system that produces religious belief, because it applies to the system that produces *all* belief, but the advocate falls prey to a strong version of "Darwin's Doubt."[13]

So we could just reproduce a version of the argument above but replace "the tendency to adopt the meaning stance" with "the system that produces *all* belief." Then, if the argument is successful, the conclusion at #5 would then read "The noetic system that produces *all our beliefs* is unlikely to reliably track truth." And if *that* is true, then the naturalist has just undercut every belief she holds, including the premises of her argument.

On a narrow enough reading of "our noetic system" to make Premise 4 plausible, Premise 3 becomes implausible. For if the system that produces religious beliefs is just the system that performs (tacit) inductive inferences, then the naturalist would have to show that religious belief is not the result of (tacit) inductive inferences. There is good reason to believe that religious belief *is* such, though.[14] Evans argues[15] that nature is full of "natural signs"

---

[13] See James Beilby, *Naturalism Defeated? Essays on Plantinga's Evolutionary Argument against Naturalism* (Ithaca, NY: Cornell University Press, 2002); Richard Taylor, *Metaphysics* (Saddle River, NJ: Prentice Hall, 1991); Lewis, *Miracles*: chapters 3 & 5; William Hasker, *The Emergent Self* (Ithaca, NY: Cornell University Press, 2001); and Victor Reppert, *C. S. Lewis's Dangerous Idea: In Defense of the Argument from Reason* (Downer's Grove, IL: IVP Academic, 2003).

[14] See Evans, *Natural Signs and Knowledge of God*.

[15] Evans's book is one way to fill out the point I made here: http://prosblogion.ektopos.com/2009/07/31/that_the_eviden/

of God (in a way connected to the work of Scottish philosopher Thomas Reid). These signs are "natural" in that one doesn't even have to think about them explicitly for the mind to draw the natural conclusion. Philosophers can come along and think about these things explicitly and construct models which attempt to state subconscious reasoning processes in the form of regimented arguments. To dispute this picture is to move away from debunking and explaining away and to engage in the first-order question of what is true, but the debunking argument was supposed to save the skeptic the trouble of actually engaging the arguments.

Even if we define natural selection so that it is not aimed at truth, it can still *be* aimed at truth. That is, God can *aim it* at truth. A gun is not intrinsically aimed at any target, but it can *be* aimed at a target. God can aim natural selection at truth in a number of ways. He could introduce some nonrandom mutations or manipulate the environment. So either Premise 1 would have to be modified to say that natural selection pressures are neither intrinsically aimed at truth nor ever "rigged" for truth in any case or Premise 4 would have to be modified to say that the system which produces religious belief is *wholly* the result of natural selection. But of course it is consistent with all the empirical evidence regarding natural selection that both these premises are false. Furthermore, none of the empirical evidence provides support for these metaphysics-laden versions of the premises.

Some would-be evolutionary debunkers of religion actually make a stronger claim. They claim not just that there exist plausible evolutionary explanations of how religious beliefs and practices are brought about (that's still too strong a phrase) by evolutionary mechanisms, but rather go on to make the stronger claim that such beliefs and practices are *expected* given evolutionary theory. In a recent and particularly egregious example,[16] the author claims that evolutionary psychology "predicts the occurrence of" religious beliefs (and all that he says seems to apply equally well to the belief that life has meaning) and appears to take "predicts" very strongly indeed. In an example,[17] the author actually assigns the likelihood of religious belief (which entails belief that life has a meaning) on naturalism the value 0.99. He rates this *higher* than the probability that people would believe in God if there were a God (you read that right)! One is initially tempted to think that this is a typographical error or used only as an example, but his example doesn't seem to work the way he seems to want it to work without that being close to the number he actually wants. So on his account, your confidence that creatures will evolve

---

[16] J. Bublia, *The Evolution of Religion: Studies, Theories, & Critiques* (Santa Margherita, CA: Collins Foundation Press, 2008), 237.
[17] Ibid., 228.

the disposition to believe in God should go *down* if you discover there is a God. Something has gone terribly wrong in the world of the so-called cognitive science of religion. In the next section, we will look at an initially better version of a specific theory, though it will come to nothing as well.

6.2 If only they HAAD a better idea: A particular EDA

Finally, we will look at one relevant version of a debunking argument that seeks to undermine the rationality of the main belief that underwrites belief in meaning. Recently, there have been both data suggesting that belief in some kind of deity agent comes naturally to humans,[18] and arguments that this actually *undercuts* the rationality of religious belief in a manner similar to the evolutionary debunking argument in moral theory.[19] Part of the latter argument notes all the many ways in which children *over* ascribe agency (to, say, balls with faces and such). On the basis of this alleged tendency to over ascribe, some people who practice what they call the "cognitive science of religion" have postulated a "Hyper Active Agency Detector" (HAAD) in humans. It is called "hyper active" due to this alleged tendency to over ascribe agency. Because it chalks up lots of things to agency that aren't really due to agency, say proponents of this argument, the HAAD is unreliable. The argument against belief in an agent behind life goes something like this.

1. HAAD is the basis for belief in a supernatural agency.
2. HAAD is unreliable.
3. The basis for belief in a supernatural agency is unreliable.
4. If the basis for belief in supernatural agency is unreliable, then religious belief is unreliable, and so religious belief is not rational.

This is not an argument to be proud of. However, it is hard to see how foes of the rationality of belief in supernatural agents of the sort included in or presupposed by the belief that life has meaning could improve it in any substantive way.

If Premise 1 is read as

1a. HAAD is the *sole* basis for belief in supernatural agency

---

[18] See Barrett, *Why Would Anyone Believe in God?* and *Born Believers*.
[19] See Jesse Bering, *The Belief Instinct: The Psychology of Souls, Destiny, and the Meaning of Life* (London: Brealing Publishing, 2010); and Pascal Boyer, *Religion Explained: The Evolutionary Origins of Religious Thought* (New York: Basic Books, 2002).

then it is surely false. For there are all kinds of bases for people's belief in supernatural agency: religious experience from the sublime to the mundane, common sense natural theology,[20] explicit natural theology (Aquinas is not without his fans these days), testimony, and more.

And even whether Premise 2 is true depends on just how we slice HAAD. Suppose it is the reason we first came to believe our parents and pets were agents. Either it continues to be the reason for such beliefs or else reasons for those beliefs are taken over by other mechanisms and thought patterns. If the former, then it doesn't seem unreliable at all, for I take it that the *vast* majority of agent ascriptions I make are accurate. And if the latter, then the same mechanisms and thought patterns may support belief in a transcendent agent. At least the foe of reasonable belief in transcendent agents would need to show that that isn't so in order to make a positive case for the irrationality of religious belief. Until such arguments are forthcoming, HAAD-based considerations seem poorly situated to challenge the rationality of this key component or presupposition of belief in life's transcendent meaning. (I suppose you could say I *dare* people who identify with the cognitive science of religion to show how their empirical results can be parlayed into a better philosophical argument than I have put forth here.)[21]

A related point is worth noting here. It is easy for the sensational failures of HAAD (speaking for the moment as if I believe in such a critter) to create a spotlight effect, biasing observers toward exaggerating the failure rate. (It's far more interesting and entertaining to point out errors—and the more extravagant the better—than boring old accuracy.) But the more important fact about its extravagant failures is the way that they don't stand up to the test of time. Agency ascriptions to balls, dolls, and shadows in the halls tend to fall away quite easily. Belief in supernatural agents tends to be amazingly durable. So if the relevant reference class is agency ascriptions that stand the test of time, then it seems that supernatural agency belief is in very good company. And if *that* is the case, then we have the makings of a bit more confirmation of Theism here. For is the existence of a cognitive mechanism that predisposes people toward belief in a supernatural agent more surprising on a form of supernaturalism or on naturalism? Well, the answer is obvious. It's not the least bit surprising on supernaturalism, yet it is quite surprising on naturalism. Therefore, not only is there a failed "judo" move here against

---

[20] See Evans, *Natural Signs and Knowledge of God*.
[21] In several long conversations with Jesse Bering—whom I personally got along with swimmingly—at the 2012 St. Thomas Summer Seminar, I was never able to see even a glimmer of hope for an argument against the rationality of belief in a transcendent agent in the neighborhood.

the argument I've set forth, all it does is provide a more concrete form of the original argument. Thanks, guys!

Objection: But in many cases, such as in most aboriginal cases, HAAD has led to belief in forms of supernatural agents that are inconsistent with that implied by the Abrahamic faiths. Isn't it surprising that that God would implant a device that would lead to such skewed belief? Reply: I see no very good reason to think this is surprising, for it is sensible to assume that God would want to predispose people to supernatural belief without forcing them to a specific form of belief. Nevertheless, if it is mildly surprising on Theism, it is much more surprising on naturalism, and that is what is relevant for determining the evidential balancing between competing hypotheses.

6.3 Structural problems for debunkers

What the debunker needs to do to undercut the Bayesian argument for God from the data I've considered is to show that some relevant set of facts probabilistically "screen off" my data. More formally, they need to provide a set S of facts that satisfy this formula, where 'D' is the datum concerning the ease with which humans form belief in life having meaning:

$$\Pr(T \mid D) > \Pr(T) \text{ but } \sim \left(\Pr(T \mid D \,\&\, S) > \Pr(T)\right)$$

When such a condition holds, then, in light of S, D is at best irrelevant to T (it could be negatively relevant).

For example, take the hypothesis R that a table is red. Let the evidential datum L be that it looks red. Clearly enough in ordinary background conditions $\Pr(R|L) > \Pr(R)$. So L counts as an epistemic reason to believe R. But now suppose we learn G that there are red gels on the lights in the room. It's not the case that $\Pr(\sim R|G) > \Pr(\sim R)$, so G doesn't count *against* R. However, it does appear to "neutralize" the evidential force of L for R. That is, it seems that $\Pr(R|L\&G) = \Pr(R)$.[22]

So what the debunker needs is some relevant set of facts S that "neutralizes" D's confirmation of T. That is, some S in the light of which D no longer supports T. This is going to be very hard to do, for consider how we came to the conclusion that D supported T. It followed from our general theory of how *any* proposition comes to confirm T. This, in turn, followed from how we defined T. Our definition of T (plus one metaethical lemma) entailed that

---

[22] Technically, plausibly, the discovery of red gels would give you evidence someone wanted the table to look red even though it wasn't, so it would give you some evidence that it was not red. We'll ignore this epicycle, and related ones, here.

God would know the value of every state of affairs (from omniscience), have an inclination to bring about any state of affairs in proportion to its goodness (from motivationism), and never suffer from akrasia (or anything like it) in this tendency (from omnipotence). There might be many-way ties for goodness and there may be incommensurability issues, but it will make any good *kind* of state of affairs unsurprising[23] on Theism. Thus, states of affairs are probable on Theism just in case they are good ends or good means to good ends. To put it more narratively, events are more probable insofar as they fit into a story we'd expect God to want to tell in the language of actuality. Such a story is one in which lots of things happen from lots of kinds of goodness. One feature of a good story is coherence. Does it fit with the character of God that he would see to it that we had a concept of purpose? Indeed, it does. Would a lack of a sense of purpose seem to be out of step with the story we'd expect God to unfold? Yes, it would. So such things are what we expect in a world such as ours (i.e., with the beings our background evidence tells us there are: intellectual apes).

So given that this is the way in which we came to the conclusion that Theism predicts the meaning of life data—and thus their observation confirms Theism—it's hard to see how debunking arguments could even get off the ground. Given the *wholly* theological and metaethical explanation, no psychology, sociology, or other soft science seems to have anything relevant to say.

7. Conclusion

Given the particular form of Theism considered and the particular kind of belief in meaning considered, it is clear that using the Bayes factor method, generically religiously oriented behavior very strongly favors Theism. Previously, it had been argued by certain naturalists that this fact actually undercut the rationality of religious belief. These arguments fail utterly. Belief that life has meaning is but one of a large number of behaviors that make more sense given Theism than naturalism, so the prospects for a cumulative case for Theism expand rapidly (and I have suggested that people have been tacitly gaining credence from these facts all along). Given that the probability of life's having meaning skyrockets if Theism is true, the widespread belief that life has meaning itself provides evidence that that belief is true.

---

[23] I here gloss over trivial nuances relating surprise to probability. It is a fun topic, but need not be gone into here.

5

Can the Demands of the Perfection Thesis be Trivialized?

Nicholas Waghorn

1. Introduction

Some philosophers believe that the reason Theism seems to offer peculiarly effective resources for answering the question of life's meaning is that our standards for what could be a satisfactory answer to this question are too high. Indeed, some have claimed that the main motivation for being attracted to theistic accounts of life's meaning is that our standards demand no less than perfection, that we feel that "meaning in one's life requires engaging with a maximally conceivable value" or superlative condition, in the words of Thaddeus Metz.[1] Following Metz, we can call this the "perfection thesis." One of his examples, which I shall take up, is the view that meaning in life is a matter of gaining an unsurpassable reward to enjoy upon having achieved moral purity. This is clearly close to a theistic notion of heaven; dropping, for simplicity's sake, the moral criterion, we might say that the meaning of life on this account is to attain the beatific vision, or enter heaven in the afterlife, where these bestow upon us perfect happiness.

I think that the perfection thesis is plausible, understood in a certain way. I would not want to say that the pursuit (or attainment) of nonsuperlative conditions would fail to bestow any meaning on our lives at all; I think it would give us a certain amount of partial meaning. But I do not think that our lives, orientated in such a way, would be *ultimately* meaningful. It seems to me that, if I isolate something the attainment of which will endow my life with some meaning, I will, *all other things considered*, want to attain that object to its maximal extent, however we cash that out. To the extent that I fail to attain that object, the meaning of my life will be vitiated. Nearly everyone agrees that there are some additions to a life that will make it more

[1] Metz, *Meaning in Life*, 120.

meaningful, and in the absence of these it will become less meaningful. All I want to say is that, all things considered, for a life to be ultimately meaningful, it will have to attain those things maximally. Of course this "all things considered" clause covers a great deal. It may be that a life that attains one object maximally is nevertheless less meaningful than a life that attains two different objects to a great extent but not maximally. It may be that maximal attainment of a given object is incompatible with attaining other meaning-bestowing objects. But I want to lay aside such concerns.

While I am laying aside concerns in this rather carefree manner, I would also paraliptically note that the plausible (to me, at least) suggestion that if the attainment of an object bestows meaning on our lives, then for our lives to have ultimate meaning we must attain that object maximally, has been subjected to criticism in the literature. The fullest and most recent development of this criticism can be found in Metz, but also of interest are Trisel and Baier.[2] Metz for his part seeks to show how life can be meaningful even if we adopt a standard for attaining meaning-giving objects that falls short of perfection. Strictly speaking, I might not disagree with this; as I say, I think life can have some meaning if it meets such a standard, even though it is ultimately meaningless.[3] In any event, evaluation of the aforementioned critiques of the perfection thesis is necessary, but I will not attempt it here; I have another criticism in my sights.

Let us turn to that criticism by way of an examination of where the theistic proponent of the perfection thesis goes from here. If the perfection thesis is adopted, and ultimate meaning is seen as something that is important to attain (and I think it should be seen as such), the theist is liable to claim that only Theism, or, more broadly, a theistic worldview, has the resources that make it plausible that we can meet the perfection thesis' standards. These resources include a benevolent, omnipotent being, the identification of each of us with an immortal soul, and so forth. It is not clear to me that Theism does have resources to discharge this duty; its resources may be more suited to increasing the amount of meaning in our lives than allowing us to attain ultimate meaning. Nevertheless, some are interested in linking Theism and

[2] Cf. Metz, *Meaning in Life*, chapter 8, and Thaddeus Metz, "Imperfection as Sufficient for a Meaningful Life: How Much is Enough?," in *New Waves in Philosophy of Religion*, eds. Yujin Nagasawa and Erik Wielenberg (New York: Palgrave Macmillan, 2009), 192–214, Brooke Alan Trisel, "Futility and the Meaning of Life Debate," *Sorites* 14 (2002): 70–84 and 'Human Extinction and the Value of Our Efforts', *Philosophical Forum* 35, no. 3 (2004): 371–391, and Kurt Baier, 'The Meaning of Life', in *The Meaning of Life*, ed. E. D. Klemke (Oxford: Oxford University Press, 1981), 81–117.

[3] This, of course, assumes that the distinction between ultimate and partial meaning makes sense. It may not. I discuss this distinction in Nicholas Waghorn, *Nothingness and the Meaning of Life* (London: Bloomsbury, 2014), chapter 7.

the perfection thesis, and I find the perfection thesis plausible and wish to support it. Specifically the criticism from which I want to defend it is that the demands of the perfection thesis can be trivialized. That is, rather than having maximally high standards that we desire to meet, and requiring that a benevolent, omnipotent being step in to help us meet them, we alter our desires, and hence those standards become much less difficult to meet. So, to return to our concrete example of the attempt to attain perfect happiness, which the theist will claim can only be attained by entering heaven, the alternative may be to alter our desires to desire precisely the state we are currently in; in this way we will have already attained perfect happiness. I will elaborate on how specifically this alternative could be effected toward the end of this chapter. For now, it suffices to note that such an alternative is only a live one if we believe that desires can be dropped or adopted at will. This does not appear to be a widely held view among philosophers, although its rejection is perhaps more assumed than argued for; most extended treatments seem to be from philosophers arguing for the view in question. Very little has been said on the topic of dropping desires at will, the discussion focusing more on whether we can adopt desires at will. For my purposes here, I simply assume that, if it can be established that we can adopt desires at will, it has likewise been established that we can drop them at will.

In what follows, I would like to elaborate some concerns that I have about this view and whether it can provide a way to trivialize the demands of the perfection thesis. The thought will be that, if desires can be adopted or dropped at will, then we can easily guarantee the satisfaction of all our desires at will, and so attaining a perfect existence will be a trivial matter. There will be no need to appeal to Theism or any other specific metaphysics in order to meet the demands of the perfection thesis. However, I will suggest that there is some evidence that we cannot desire at will directly, and little evidence that we can; moreover, the claim that we can desire at will indirectly, while more plausible, may commit us to specific views about the nature of practical reason that are not universally shared. Even if we do adopt the view that we can desire at will indirectly, I will outline some reasons to believe that the contingency of the match between our desires and the state of the world means that trivializing the demands of the perfection thesis in this way will be a matter that is ultimately out of our control.

2. The case against desiring at will

Let us begin with a positive case for the position that we cannot desire at will. That most philosophers, and, indeed, most ordinary people, assume that we cannot adopt/drop desires at will is striking. Whether we can will to adopt or drop desires would seem to be an empirical fact about our psychology. If this is so, and if we agree that we should be able to observe such an empirical fact about ourselves were it the case, the general consensus that we cannot desire at will seems to be some prima facie evidence for the truth of that position. Two further observations support this.

First, it is surprising to note that, if we can change our desires at will, we do not appear to do it more often. Often we are tormented due to having desires that we cannot satisfy, or by not desiring what we think we should. If we can assuage this suffering by altering our desires by an act of will, why do we not do so? If I am not looking forward to the long commute I have tomorrow, why not just adopt the desire for it?[4] Proponents of desiring at will often point to the fact that, though we may be able to will some desires, it does not follow that we always can do this—just as one does not succeed every time in other things one wills.[5] But at least with the objects of these analogies, such as willing (and failing) to turn a pirouette, or willing (and failing) to concentrate on work, we understand the mechanism by which such failures happen. Unless proponents of desiring at will are able to elaborate on the mechanism by which we fail to desire at will, then *why* we fail or succeed to desire when we will to do so will be left crucially unexplained.

Secondly, we have the well-known observation of Revd. Francis Hutcheson that, if we could desire at will "we could be bribed into any Affection whatsoever toward any Object";[6] that is, we could sell our desires to the highest bidder. But, in fact, there is no market for desires—we all know this would be impossible. So why think we can desire at will? This argument has been responded to in depth by Yonatan Shemmer.[7] His first claim is that "[m]arkets for desires exist all over the place," citing marriages, the workplace, and the army as examples of situations in which people acquire love or hatred. As it stands, this point seems insufficiently supported; Shemmer does not provide any reason to suggest that these desires are (i) acquired in pursuit of recompense, (ii) acquired at will. Certainly it does not seem to me that any of the situations he cites are most plausibly construed even partially as markets for desires.

---

[4] Cf. Elijah Millgram, *Practical Induction* (Cambridge, MA: Harvard University Press, 1997), 14.
[5] Cf. Gilbert Harman, "Practical Reasoning," *The Review of Metaphysics* 29, no. 3 (1976): 461, Yonatan Shemmer, "Desiring at Will and Humeanism in Practical Reason," *Philosophical Studies: An International Journal for Philosophy in the Analytic Tradition* 119, no. 3 (2004): 285.
[6] Revd. Francis Hutcheson, *An Inquiry into the Original of our Ideas of Beauty and Virtue; in Two Treatises. II. Concerning Moral Good and Evil* (London, 1726), Section 2.
[7] Shemmer, "Desiring at Will and Humeanism in Practical Reason," 279–281.

Shemmer himself agrees that his response is not dispositive against Hutcheson's observation; he notes that, even if we agree such markets exist, this does not show that the desires are acquired at will *directly*. That is, in such cases we are only putting ourselves intentionally in the way of acquiring the desires, as it were, which we may or may not then acquire involuntarily.[8] But he thinks that the existence of such indirect processes of acquiring desires neither entails that there are *no* direct processes, nor that there is no explanatory work for these direct processes to do. Why not?

Shemmer believes that the claim that no desire acquisition is direct is grounded in the superior explanatory power of the indirect processes of such acquisition, but, given that the mechanisms that are operative in both processes are equally unknown to us and equally likely to be simple or scientific, the superiority of the latter's explanatory power is illusory. But I do not think Hutcheson's objection relies on the mechanisms underlying indirect processes of desire acquisition being simpler than those of direct desire acquisition. The claim was that if we had the ability to directly will desires, we would expect to have a market for them. In the face of the claim that we do have such markets, the response was that these involve indirect desire acquisition, which everyone admits occurs. Now, the fact that indirect desire acquisition exists does not prove that in these markets such acquisition is the only one operative. But it is the simpler, and thus preferred, explanation insofar as we need not postulate a whole new process of desire acquisition to explain those markets. Moreover it is suspicious, to say the least, that the only cases of markets in which direct desire acquisition might be operative are cases in which indirect desire acquisition is also possible. Why are there no cases of markets for desires in which the acquisition is clearly direct?

As for Shemmer's claim that indirect processes cannot by themselves account for the acquisition of desires, this is based on the observation that putting ourselves in the way of acquiring a desire does not always lead to us acquiring the relevant desire. Shemmer thinks the relevant difference consists in the fact that in the case in which we do acquire the desire we decide to have that desire. Thus he says: "It therefore seems that without the direct effect of our decision the indirect means for acquiring desires would be inert."[9] But, even if we accept Shemmer's diagnosis (and I am not sure we should—after all, even when we add the decision to have the desire we nevertheless sometimes fail to acquire the desire, and sometimes we can "accidentally" acquire

---

[8] It is this interpretation that I think we should give of two of Harman's examples of desiring at will (Harman, "Practical Reasoning," 459), which Shemmer also adduces as evidence that we do so. I will consider another way of looking at Harman's examples below.
[9] Shemmer, "Desiring at Will and Humeanism in Practical Reason," 281.

the desire by inadvertently putting ourselves in its way without deciding to have it, so it does not seem to be the decision that makes the difference), all this shows is that the indirect means of acquiring desires has a decision that has some direct effect as a part of it. But that does not make an indirect means of acquiring desires into a direct means of acquiring desires. Nor does it show that there is a direct means of acquiring desires.

Having defended Hutcheson's observation and added some others, I believe that there is a fair amount of prima facie evidence in favor of the view that we cannot desire at will. But now we must turn to the positive case for the belief that we can. If, overall, that view is better supported, it will overwhelm the aforementioned evidence.

3. The case for desiring at will

Gilbert Harman offers two reasons to believe that we can adopt new intrinsic desires at will. Firstly Harman claims that, given that we sometimes hold people responsible for their attitude toward what they are doing, we must be supposing those attitudes to be under their control. Not everyone is convinced that we cannot hold someone responsible for a situation if that person has no control over that situation. But I do not want to base an objection on such a controversial view as that. It seems more promising to object that Harman's argument is merely descriptive: it may be true that, as a matter of fact, we do sometimes hold people responsible for their attitudes, and that, if we do that, it follows that we must also suppose that their attitude is under their control (although perhaps the issue does not occur to most of us). But why believe that we are rational to hold people so responsible? In our day-to-day dealings with others, we may take up stances which, on reflection, are in conflict with other beliefs we hold. But that observation in itself does not tell us whether we should get rid of those beliefs on the one hand or stop taking up those stances on the other. Perhaps the moral of Harman's argument is that, on reflection, given that we know people cannot desire at will, we should not hold them responsible for their attitudes. I think we tend to be much more wedded to the idea that desires cannot be willed than to the idea that we can rationally hold people responsible for their attitudes. To see this, take Harman's example of our blaming someone playing Monopoly with us for not being interested in winning, for not having the right attitude. I can imagine my doing this to someone. I can also imagine their response: "Well, I'm sorry—I can't *make* myself interested! I just don't like Monopoly that much." My reply might show what is really bothering me: "You could at least *pretend* to be interested. You know how much games night means to me!" My response would show that

I agree that my opponent cannot desire at will; what is really bothering me (justifiably or not) is the lack of respect for my feelings he or she displays. There is a difference between taking an interest and being interested (I can take an interest in the state of a friend's gout, asking questions and making soothing noises, while remaining thoroughly *un*interested throughout[10]), and I am blaming my opponent for failing with regard to the former, which is subject to the will. I think that when Harman talks about holding people responsible for their "attitudes" the most plausible construal is that we are blaming them for something like not taking an interest.

Harman thinks his second reason for believing that we can will some of our desires is more important. If we can acquire new desires via an act of will, then we can explain our acquisition of dispositions to have new desires in terms of habit formation; repeated such acts of will are what lead us to acquire such dispositions. Harman's claim is that, without our ability to will desires, we must postulate some "new ad hoc mechanism" to account for new desires and dispositions, where this will add unwanted theoretical complexity. This argument appears to lack dialectical force. If I have prima facie reason to believe that desires are not (sometimes) subject to our will, considerations of theoretical simplicity are unlikely to move me to reject that belief. It may be a virtue to posit as few mechanisms as possible, but it is necessary to posit enough to explain all the data I believe there to be. For this reason, it seems unfair for Harman to call the postulation of such an additional mechanism "ad hoc." If we believe desires to be acquired involuntarily then the positing of a mechanism to explain this is not added into our theory of mind in an unmotivated fashion in an attempt to save that theory from refutation. Rather, such a mechanism just needs to be part of an adequate theory insofar as a measure of its adequacy is that it explains all the data. In any case, Harman's argument is weakened by the recent proposal of a number of other mechanisms of desire acquisition in the literature which do not rely on desires being adopted at will.[11] There is insufficient space to discuss these various proposals here, but, if any of them should account for desire acquisition without being committed to any view equally or more controversial than that we can desire at will, Harman's point will be ineffective.

---

[10] Some may prefer to think of this as faking an interest rather than taking an interest. If these are distinguished by the latter's involving genuine interest on one's part, then taking an interest will be just as irrational to require another to will as being interested. This does not tell against the reconstructed conversation I have just given.

[11] Cf. the references to proposals from Michael Smith and from Timothy Schroeder in Timothy Schroeder, "Desire," Section 3.2, *The Stanford Encyclopedia of Philosophy* (Spring 2014 Edition), ed. Edward N. Zalta. http://plato.stanford.edu/archives/spr2014/entries/desire/.

Steven Luper has argued that we have a limited ability to adopt and drop desires voluntarily, although in the interests of fairness I should note that he seems less interested in giving conclusive reasons to accept that view, instead wanting to assume that it is correct in order to see what consequences it may have. He believes that our ability is limited insofar as we cannot drop or add desires by brute force of will. Moreover, there are some desires, such as fondness for gastronomic pleasures or the desire to avoid pain that we cannot control, no matter how much we may want to do so. So what does Luper have to say in favor of our changing our desires? He makes three points. Firstly, he notes that some desires are less deeply rooted than, say, the desire to avoid pain. With regard to such desires, we can "coax ourselves into dropping or adding desires by thinking about the merits of their objects."[12] Luper gives the example of his desire for a cat; he can, he claims, easily abandon this desire by discovering that he is, say, violently allergic to fur. There are a few things to say about this point. One thing is that this does not seem to be a case of *voluntarily* abandoning a belief. For, although one can will whether or not to investigate whether one is allergic to fur, it is not within one's power to decide whether one is or is not so allergic (hence Luper's use of the word "discover"). But it is the discovery that one is allergic that leads to the dropping of the desire, not the investigation of the matter. Hence the dropping of the desire is not voluntary. Moreover, I do not think that if I wanted to get a cat, but turned out to be allergic, that I would cease to desire the cat. I might still desire to get a cat, but have a stronger desire to avoid unpleasant allergic reactions, and just have to live with the sadness of not being able to fulfill the former, still present, desire. Or maybe my discovery of the allergy would not rid me of my desire to get a cat, but instead refine it to a desire to get a hypoallergenic cat or a desire to get both a cat and a wonder cure for my allergy.

Secondly, Luper notes that motivations such as aggression are "malleable and unspecific."[13] For example, we can decide to channel our aggression into violence, or a rigorous form of self-denial, or a fervent attempt to better humanity in some way. The malleability of our drives means that they do little to decide our life plan. I take Luper's point here to be that, although we cannot get rid of the desires imposed on us by certain drives, we can decide how our attempt to meet these desires manifests itself, for example, by violence or by self-denial, etc. But I do not see how this establishes that we can desire at will. The idea may be that, although the fundamental motivation provides us with certain general desires, we can select at will the more

---

[12] Steven Luper, *Invulnerability: On Securing Happiness* (Chicago and La Salle, IL: Open Court, 1996), 55.
[13] Luper, *Invulnerability*, 55.

specific desires that are the manifestation of this motivation. But, even if the general desires a motivation provides us with are manifested in a range of more specific desires, a subset of which are present in any individual who has that motivation, this does not mean that the presence of any specific subset in a given individual is a result of an act of will on that individual's part. This needs arguing for, but the considerations adduced here do not seem to get us any nearer to such a conclusion.[14]

Even if we do accept this second point, though, I do not think it can be used successfully to criticize the perfection thesis. Luper compares fundamental motivations with parents who tell their children to go out and do the best they can, without giving any specific advice on what the children should do—and the problem here is that, whatever desire we do choose, we are still beholden to do the "best we can," as per the perfection thesis.

Finally, and most persuasively, Luper suggests that we might modify our desires by artificial means—say, by the chemical or surgical manipulation of our brains. In discussing this point, I want to turn to some arguments made by Elijah Millgram and examine them at length.

4. Millgram on desiring at will and at pill

In his *Practical Induction*, Millgram argues against desiring at will as well as "desiring at pill," that is, acquiring desires via chemical manipulation such as taking a desire-producing pill. He thinks that our inability to do so is a necessary fact, and wants to use this fact to show that a certain view of practical reason, instrumentalism, is mistaken—instrumentalism being, roughly, the idea that desires are reason-giving in their own right, rather than mere indicators of facts about the world that are reason-giving. Put very abstractly, his argument is that instrumentalism requires that we be able to desire at will (at least sometimes), but we cannot desire at will, therefore instrumentalism is false—there is more for practical reason to do than the instrumentalist thinks. I shall bracket the question of the truth of instrumentalism for now and look at how Millgram supports the claim that we cannot desire at will. Firstly, Millgram helpfully distinguishes between willing desires directly, on

---

[14] Elijah Millgram, "Practical Reasoning: The Current State of Play," in *Varieties of Practical Reasoning*, ed. Elijah Millgram (Cambridge, MA: MIT Press, 2001), 10–11 discusses various forms of "specificationism" about practical reasoning by which we further specify our indefinite ends. But he contrasts this view (largely) with instrumentalism, and, if we accept this contrast, by accepting specificationism we will find ourselves without recourse to instrumentalism to rebut Millgram's own argument against desiring at will (discussed below).

the one hand, where the paradigm of willing directly would be a case where I, say, will my leg to move and my leg then moves as a result of my so willing, and on the other hand willing desires indirectly, whereby I will the use of indirect means, such as a pill or hypnotic suggestion, to attain a desire. Analogizing with belief, Millgram holds that we can only desire at will using indirect means if we "cannot take it that one has acquired and is maintaining [the desire] in a way that one takes to provide no reason to hold it."[15]

The case against desiring at will is supported by some examples. As Millgram wants to claim that our inability to desire at will (in most cases) is a necessary fact, he recognizes that he cannot just give examples of cases where we attempt to directly desire at will and fail. This would only establish a de facto inability, perhaps contingently bequeathed to us by our evolutionary past. Millgram must go further, and give examples that indicate that there exist restrictions on our ability to desire at will by indirect means, such as desiring at pill. One such example runs as follows. I want to become a car salesman, but I know that I will only be able to convince my customers to buy the cars (and so get the job) if I too possess a genuine desire for the various fripperies the cars come with (such as a rotating bonnet ornament). So I take a pill that makes me desire such things. Unfortunately I lose the job due to a recession, and then, a few weeks later, am offered a car with all the fripperies, with the latter coming at a much reduced price. I can afford the car with all the extras, if I really want them (and I do, having taken a pill to give me a very strong desire). Should I put down the money for it?

While thinking this, Millgram suggests, I may remember that I only desire the fripperies because I took a pill, which I did solely to get the job—previously I had thought they were a waste of money. Given that the money I would pay is considerable, not a sum to be thrown away, surely I would think it insane to act on my pill-given desire and so decline the offer of the car? As true attribution of desires involves inferential commitments in practical reasoning that attend those desires, the pill can be seen not to have induced desires in me after all, as I do not have those commitments. This case can be seen to be susceptible to Millgram's diagnosis that, as I become aware that I do not have a reason to possess this desire, I cannot maintain it. That is, my desires must involve "backward-directed inferential commitments"[16] to the effect that they were acquired/maintained in ways that support the inferences made from them in the future—there must be adequate reasons for acquiring and maintaining my desires. Were this not the case, Millgram claims, agents

---

[15] Millgram, *Practical Induction*, 15. Millgram is actually talking about beliefs here, but is drawing an analogy with desires.
[16] Ibid., 27.

would, for all practical purposes, acquire and lose desires randomly leading to a disintegration of agency: "planning, projects, and continuity would all be rendered impossible."[17] As these necessary backward-directed commitments are "a matter of the origin and reasonableness of the psychological states from which [our] inferences are going to proceed"[18] there must be more to practical reason than simply means-end reasoning, and thus instrumentalism is false.

If the argument above is correct, Luper's suggestion that we might use chemical or neurosurgical manipulation of our desires, desiring at will by indirect means, will not work—at least not unless we meet the restrictions imposed on it by Millgram's theory. It also provides a further argument against desiring at will directly. But is it correct? I will not consider criticism that purports to show that, *pace* Millgram, instrumentalism can accept that we are unable to desire at will, as such an acceptance will not cause problems for the perfection thesis. The most extended critical discussions of Millgram's argument that purport to rebut his claim that we cannot desire at will, directly or indirectly, have come from Sydney Shoemaker and Yonatan Shemmer.

Let us look at an objection from Shoemaker first. Shoemaker offers an example of his own: someone who does not like broccoli, but wants to in order to reap the health benefits, takes a pill which produces the desire to eat broccoli, the belief that it will taste good, and which will make broccoli actually taste good to him.[19] Such a pill does not seem conceptually impossible. Moreover, were one to take it and acquire the taste for broccoli, it does not seem that the realization that one's liking for it was merely due to having taken a pill to produce this effect would cause one to cease having a taste for and desiring broccoli. Millgram recognizes that, given that many of our desires are supported by our tastes, the ability to alter our tastes at pill would give us considerable control over our desires by indirect means.[20] His own response to it is delicate. He claims that certain tastes can lead us to the practical observation that a given object is desirable, this being indicated by our deriving pleasure from it, but the judgment consequent on that observation still involves backward-directed commitments. If these commitments are not met, the judgment will be discredited—such as when one realizes that the

---

[17] Ibid.
[18] Ibid., 26.
[19] Sydney Shoemaker, "Desiring at Will (and at Pill): A Reply to Millgram," in *Preferences*, ed. Christoph Fehige and Ulla Wessels (Berlin: Walter de Gruyter, 1998), 27.
[20] Millgram, *Practical Induction*, 32. Note that Shoemaker believes that there are still desires that cannot be altered, either at will or at pill; this is, to his mind, because the impossibility of desiring at pill is a consequent of the impossibility of believing at pill or because it would require a change in the subject's system of values that is not possible (Shoemaker, "Desiring at Will (and at Pill)," 28–29).

pleasure in the depth of a rock song's lyrics is an artifact of the drugs consumed while listening to it. Nevertheless (as Millgram admits), it is hard to see what backward-directed commitments we have in the case of our taste for, say, broccoli. Our lack of reaction to realizing that our taste for it was endowed on us by a pill indicates this. However, Millgram wonders whether such pill-induced desires are as stable as they appear, asking rhetorically what we would think of a pill that made one prefer, say, a box of supermarket red to a bottle of Châteauneuf-du-Pape 1998. But the question is, presumably, not what we would think of the pill, whether we would think it bad or good, but rather, whether we think the realization that we had taken the pill would cause our taste for the economy wine to be replaced by a taste for the good stuff. I do not think that it would. Millgram asks how stable the effects of the pill would be "on someone who bothers to notice their food?"[21] Now, I have a taste for cheap commercial chocolate over the 85% cocoa luxury bars. Moreover, my taste is impervious to my recognition that I prefer what is widely thought to be a less high-quality product (I assume that this is what Millgram means by "noticing one's food")—the fact that a gourmet might say that I have an unrefined palate does not worry me. So, again, I do not see that such recognition would change my tastes if they had come about via a pill (unless, perhaps, the idea is that satisfying my desire for good chocolate will give me greater subjective satisfaction than satisfying my desire for bad chocolate). But, even if one does not share my intuitions, and thinks that such recognition would alter one's desire, there are still cases in which realization of the etiology of a pill-induced desire would not matter, such as Millgram's own example of preferring chocolate to vanilla ice cream, or a switch from liking broccoli over cabbage to making cabbage the preferred option. While I do not think Millgram would be overly worried by such an example,[22] the ability to select desires under such conditions may still provide a problem for the perfection thesis.

Millgram's second line of response to Shoemaker's argument is to remind us of his view that, if we are able to induce desires at pill in this way, and desires like this purport to have no backward-directed commitments, the pill user's unity of agency will be fractured. Suppose I took a pill which induced in me an extremely strong desire for cheap chocolate, such that my life became devoted to the eating of it in the same way that a drug-user's might be devoted to their narcotic of choice, with predictably disastrous results. If such a desire is insensitive to those results, I am liable to regard my behavior driven by it as compulsive, and myself *qua* agent alienated from it. I have two concerns about this response. It will not work against someone who is

[21] Millgram, *Practical Induction*, 133.
[22] For reasons he gives at Millgram, *Practical Induction*, 31.

prepared to just bite the bullet and say that they are not worried about their agency being fragmented in this way. In addition, it may be that I would not find my behavior compulsive, but would rather judge myself to be striving sensibly for that which I find most worthwhile, unhindered by comparative trivialities.

Unfortunately, even if we set aside these concerns, this second response will be of little help to the perfection thesis for several reasons. Firstly, Millgram, in giving this response, seems not so much interested in rejecting desiring at pill per se, but rather in attempting to show that, even if it is possible to desire at pill, considerations of the unity of agency will mean that our ability to use pills to induce such desires will presuppose his specific theory of practical reason.[23] But that conclusion is no comfort to the proponent of the perfection thesis who is worried about the possibility of desiring at pill. Secondly, Millgram concedes that "a few such tastes can perhaps be accommodated." Thirdly, the proponent of the perfection thesis is liable not to be too interested in maintaining unity of agency, insofar as the perfect state envisaged as one's final end will leave no room for agency, unified or not.[24] Moreover, in my own earlier discussion I stipulated out the possibility of conflicting desires which might lead to a fragmenting of agency in order to sideline problems for the perfection thesis based on such conflict,[25] but such a stipulation also means that unity of agency will be easy to come by.

Shemmer also disagrees with Shoemaker, for a different reason. As I read him he thinks that, if we alter our desires by altering our tastes, this does not show that we can desire at will or at pill. Rather we are altering the states of the world that our desires track (i.e., whether *x* tastes good or not), which carry our desires involuntarily along with them. If this is correct, this disqualifies Shoemaker's objection as indicating a way of trivializing the perfection thesis by desiring at will/pill. However, this is cold comfort for the perfection thesis: it still allows there to be a way of trivializing it by "internal" self-directed means, rather than external world-directed means.

Let us now turn to Shemmer's own criticism of Millgram's argument against desiring at will or at pill.[26] Shemmer is skeptical of the moral drawn from the car salesman thought experiment. His own instrumentalist assessment is

---

[23] This, I take it, is the intent of Millgram, *Practical Induction*, 134, footnote 43 and his claim that "pills of this kind are not a way of *replacing* practical observation and practical induction" [emphasis added], Millgram, *Practical Induction*, 133.

[24] Of course, if we claim the destruction of (the unity of) agency leads to a destruction of self, there will be room here to argue that this idea of ultimate meaning precludes *me* from attaining it.

[25] Cf. Waghorn, *Nothingness and the Meaning of Life*, 182.

[26] Cf. Yonatan Shemmer, "Instrumentalism and Desiring at Will," *Canadian Journal of Philosophy* 35, no. 2 (2005): 269–288.

that the scenario is insufficiently detailed; for us to decide whether the pill-induced mental states give us reason to act on them, we must know whether they are desires. If they are not, then no doubt one will not act on them, but this does not show that desiring at pill is impossible—rather, it shows that the pill did not do what it was supposed to do, that is, induce *desires*. If they are, then it is perfectly rational to act on those desires, and realization of how we acquired them will not render them ineffective in moving us to act on them.

Now it may be true that, prepill, the salesman did not desire the fripperies, and so would be irrational to try to obtain them. But, Shemmer asks, what has that fact got to do with his postpill desire? Now that he has the desire, he *does* have a reason to obtain the fripperies; just the same reason that anyone who happened to come by that desire in a "normal" way would have. Moreover, if one antecedently believes, with the instrumentalist, that the etiology of the desire need not negate the reason-giving nature of desires (as the instrumentalist conceives them), then realization that the desires were induced at pill for reasons which are no longer present (employment) will not mean it is irrational to act on those desires.

How should we assess Shemmer's response? It seems to me that whether we accept Shemmer's reading of the thought experiment or Millgram's will depend on our prior beliefs about whether instrumentalism is true or false. If we accept the instrumentalist view that desires can give us reasons for action by themselves, then we will favor Shemmer's, if we think of desires as merely indicating that certain states of affairs are desirable and thus rational to pursue, we will be drawn to Millgram's. Millgram's original aim was (roughly) to show that, because desiring at will/pill is absurd, instrumentalism is false. Shemmer's reply is to say that, because instrumentalism is true, it is possible to desire at will/pill—having accepted instrumentalism, we will understand desires in such a way that there is no absurdity in attaining them at will/pill. Now, it may be that how we react to Millgram's thought experiment will give us some indication of how intuitive we find instrumentalism or its denial. But Shemmer's response to Millgram at least tells us this much: in order to defend desiring at will/pill, we must sign up to instrumentalism, so the former carries a certain theoretical cost.

It seems to me that Shemmer's view also requires us to say that our taste for, say, a given food, that is, whether the sensations we get from eating it are pleasurable, depends on whether we desire it (rather than vice versa). Although this claim is controversial (especially, I imagine, to hedonists) I will just grant it here, as there is insufficient space to discuss it. It is worth noting, though, that Shemmer thinks "that there are some sensations that we cannot but experience as pleasurable or non-pleasurable and that no attempt to change our desires would affect that. I wouldn't be surprised if some terrible pain has that feature" (personal correspondence). This would indicate that even on Shemmer's instrumentalism it will not be possible to wholly trivialize the perfection thesis.[27]

Shemmer has attempted to motivate those already beholden to instrumentalism to accept that we are able to desire at will on the basis that such acceptance provides a solution to the farmer's dilemma.[28] (The farmer's dilemma: two farmers, one with a September harvest (F1) and one with an October harvest (F2), who each cannot harvest their crops alone, could help one another—and it would be worth the effort for each to do so. But the farmers have no desire to help each other; they only want to maximize their crop production. So F1 will realize that it is best for F2 to help him, and for him then not to help back, and F2 will realize that F1 has realized this, and so will not help F1 in the first place. Thus, neither will help the other, even though they would be better off if they cooperated.) For reasons of space I will only say that I agree with the line of argument, referred to by him, of saying that there is nothing paradoxical about the farmer's dilemma; it just indicates that certain behavior would be irrational.[29] Shemmer appeals to the assumption that people do cooperate in farmer's dilemma situations and that their lives go better as a result, but this (questionable) assumption does not establish, as he suggests, that their cooperation is "in some sense" rational. All it need establish is that sometimes people act irrationally, and that irrationality need not always result in adverse consequences (especially if other people react irrationally in their turn). If this is right, the farmer's dilemma does not need a solution, still less one that involves a counterintuitive commitment such as to our ability to desire at will.

5. Implications for the perfection thesis

Let us take stock. I began by outlining some observations that I took to constitute reasonably strong prima facie evidence that we could not desire at will, defending them from criticism. I then offered criticism of my own of the positive case for desiring at will given by Harman and Luper. Regarding the idea of desiring at pill, whereby we intentionally induce desires in ourselves by indirect means, I considered an argument from Millgram against this (and a fortiori, against desiring at will) and concluded that it was

---

[27] My thanks to Dr. Shemmer for helpful discussion of footnote 16 of his "Instrumentalism and Desiring at Will."
[28] Shemmer, "Desiring at Will and Humeanism in Practical Reason."
[29] Ibid., 269.

less effective in cases whereby we might change fundamental tastes at pill (and thus change any desires dependent on those tastes); moreover those already predisposed toward instrumentalism would be liable to interpret the thought experiment at the heart of Millgram's argument differently. My conclusion is that there is a good case for rejecting the view that we can desire at will directly, but that some, particularly instrumentalists, might be on firmer ground in believing that we can desire at will indirectly, such as by means of a pill.

So this provides the opportunity to criticize the perfection thesis thus. Let us be crude and represent our phenomenal field using a 4×4 grid (apart from irrelevant relational properties, the squares are conceptually indistinguishable). Now suppose that what I desire most is the pleasant sensation of eating ice cream. In all squares but one (i.e., in the vast majority of my phenomenal field) I am enjoying the pleasurable sensation of eating ice cream. My reason for "filling the squares" (i.e., filling the parts of my phenomenal field with the sensation of eating ice cream) in this way is the pleasurable taste of ice cream (or my desire for it), which outranks its competitors. If this is my reason for "filling the squares" in this way, then the one square that represents part of my phenomenal field that is not occupied by the pleasant sensation of tasting ice cream requires some explanation. Given that, ex hypothesi, the squares have no significant differences between them, and that my desire for the sensation of eating ice cream outranks any competitors, the most plausible explanation seems to be that I have been unable to fill the square as I have its gridmates, and this frustrates my desire, causing me a certain amount of unhappiness. The perfection thesis dictates that, given my desires and their ranking, I should, from my point of view, perfect the makeup of my phenomenal field or else feel some unhappiness.

Now suppose we can control our desires by means of a pill or neurosurgery. If this is so, we need not worry that our phenomenal field is imperfectly filled, or that, once perfectly filled, it is subject to contingency. For instead of altering the makeup of our phenomenal field, which may be quite difficult to do, we might alter our desires. Faced with the aforementioned recalcitrant square we may simply change our desire for that part of our phenomenal field to be filled with the pleasurable sensation of tasting ice cream to a desire that it (i.e., that specific part) be filled with the sensation of x, where "x" describes the sensation that already fills that part. According to our new set of desires, our phenomenal field is now perfect. Given that, for any change in that field we can simply change our desires to fit the new makeup of that field (I assume very advanced neurosurgery that can cope with any practical problems that may arise), the perfection thesis is trivially satisfiable. We learn not to seek perfection, but to see what we have as perfection. So trivialized, the perfection thesis is not liable to motivate a specifically theistic answer to the question of life's meaning.

But does this scenario really wholly trivialize the perfection thesis? I am inclined to think it does not. For, although it is true that if we control our desires we need not worry about the makeup of our phenomenal field being subject to contingency, our worry will merely transfer to the contingency of our desiring the contents of our phenomenal field. That is, we must make sure that our desires correlate with the contents of our phenomenal field when the latter change, and that our desires do not vary when the contents stay the same. Otherwise we will end up with unsatisfied desires.

Now, it may be true that this new contingency worry, pertaining as it does to our desires rather than the existents in the world, is less of a worry than the old one. There appear to be fewer factors that might act on our desires (or our willing of those desires) such that they do not tally up with the existents in the world than there are factors that might act on things in the world in general. But this will not save the attempt to trivialize the perfection thesis, which targets the imperfection of states of affairs insofar as they allow *any* room for undesired contingency.

Maybe this phrase "undesired contingency" provides a clue to a possible answer. For, if it is the worry of contingency that precludes us from being perfectly happy, we could alter our desires such that we *desire* that our desires only contingently (but nevertheless do actually) match the contents of our phenomenal field.

Then our question becomes: do we desire that this meta-desire be one that we have only contingently, or necessarily? Obviously, desiring that we have it necessarily will leave us back with the contingency problem (since we do only have it contingently), and desiring that we have it contingently will merely push us back to the question of whether we desire that this meta-meta-desire be one we have only contingently or necessarily. An infinite regress thus beckons. Note that choosing to desire the regress will not help; it is not that we find the regress undesirable that is the problem. Rather, the problem is that we ultimately are at the mercy of contingency.

One answer to the regress may be just to opt to desire the contingency of our desires in general, rather than piecemeal. This will then apply reflexively to that very desire, and, assuming we have no necessary desires for contingent states of affairs (which the proponent of a desire alteration response to the perfection thesis will have to assume anyway), any meta-desire that could be produced.

Let us assume that this is possible. Have we found a way to trivialize the demands of the perfection thesis? I do not believe so. If we recognize that the choosing of our meta-desires to match up with the contingency of their object desires is just another example of our choosing to match our desires with their objects (where the latter is a state of affairs involving desires on the level "below"), then we must also accept that this response requires the brute occurrence of an unspecified number of contingencies. In response to the worry that our desires may not necessarily match up with the objects of our phenomenal field, our response was to change our attitude rather than the world, and desire that they match up only contingently. But by doing this, we leave it in large part up to chance whether they do so match up. Wanting a desire to match up with an object in one's phenomenal field is, obviously, not a way of securing that this happens (although it does help). There are all sorts of things that can happen, that, despite one wanting that one's desire matches a given object in one's phenomenal field, can bring it about that this is not the case. But furthermore, if one's desiring of this (and, even more importantly, one's desiring that one not desire a mismatch between desire and object) is itself contingent, then one is leaving it to chance that this desire remains as it is also. Of course, one's meta-desire that this desire should actually but contingently hold in part secures it, but it derives what security it does have from the security of the next meta-desire along, which derives its own security from the next along, and so on. Since this regress has no end, we ultimately enjoy no security at all (although, of course, this will not make us unhappy).[30]

The root problem is that, by making desires ungrounded and so easy to drop and adopt, the instrumentalist way of trivializing the perfection thesis ceases to become a "way" of achieving something at all. Any attempt to achieve an end needs some stable desire at its ground superintending that attempt. If the capacity of desires to fluctuate leads to the view that, ultimately, it does not matter what the end of our efforts is, we cannot develop a methodology to achieve a specific end. It will just be left to chance what end we finish up with.[31] Now, in one sense there is no problem with this.

---

[30] Both Millgram and Shemmer discuss whether, on instrumentalism, our desires would end up being arbitrary and thus our happiness would be a matter of good fortune rather than rational action. Millgram claims that the instrumentalist might point to a meta-desire as providing reason to adopt or drop desires, but objects that, as desires cannot be adopted or dropped at will, this response is not open to the instrumentalist. Shemmer replies that this objection is only successful if we accept that we cannot desire at will, which he does not (and I am currently following him in this regard). But my worry is rather that, unless we argue that the meta-desire is not arbitrary (and, if we punt to a higher meta-desire, that *that* meta-desire is not arbitrary), we have not made any progress—the object desire is still ultimately arbitrary, and so our happiness is hostage to fortune.

[31] In Luper's terminology, the position here is one that is not "self-supporting" (Luper, *Invulnerability*, 100). (Note that this problem bears interesting resemblance to Millgram's claim that agency disintegrates if we can desire at will.) Somewhat oddly, Luper thinks that the subvariety of conformism he calls "malleabilism," which is probably the

One might end up fulfilling the perfection thesis trivially by chance—all these contingencies might "go one's way."[32] However, this cannot be a way of achieving ultimate meaning or perfect happiness or whatever, as it cannot be a way of doing anything at all, if by that we mean a method guided by a given end. All that it amounts to is a nice story where everything works out (and, given that everything works out by chance, it is a story which gets less plausible the longer it goes on), but which is isolated from any attempt to solve the issue of life's ultimate meaning for one who is struggling with it.

Now, it is true that one might be able to get into this state from being outside it; the problem is remaining in it. The inability to develop a method of remaining in the state is the problem (all the time one is outside it, and trying to get into it, one is susceptible to frustrations and unhappiness). Moreover, even if we *could* get into this state from being outside it, would we with our current set of desires and values, even *want* to enter into this sort of life? From an instrumentalist perspective, Luper's claim that, if we cannot achieve perfect happiness with the desires we have, a change to a set of desires which we can fulfill perfectly will seem more attractive, may appear plausible.[33] But, given the switch of desires we are considering will involve us altering our desires when life-threatening circumstances arise to desiring those circumstances, rather than trying to get ourselves out of such circumstances, it may well be the case that we could never wish to make such a switch. From a position of inevitably imperfect happiness, it may be attractive to switch to a state of perfect happiness, even though it relies on some upheaval of one's current values, but if that switch also leads to a much increased risk of a state of having none of one's desires fulfilled (i.e., death), that is, of being unable to feel happiness at all, the proposed upheaval is likely to be much too great. Even worse, suppose a set of circumstances were to obtain such that remaining in them would result in one being robbed of happiness and never experiencing it at any time in the future. A switch to the desire set that trivializes the

closest he comes to discussing the position I am outlining here, *is* self-supporting. But malleabilists, according to Luper, "[M]ust not have … any desires about the future" (Luper, *Invulnerability*, 86), and this will include the desire to be or remain a malleabilist in future, so I do not see how this can be so. Maybe Luper wishes to combine malleabilism with autarchy, the view that we can have desires as long as the satisfaction of those desires is completely within our control—then we could say that the desire to be a malleabilist is completely within our control, and so we can desire it. But this will not help. Our control of any given desire will be contingent on our desire to control our desire, and our control of *that* desire will be contingent on a further desire to control it, and so on. Hence, as I indicated above, none of our desires are ultimately in our control.

[32] This would be to see meaning as evaluative rather than normative: cf. Metz, *Meaning in Life*, 142.
[33] Cf. Luper, *Invulnerability*, 138–139.

perfection thesis would mean that one would simply alter one's desires to desire that one be in that set of circumstances. Putting oneself in a position more vulnerable to such a possibility by making such a switch is liable to seem too high a price to the outsider.

6. Conclusion

Let us sum up our findings. I suggested at the beginning that one reason to believe that Theism might be thought to offer peculiarly effective resources to answer the question of life's meaning is because of the plausibility of the perfection thesis. The perfection thesis claims that if we take the fact of our lives' exemplifying a certain property as bestowing meaning on those lives, then, ceteris paribus, we will wish our lives to exemplify that property maximally. Theism, with its postulation of a benevolent God, makes it prima facie more likely that our lives will exemplify that property maximally. So, for those of us who find the perfection thesis plausible, theistic answers to the question of life's meaning will likewise seem more plausible. However, the link between the perfection thesis and Theism can be broken if the demands of the former can be trivially satisfied; if this is so, we will not need some powerful divine benefactor to help us satisfy those demands. The demands appear to be susceptible to trivial satisfaction if it is possible for us to directly or indirectly alter our desires at will.

This is because, rather than being stuck with a set of desires that we need to alter the state of the world to satisfy, we can take the current state of the world and alter our desires so that the resultant set of them are satisfied by that state of the world. In response to this possibility, I have argued that there is some positive evidence against the view that we can desire directly at will, and that the evidence in favor of such a view is insufficient to establish it. With regard to the weaker claim that we might be able to desire at will indirectly, by means of chemical or surgical manipulation of our brains, I have argued that it may be necessary to defend instrumentalist accounts of practical reason to support this, where such accounts are controversial. Finally, I have argued that, even if we do accept the possibility of indirectly desiring at will, this will not provide much succor to those who wish to trivialize the perfection thesis' demands. Our desires and the states of the world for which they are desires will only tally contingently, and there is no way of guaranteeing that these contingencies will hold. If this is so, then, for those who find the perfection thesis plausible, attempts to trivialize its demands will live under the shadow of this contingency; moreover, as time goes on, the chances of matters going awry will approach certainty. Hence, answers to the question of life's meaning that trade on the plausibility of the perfection thesis for their attractiveness, whether they are theistic or of another type, will have little to worry about from attempts to trivialize that thesis' demands.

Part Three

Meaningfulness, Time, and Eternity

6

Meaningfulness, Eternity, and Theism[1]

John Cottingham

1. Theism, meaning, and contingency

We all want our lives to be meaningful: the sense of futility or absurdity that haunted the French existentialists of the twentieth century, and finds expression as early as the book of Ecclesiastes (third century BC), is something we all dread. Religious believers typically find that their faith is a great alleviator of this sense of futility; and even those who deny the truth of Theism often grant that if Theism *were* true, believers would be right to be comforted. For if our lives take place against the backdrop of a cosmos that reflects the purposes of a supremely good and benevolent creator, then (so it is felt) there would be a point to them. Instead of being here accidentally, through a blind contingent chain of circumstances that is utterly neutral and impersonal and indifferent to our concerns, we would have the assurance that our existence has a meaning and a purpose.

There are, however, all sorts of objections that can be raised against this view of the reassuring implications of Theism as regards meaningfulness. One line of thought (which might be called "the concessive line") starts by accepting that the theistic picture may be reassuring, but denies that it is *uniquely* reassuring. It concedes that a theistic worldview is hospitable to the idea of our lives as meaningful, but goes on to point out that even on a secularist or naturalistic worldview there are plenty of ways to salvage meaningfulness. Even allowing for the radical contingency of our origins, and the fluidity of the historical and cultural circumstances that have happened to shape us, it nevertheless remains true, on this secularist view, that we can still find meaning in the projects we choose to pursue and the goals we find it enriching and satisfying to set ourselves. An *internal* or *self-generated* teleology, on this

---

[1] Originally appeared in Beatrix Himmelmann, ed. *On Meaning in Life* (Boston/Berlin: De Gruyter, 2013): 99–112. Copyright © 2013, Walter de Gruyter GmbH.

picture, is quite sufficient for meaning, even once we have abandoned the idea of an external or divinely ordained teleology.

Such a defense of the idea of meaningfulness-without-God commands widespread support, and is probably the dominant or majority view on the contemporary philosophical scene. But it does have problems of its own. Ever since Nietzsche raised the subversive idea of the "genealogy of morals"—that once we see the contingent origins of our value system, we can begin to ask "*what value those values themselves possess*" (Nietzsche 1887, Preface, §3)— moral philosophy has been living under the shadow of the "radical contingency of the ethical," as Bernard Williams once called it:[2] I may earnestly pursue my "projects," and earnestly declare the importance of my values, or of the values held by my culture group, but at the back of my mind I am aware that these projects and values might seem highly questionable, or even absurd, to those of other cultures, or might even have seemed absurd to me, or to my society, had things in the past gone slightly differently. Against this, it might be objected that these supposedly subversive implications of contingency are being overdone: might not there be over time a tendency toward ethical *convergence*, based on fundamental aspects of the human condition that do not change (except perhaps extremely slowly), so that there is hope for ethical progress? In due course, then, might we not have reason to suppose that a sufficient consensus can arise to allow a stable and enduring set of values to be the focus of human striving, so that our lives can be good and meaningful against this backdrop?

This is in many ways an attractive position, and has found eloquent defenders. Moral philosophers such as David Wiggins and John McDowell have suggested, in different ways, that the steady process of human acculturation allows us to gain access to a sufficiently stable ethical domain within which good and meaningful lives can be lived.[3] Against this, Bernard Williams was a (perhaps sometimes reluctant) defender of the more subversive Nietzschean line. Contrasting the ethical with the scientific case, Williams offered powerful reasons for doubting that there is any reasonable hope of convergence in the ethical sphere, of the kind that we aspire to in science.[4] And if this worry cannot be neutralized, then there will always be the anxiety that building our system of value and meaning within the parameters of the particular culture of which we happen to be members will risk incurring the charge of ethical

---

[2] Bernard Williams, *Truth and Truthfulness* (Princeton, NJ: Princeton University Press, 2002), 20.
[3] David Wiggins, *Ethics* (London: Penguin, 2006); John McDowell, *Mind and World* (Cambridge, MA: Harvard University Press, 1994).
[4] Bernard Williams, *Ethics and the Limits of Philosophy* (London: Fontana, 1985), chapter 8.

complacency or quietism. If, on the other hand, we rely solely on our own individually chosen "projects" to generate meaning, then there is the risk of falling into too "voluntaristic" a conception of meaningfulness. This would come close to the solution offered by Nietzsche himself, when he supposed that a certain kind of heroic and exceptional human being has the power to bootstrap value into existence, to *create value* by a supreme act of will;[5] but that solution, even if it could be shown to be philosophically coherent,[6] appears altogether too arrogant and individualistic to form a framework for meaningfulness that could command widespread acceptance.[7]

These arguments and counterarguments provide rich food for philosophical reflection, and indeed are an essential prerequisite for any serious contemporary study of meaningfulness in human life. For the purposes of the present chapter, it will be useful to keep these debates in mind; but I want to turn the main spotlight on an alternative strategy for vindicating the idea of meaningfulness-without-God. Instead of the concessive line—accepting the premise that Theism would underwrite meaningfulness but attempting to show that there are viable secular or naturalistic ways of underwriting it— I want to consider a more radical approach, which makes the prior move of challenging the premise itself, and raising the question of why a theistic worldview should be hospitable to meaning in the first place. On this more radical strategy, there is a challenge to the very idea that an "external teleology" might do the job of supporting the meaningfulness of human life.

2. Euthyphro-type problems

The very expression "external teleology" should perhaps already raise alarm bells for those who want to claim that meaning can be found within the wider picture of a cosmos that is the work of a divine creator. For if the purposes of such a creator lie outside the domain of human choices and goals, what have they to do with us, and with the meaning of our human lives? Many of the ancients, to be sure, seem to have felt that being a small part of a much greater

---

[5] Nietzsche, in *On the Genealogy of Morals*, (§203) envisages a "new philosopher" with a spirit "strong enough to revalue and invent new values."

[6] The obvious problem is that it is hard to see how mere choice can generate value; on the contrary, our choices seem valuable only when their objects have value antecedent to our making them. See further John Cottingham, "The Good Life and the 'Radical Contingency of the Ethical,'" in *Reading Bernard Williams*, ed. D. Callcut (London: Routledge, 2008), 25–43.

[7] Compare Martha Nussbaum, "Mercy and Pity," in *Nietzsche, Genealogy, Morality*, ed. R. Schacht (Berkeley, CA: University of California Press, 1994), 139–167, on the conspicuous lack of a sense of fellow-feeling for others in Nietzsche's ethical outlook.

process somehow bestows significance on human life: "In the thought that I am part of the whole," said the Stoic Marcus Aurelius, "I shall be content with all that can come to pass" (Aurelius, AD 85, VI 42). But a life of Stoic contentment is not quite the same as a meaningful life in the sense in which most people understand the latter phrase. The Stoics cultivated *apatheia*, a state of calm, rational detachment from the passions and drives of our human nature; and although they saw a certain harmony between our rational nature and the principles that they took to govern the cosmos as a whole, the life they advocated seems to be more one of endurance of the vicissitudes and misfortunes of human existence, and a detachment from the joys and sorrows of human love, than a life in which there is any ultimate meaning in all of this.

Even for those, such as adherents of the great Abrahamic faiths, who see ultimate reality in much more personal terms, attributing to God not only predicates like "rational," but ones such as "merciful," it is still not entirely clear why a divinely ordained cosmic teleology automatically generates meaningfulness in human life. Examples like the hapless talking cow in the *Hitchhiker's Guide to the Galaxy*, who is delighted to provide meat for the dinner table, are funny precisely because they highlight how subserving the purposes of a higher being, even willingly and joyfully, does not defuse the threat of futility and absurdity.[8] Or perhaps the cow's existence is not *futile*, since it meets the needs of the masters who have bred it; but meaningfulness of a life seems to require more—it demands some match between the goals toward which someone's life is tending and the ultimate good of the one who is actually living the life. In short, the objection (what I have elsewhere called the "alienation objection") is that an external teleology estranges us from what is good *for us*, and so forfeits its title to be a valid generator of true meaning. And finally, even in the case where the higher power may be kind and benevolent, as in the "Truman Show" example, where the protagonist of the film is the unwitting star of a popular TV series orchestrated by an unseen director, who has concealed cameras filming every day of his life from birth onward, the supposed benevolence of the director does not make any difference to the argument: the point is that the hero discovers to his horror that he is living to serve the purposes of *someone else*, and this seems profoundly corrosive of meaning.[9]

The theist, I think, has a viable answer to the alienation objection, namely that unlike the Truman case (where the director has at the very least mixed

---

[8] Douglas Adams, *The Restaurant at the End of the Universe* (London: Pan Books, 1984). Cf. John Cottingham, *The Spiritual Dimension: Religion, Philosophy and Human Value* (Cambridge: Cambridge University Press, 2005), chapter 3.

[9] Cf. John Cottingham, "Meaningful Life," in *The Wisdom of the Christian Faith*. eds. Paul K. Moser and Michael T. McFall (Cambridge: Cambridge University Press, 2012).

motives) the purposes of a truly loving and supremely good God are such as to allow the human subject to identify completely with the goals that have been divinely ordained. In other words, there is a complete harmony between internal and external teleology: our deepest desires, when purified of distortions and confusions, and our clearest rational perceptions, when properly focused, take us toward the supreme good where our true fulfilment lies. Our divinely ordained destiny is precisely that which we ourselves would strive for when our reason is unclouded and our will is unconstrained by anything but the light of truth and goodness.[10]

There are some structural similarities between the issues raised in the alienation objection and a cluster of more abstract concerns that may as a convenient shorthand be labeled "Euthyphro-type problems." Plato's original question, in the *Euthyphro*, was whether something counts as pious because it is loved or approved by the gods, or, on the contrary, whether it is loved by the gods because it is pious (Plato 390 BC). The core of the dilemma, as it has mutated down the generations to current debates about the relation between morality and religion, is this: we cannot, it seems, say that what makes something good is *simply* its being commanded by God, for that would lead to the repugnant conclusion that if God were to command some morally horrible act it would be good; but if on the other hand we take the other horn of the dilemma and say that God commands things because they are *already* (as it were) good, this seems to make God in a certain sense redundant to morality. For the features which make actions good, and in virtue of which God has good reason to command them and we have good reason to obey, are features which presumably obtain *independently* of the fact that God commands them.

It should already be clear how this bears on the problem of meaningfulness. The dilemma for the theist is that our lives cannot be meaningful *simply* insofar as they serve God's purposes for the cosmos; for that would lead to the repugnant conclusion that if God's purposes were, for example, cruel or capricious, serving these purposes would *eo ipso* make our lives meaningful. But on the other hand, if we say that God lays down the goals for human life in light of the fact that such goals are *already* (as it were) such as to give our lives meaning and value, then God turns out to be in a certain sense redundant to the question of meaningfulness in our lives. For the meaning-bestowing features of our actions or projects, in virtue of which God has good reason to ordain them as the proper goals of human life (e.g., the fact that a

---

[10] For an excellent discussion of love and desire for union with the good, based on some key ideas in Aquinas, see Eleonore Stump, *Wandering in Darkness* (Oxford: Oxford University Press, 2011).

life is devoted to the service of others), are presumably features that count as meaning-bestowing *independently* of the fact that he approves them as goals to which we should devote ourselves. The upshot is that the "external" teleology invoked by bringing God into the question of life's meaning would appear to do no real work. The work is done by the meaning-bestowing features themselves (e.g., the altruistic or self-sacrificial character of the relevant acts). Of course God may be the *source* of the very possibility of these features, if only in the sense in which, for the theist, *all* that exists or can exist flows ultimately from the divine nature. But this does not seem enough to vindicate the invocation of God as some sort of "answer" to the question of what it is that makes for meaningfulness in human life, except in the very general sense that he is, for the theist, the "answer" to questions about the ultimate source of *any* existing phenomenon, whether the corrosive features of acids, or the gravity-making features of stars and planets, or whatever.

Now in current discussions of the standard Euthyphro problem about the relation between God and morality, it has become common for the theist to defend a "modified" divine command theory: goodness is identified not with what is commanded by God *simpliciter*, but rather with what is commanded by God *qua* one whose essential nature is supremely merciful, just, and loving.[11] Applying this kind of move to the issue of meaningfulness, the theist might well point out that God's purposes for the cosmos and for human life are, necessarily, the purposes of a supremely loving creator. And one might go on from there to argue that an "external" divine teleology is not therefore redundant to the question of meaning in life: for if we add the point that God is also all-knowing and all-wise, then the purposes and goals that he ordains for us in love may well exceed our human power to fully understand from our own resources alone (compare the "external" teleology that guides a loving parent to direct a child toward goals which the child cannot yet properly grasp or internalize). So an "internal teleology," based on our own conception of the projects and purposes that make for meaningfulness in life must indeed (so the argument runs) be supplemented by appeal to the "external teleology" deriving from the wisdom and love of God's purposes for our lives.

This does not seem to be in itself an inappropriate line for the theist to take about meaning. But it does have the effect of shifting the discussion from the ontological to the epistemological sphere. Instead of raising questions about what *makes for* meaningfulness in human life, and how far the truth (or otherwise) of a theistic worldview might *contribute* to answering

---

[11] Cf. Robert Merrihew Adams, "A Modified Divine Command Theory of Ethical Wrongness," in *Religion and Morality*, eds. G. Outka and J. P. Reeder (Garden City, NY: Anchor, 1973).

these questions, the effect of stressing God's presumed infinitely superior knowledge will inevitably move the debate on to the *evidential* question how, if Theism is true, we might know, or reasonably believe, that such and such human actions contribute to the plans of a supremely wise and loving creator. And this in turn gives rise to a dilemma. If we are fully competent to judge which goals are indeed benign and meaning-bestowing simply from our own natural resources—our power of discerning in natural human terms that such and such actions do indeed make for a meaningful life—then we are back with the "redundancy" objection: why bring God into the matter at all? If on the other hand it is replied that God is all-knowing and all-wise, so may know truths about the real meaning of our lives that are beyond our ken, then it seems that the only way for such a meaning to make a significant difference to our view of human life would be to suppose that God might directly disclose to us goals that we *would not otherwise recognize* as the locus of ultimate meaning and value in our lives; but such a supposition would of course take us into the area of revealed truth. We (or perhaps divinely inspired prophets or priests) will have to rely on such divine disclosure to know that *these* are the goals that give meaning to human life; such knowledge or belief will not be based on our being able to point to meaning-bestowing features that are accessible to natural human discernment, but will depend on the supposed revelation by God of his plans for us. The status of such appeals to revelation is a highly complex matter that cannot be evaluated here. But the point for present purposes is not to pass judgment on revelatory accounts of meaning in human life, but simply to note that they take us outside the domain of what can be established by natural philosophical reason alone.

3. What difference does eternity make?

In the remaining part of this chapter, I want to consider a particular feature of the theistic worldview that might be thought especially relevant to the question of human life and its meaning, namely the "eternal" dimension which is so central to many forms of religious belief. The theist typically views our human existence *sub specie aeternitatis*. God himself is taken to be immortal and everlasting, either in the sense that he had no beginning in time and he will continue forever, or perhaps in the sense that he transcends time altogether (the difference between these two analyses of God's "eternal" nature will not need to be unpacked for the purposes of the present inquiry).[12] God

---

[12] "God is eternal. But this has been understood in two different senses: either as the claim that God is timeless (he does not exist in time, or at any rate in our time) or as the claim that God is everlasting (he existed at every moment of past time, exists now, and will exist

himself, then, is eternal: "a thousand ages in thy sight are like an evening gone."[13] In addition to this notion of *divine* eternity, many theistic faiths, such as Christianity and Islam, and some forms of Judaism,[14] hold that all or some humans will enter the "life of the world to come" (ζωὴν τοῦ μέλλοντος αἰῶνος), to quote the words of the Niceno-Constantinopolitan Creed [AD 381]; and this is generally taken to mean eternal life after death.

Both these two ideas, that of the eternity of God and that of our own possible eternal future existence, might be thought relevant to the meaningfulness of human life. Let us take the second first. The erosion of meaning in human life is by many people connected with the thought that in a thousand years, or certainly in ten thousand, all our struggles and achievements, such as they are, will be *as if they had never been*. The Roman poet Horace, in his celebrated poem *Exegi monumentum aere perennius* ("I have raised a monument more permanent than bronze")[15] sees meaning and value in his poetic achievement precisely insofar as it will not fade with the years, but will continue on into the remote future. But of course we know that even bronze, along with "the cloud-capped towers, the gorgeous palaces, the solemn temples, the great globe itself,"[16] will one day perish; and indeed the universe itself will descend into the ultimate stasis of heat-death. As William Lane Craig, an eloquent exponent of this theme, puts it:

> Mankind is a doomed race in a dying universe. Because the human race will eventually cease to exist, it makes no ultimate difference whether it ever did exist. Mankind is thus no more significant than a swarm of mosquitoes or a barnyard of pigs, for their end is all the same. The same blind cosmic process that coughed them up in the first place will eventually swallow them all again.[17]

---

at every moment of future time)." Richard Swinburne, *Was Jesus God?* (Oxford: Oxford University Press, 2008), 12. Swinburne favors the latter view.

[13] From the hymn "Abide with me," by the Scottish Anglican Henry Francis Lyle (composed 1847).

[14] The Jewish sacred texts do not appear to lay much stress on the notion of the afterlife, and it is often said that the main focus of the religion is on performing one's duties to God and one's fellow men in *this* life. Jewish sects during the lifetime of Christ were divided over the question of the Resurrection of the dead, the Pharisees (followed in later Rabbinical tradition) affirming it, and the Sadducees denying it (cf. Luke 20:27, Mark 20:18).

[15] Horace, *Odes* [*Carmina*, 23 BC], Bk III, no 30.

[16] William Shakespeare, *Tempest* [1610], Act IV, scene 1.

[17] William Lane Craig, *Reasonable Faith, Christian Truth and Apologetics*, rev. ed. Wheaton, IL: Crossway, 1994), 58.

Would it help to dispel this futility if we live forever? As Bernard Williams pointedly argued in a celebrated paper, it seems not—indeed, to the contrary. For although it might initially seem nice to continue with our satisfying activities for many centuries without the fear of extinction, the lesson (as drawn from Bernard Williams) from the Janacek opera *The Makropulos Case* is that an *indefinitely* prolonged future existence could only produce a sense of tedium.[18] Nor would an "eternal recurrence," Nietzsche-style, seem to do much to help;[19] on the contrary, it might actually *detract* from meaningfulness, by the grinding cycle of everlasting repetition, which not only removes any hope of improvement, but also erodes the uniqueness, and therefore the precarious preciousness, of our human struggles and choices here and now.

In light of these difficulties, it seems that the better way of approaching the possible link between eternity and meaning will be to connect meaningfulness not so much with *our* eternal future existence, but with God's. If standard Theism is true, then our actions will be held forever, or are eternally present, in the mind of a supremely good and loving and wise God, and so will have ultimate significance.

On the naturalist picture, as portrayed in the above quotation by Craig, there can be no such permanent significance, given that the universe is destined for total extinction. But it seems there could be an alternative, but still naturalist, picture in which the structure of the natural cosmos is one where (as it were) "nothing ever goes away": each action is a permanent or timeless part of the complex web that is the space-time continuum.[20] But even were one to grant this, or something like it, it doesn't seem enough for meaningfulness, if the "continuum" is taken to be simply an abstract web or impersonal matrix. What meaning is conferred by the permanent place my actions have in this blank space-time complex, along with every other event in the universe? But if, by contrast, reality is ultimately personal, and, in particular, if it is as envisaged on the theistic view, then our lives remain forever enfolded in the presence of a supremely loving God.

The poet Alfred Tennyson found his belief in such a benign cosmic order deeply shaken, when in the mid-nineteenth century he confronted the horror of the blank and purposeless processes of nature disclosed by the emerging

---

[18] Bernard Williams, "The Makropulos Case: Reflections on the Tedium of Immortality," in *Problems of the Self* (Cambridge: Cambridge University Press, 1973), 82–100.
[19] Cf. Friedrich Nietzsche, *The Joyful Science*, 1882.
[20] See Nietzsche, *The Joyful Science*. The complexities of the views on this issue offered by contemporary theoretical physicists and philosophers of time are extremely difficult for the nonspecialist to follow, but a useful overview is provided in Stephen Savitt, 'Being and Becoming in Modern Physics', *Stanford Encyclopedia of Philosophy* http://plato.stanford.edu/entries/spacetime-bebecome/#2.1, accessed February 2013.

fossil record—the long and brutal struggle for survival over vast millennia, in which countless individuals and species are wiped out. But he still clung "faintly" to the theistic hope

> that not one life shall be destroyed,
> or cast as rubbish to the void,
> when God hath made the pile complete.[21]

His faltering but eventually (by the end of the poem) reaffirmed faith was in the possibility of individual survival in an afterlife, so that the poet would again be able to set eyes on the dear friend who is the subject of his agonized lament here in *In Memoriam*. But even if Tennyson was wrong to "faintly trust the larger hope,"[22] even if we are indeed wholly mortal, our lives, on the theistic picture we are now considering, would still not be "cast as rubbish to the void" when they end, since they would retain, eternally, their moral significance by being present to God.

In another of Tennyson's famous poems, *Ulysses*, the hero reflects what remains of his own life, and tries to encourage himself by referring to what good still remained to be sought on earth: "every hour is saved from that eternal silence."[23] That phrase clearly presupposes the bleaker view that meaning must slip away forever as our short existence ends and disappears into silence. But on the theistic view, instead of "every hour is saved from that eternal silence" (which suggests a desperate clutching on to some transient spark of value and meaning in the face of our grim awareness of the eventual total extinction of everything), we would need to rewrite Tennyson and say something like "every hour is saved in that eternal *presence*"—where "saved" now means not "temporarily salvaged," but something like "preserved, protected, treasured." Whatever of the good or meaningful we manage to achieve is eternally stored and cherished in the loving presence of God.

4. Personal immortality and Averroean concerns

Some might worry that the route to meaningfulness just sketched out risks committing the "Averroean heresy," named after the great twelfth-century Islamic philosopher and Aristotelian commentator Averroes (or Ibn Rushd), who denied that the individual soul survives death. Strictly speaking, of

---

[21] Alfred Tennyson, *In Memoriam*, 1850, liv.
[22] Ibid., lv.
[23] Alfred Tennyson, *Ulysses*, 1842.

course, there are no necessary "Averroean" implications in the argument we have been considering. The question of personal survival of death is left completely open; the point is simply that *even if* there is no personal immortality, there would still be a kind of ultimate metaphysical significance to our lives on the theistic view. Nevertheless, a qualm of an approximately "Averroean" character may seem to remain. If the only meaning we can hope for is that our actions remain present in the divine mind after we die, then our lives perhaps have some "cosmic" significance, but do not have ultimate personal significance *for us*, or from our point of view.

The frequent and fierce condemnations of Averroes by the Church in the Middle Ages were in part connected with the fear that without personal survival there could be no Last Judgment; and this was not just contrary to clear Christian doctrine, going right back to the Gospels, but was also felt to be subversive of morals. This continuing fear of the subversiveness of denying individual immortality was aptly summed up by Descartes, several centuries later: "since in this life the rewards offered to vice are often greater than the rewards of virtue, few people would prefer what is right to what is expedient if they did not fear God or have the expectation of an afterlife."[24] But the point at issue goes far beyond the crude idea of the afterlife as a means of keeping people on the straight and narrow, and impacts directly on the question of meaning. The sense of responsibility, that we are truly accountable for our actions, is intimately bound up with the idea that they are morally significant, that they *matter*. But if the "mattering" is something that fades over time, to that extent meaningfulness seems to be eroded. This is particularly apparent in the journalism-dominated culture of contemporary Western politics, where the "story of the day" is frenziedly hyped up, only to disappear from view and be replaced by tomorrow's big news: politicians increasingly take advantage of this in a way that subtly but inexorably undermines the idea that personal moral conduct really matters. So when detected in corruption they will brazen things out, or if there is no other recourse, they will issue an "apology" of transparent perfunctoriness and insincerity, trusting that in a few months' time the event will have been all but obliterated by the latest brouhaha.

Politicians are (for the most part) a particularly unappetizing model to have in mind when we think about the value and meaningfulness of human lives. But for all of us there is the specter of temporariness—the fading of memories, the steadily reduced impact of our actions, like the ripples in a pond slowly subsiding; all this does seem to threaten the idea of *enduring responsibility* that is one of the foundations of meaningfulness in our lives.

[24] René Descartes, *Meditations on First Philosophy*, 1641, Dedicatory Letter to the Sorbonne.

But if it is true, as Christianity and other religions affirm (but as philosophical inquiry cannot determine one way or the other) that there is personal survival, then this would function as a further "bonus," as it were, as far as meaningfulness is concerned—a bonus to be added to the previous argument about the eternal presence of our actions in the mind of God. For if personal survival is true, then the eternal joy of God at the good deeds of his creatures would be a joy in which those who have lived well somehow share.

But an important caveat to note here is that someone's continued personal existence, if it happens, could not *in itself* confer meaning on their life; that point is already clearly established by the Makropulos example. The imagined scenario instead is one of continuing joy that must arise in significant part out of the meaning-conferring achievements and actions of the human life as it was actually lived—or out of the fact that, though all the faults are acknowledged, that life has found redemption. The religious believer might of course speculate about additional "heavenly" joys not now conceivable; but on any plausible view of the continuing ultimate responsibility that is invoked by the ideas of heaven and hell, the joys would have to have a continuing personal connection with the former life and its character—just as indeed *any* joy, in ordinary earthly life, is laden with the past that has shaped the life up to that moment. The upshot of these points is that heavenly bliss, like earthly bliss, should not be thought of as *in itself* the generator of meaning; it must instead be thought of as a somewhat similar status to pleasure on the account given in Aristotle's ethics: a kind of epiphenomenal fragrance or glow, like the bloom of youth, that sets the seal on, or is a sign of, the life well lived, or a life redeemed.[25]

In case all this seems to present too rosy and complacent an account of the religious conception of eternity, it is worth adding that the theistic idea that every single one of our actions on earth remains eternally present in the mind of God cuts both ways. Just as whatever we can achieve of genuine worth and meaningfulness somehow does not fade but endures forever, so whatever we do that undermines the value or meaning of our lives or the lives of others will also remain eternally present in the divine mind. That is indeed a terrible thought, and becomes even more fearful when we add the further idea of individual survival of death; for this implies not just that our good and evil acts retain their significance forever, but also that we shall be called to account for them. And although on the Judaeo-Christian picture (and perhaps most prominently in the Christianity of the Gospels) this insistence on responsibility is compatible with the possibility of divine forgiveness

---

[25] "Pleasure completes the activity as an end that supervenes as the bloom of youth does on those in the flower of their age." Aristotle, *Nicomachean Ethics*, Bk. X, Ch. 4.

(cf. Luke 15:11–32; Matthew 18:22), there is nothing whatever in the tradition that suggests that that possibility can or should be taken for granted.[26]

But however that may be, the crucial point for present purposes is that the inescapability of ultimate judgment on our lives—that very prospect that is so unpalatable and even absurd in the eyes of those who hold strongly deterministic versions of a secularist or naturalist worldview—turns out to be an aspect of the theistic outlook that actually *adds* to meaning. The sense that our acts are eternally subject to divine evaluation, so far from detracting from their meaning, seems deeply to enhance their significance. The responsibility that we bear for every single act that we do or fail to do during our lives is not something that fades or slips away, but retains its ultimate significance. For on the theistic view, the cosmos is not just an indifferent backdrop to our fleeting lives; it is a cosmos shot through with meaning and value, where our contribution ultimately and eternally matters.

So, in conclusion, the ultimate meaningfulness of our actions, on the view advocated here, comes from their taking their place, *sub specie aeternitatis*, as actions that eternally matter: where whatever sparks of good they contain is a source of joy to a being of supreme wisdom and love. This amplifies and as it were confirms the meaningfulness that they already had on earth, and protects them against the erosions of time and contingency, shielding them against the backdrop of impermanence against which nothing in the long term matters very much. And if we add to this the doctrine of individual postmortem survival, then the blessed who have led good lives, or received the grace of redemption, will share personally in that eternal meaningfulness, and the joy that crowns it.

Some readers may feel that the considerations advanced here at the close of our discussion can hardly bear on the philosophical understanding of the question of life's meaning, since they involve too many theological ideas whose acceptance is a matter of revelation or faith. But it would be a mistake to suppose that any argument that treats matters of religious faith will take us wholly outside the domain of rational discussion and philosophical evaluation. Part of our discussion has been about what religious claims about the existence of an eternal loving God, and of our own future existence, might coherently be supposed to contribute to the meaningfulness of our lives *if* they were true; and on any showing that kind of analysis must be counted a legitimate matter for philosophical inquiry. But more importantly, by

---

[26] This incidentally explains why one feels there is something slightly rosy or sentimental in Tennyson's thought that from the perspective of eternity our lives will be viewed from a gently indulgent perspective: "Be near us when we climb or fall:/Ye watch, like God,/The rolling hours/With larger other eyes than ours,/To make allowance for us all." *In Memoriam*, li.

unpacking the implications of the theistic worldview as regards the meaningfulness of human life, we are able to see how far these implications resonate with our powerful pretheoretical intuitions about what makes for meaning and value in our lives. If, as has been suggested here, the theistic picture is strikingly hospitable to many of those intuitions, and if it is also true that those intuitions cannot be fully and satisfactorily accommodated within alternative naturalist pictures, then if we are disinclined to accept the theistic picture we face a stark choice. We could try to give up the search for ultimate meaning, and abandon the idea that our lives can be meaningful in any but a local and temporary sense: we could perhaps try to "cure" ourselves of the idea, on the grounds that it is no more than a fantasy or an illusion born of our unwillingness to face the starkness of reality. But we may find that the yearning for ultimate meaning is an ineradicable part of our human nature, or that to try to abandon it would do too much violence to our fundamental human aspirations for it to be an option we can coherently pursue. If that is the case, and no other framework but the theistic one is available to support those aspirations, then the question arises as to whether the theistic framework is one that we can in integrity continue to dismiss out of hand.

7

The Expansion and Contraction of the Meaning of Life

Charles Taliaferro

Some philosophers locate the meaning of life in terms of the everyday evident goods we relish, and intentionally ignore or reject any extraordinary, transcendent notion of meaning or purpose. Simon Blackburn is committed to the "immanent option" as opposed to finding meaning in persons' relationship to God as a transcendent, purposive, all good Creator.[1] In a sense, Blackburn looks for meaning *in* life rather than for the meaning *of* life. While, as we shall see later, there might be an important gain in recognizing both forms of meaning, Blackburn is among those philosophers who affirm immanent meaning instead of (or in the course of denying) transcendent meaning and value.

> [A]nother option for meaning ... is to look only within life itself. This is the immanent option. It is content with the everyday. There is sufficient meaning for human beings in the human world—the world of familiar, and even humdrum, doings and experiences. In the immanent option, the smile of the baby, the grace of the dancer, the sound of voices, the movement of a lover, give meaning to life. For some, it is activity and achievement: gaining the summit of the mountain, crossing the finish line first, finding the cure, or writing the poem. These things last only their short time, but that does not deny them meaning. A smile does not need to go on forever in order to mean what it does. There is nothing beyond or apart from the processes of life. Furthermore, there is no one goal to which all these processes tend, but we can find something precious, value and meaning, in the processes themselves.[2]

---

[1] Simon Blackburn, "Religion and Respect," in *Philosophers without Gods: Meditations on Atheism and the Secular Life*, ed. Louise M. Antony (Oxford: Oxford University Press, 2007): 179–193.
[2] Ibid., 190.

Ronald Dworkin endorses a similar perspective:

> When you do something smaller well—play a tune or a part or a hand, throw a curve or a compliment, make a chair or a sonnet or love—your satisfaction is complete in itself. Those are achievements within life. Why can't a life also be an achievement complete in itself, with its own value in the art in living it displays?[3]

Philip Kitcher also seeks to find meaning and value in immanent goods and he offers a critique of those of us who seek meaning in both immanent and transcendent goods.[4]

Blackburn, Dworkin, and Kitcher all share a form of naturalism that Joshua Seachris calls *optimistic naturalism*, according to which "nothing of the transcendent sort is needed to ground those things in life that we, pre-philosophically, find to be meaningful. Supernaturalism [e.g. Theism in the Abrahamic religious traditions] sets the bar for a meaningful life too high."[5]

In this chapter, I argue that the optimistic naturalists' recognition of values should lead them to be optimistic about "supernaturalism," or what I will refer to as *Platonic theism*. So, I will *not* present arguments that the goods that optimistic naturalists recognize are not meaningful. I shall instead maintain that if these immanent goods are meaningful, then there is reason for hoping that the measure of meaning in life should be higher than optimistic naturalists can meet. People like Dworkin et al. believe that significance, and, therefore, meaning in life comes from enjoying or delighting in certain goods. Given that this is the case, it is hard to understand how continued enjoyment of these goods would not make for a more meaningful life. Who can rationally prefer the cessation of enjoying what is good over the prolongation of enjoying what is good? I hope to show that a prolonged enjoyment of immanent goods leads naturally to hope for the reality of a transcendent good that would enable such an expansion of goods.

There needs to be some stage setting to advance my line of reasoning. And so I begin with a preface and then offer, in Section 1, reasons why Blackburn, Dworkin, and Kitcher should lament rejecting *Platonic theism*. In Section 2, I challenge Kitcher's reasons for thinking that this sort of theism conflicts with our understanding of human nature.

---

[3] Ronald Dworkin, *Religion without God* (Cambridge, MA: Harvard University Press, 2013): 158.
[4] Phillip Kitcher, *Life After Faith: The Case for Secular Humanism* (New Haven, CT: Yale University Press, 2014).
[5] Joshua Seachris, "Meaning of Life: Contemporary Analytic Perspectives," in *The Internet Encyclopedia of Philosophy* (http://www.iep.utm.edu/mean-ana/).

1. A preface

In this chapter, I shall use the term *Platonic theism* to refer to the view that there is a maximally excellent, omnipotent, omniscient, eternal or everlasting, necessarily existing Creator, as revealed in the common understanding of God in classical Judaism, Christianity, and Islam. Of course, these Abrahamic faiths differ in substantial matters (about the Trinity and incarnation, for example) and have internal differences (some observant Jews affirm while others deny or are agnostic about an individual afterlife), but I shall take it that there is historically in each tradition an affirmation that God is indeed essentially good, possesses the divine attributes (omnipotence, and so on), and is revealed in human history as seeking to redeem human persons in this life and in life beyond this life. All three traditions have fostered different conceptions of how such redemption takes place and different concepts of the scope of such redemption, but they are united in holding that God is both just and merciful and seeks to transform human persons into a community that is in harmony with God's nature and will. Other terms in the literature sometimes used to refer to what I am calling Platonic Theism are *Anselmian Theology* or *Perfect Being Theology*.

Elsewhere I have argued for the coherence and plausibility of Platonic Theism and against the coherence and plausibility of naturalism.[6] If those arguments are cogent, then we have reason to think, metaphysically, that Blackburn et al. are not able to form a satisfactory foundation for the values they recognize. However, in order to keep the focus on the meaning of life, I ask readers only to assume (for the sake of argument) that the evidential cases for Platonic Theism and naturalism are sufficient such that reasonable persons can have reason to embrace (believe or assume or reasonably hope for the truth of) either Platonic Theism or naturalism and have no compelling reason to remain agnostic. This proviso is essential so that we can focus on the nature of meaning and the question of whether optimistic naturalists should hope their position is false and Platonic Theism is true.

The phrase "the meaning of life" suggests a variety of usages in this book. I prefer to use it in relationship to questions about *what exists* and *significance*. If asked about the meaning of my writing this chapter or the meaning of a talk taking place in the classroom across the hall, I take it that I am being asked what is going on and its contextual significance. The answer may or may not involve an appeal to some overriding purpose. Appealing

---

[6] See Charles Taliaferro and Jil Evans, *The Image in Mind: Theism, Naturalism, and the Imagination* (London: Continuum, 2013), and Taliaferro, *The Golden Cord* (Notre Dame, IN: University of Notre Dame Press, 2012).

to purposes, however, may be what some have in mind, as in the famous anecdote about Bertrand Russell being asked in a cab "What's it all about?" to which he was supposedly speechless. If the event occurred, he was probably speechless because he did not think any of us (nor the cosmos itself) have any purpose and this was what he was being asked to identify. But, given my usage where purposes are sufficient but not necessary for the definition of meaning, Russell would have a ready reply: life emerged from chance and necessity. There are no objective values, only conflicting desires. And all of us as individuals and life itself will ultimately perish.

It seems to me that we can reasonably refer to meaning on a scale. Just as some things have more significance than others, some things are more meaningful than others. My visiting a friend last night to express my love and gratitude for him just before he died of a prolonged illness has more significance, and thus more apparent meaning, than my deciding which cereal to have for breakfast. Given this usage, my claim is that the goods identified by Blackburn et al. have more meaning in the context of Platonic Theism than naturalism.

2. Why naturalists should hope Platonic Theism is true

At the risk of repetition, I stress that I am assuming that neither naturalism nor Platonic Theism has primacy in terms of evidence. If it turns out that I am mistaken and naturalism is more evident than Theism, I think we need to accept naturalism or, if the evidence is stronger but only moderately so, adopt agnosticism, and adopt a position more or less like Blackburn's. But here let us consider Blackburn, Dworkin, and Kitcher from the standpoint of evidential neutrality.

Consider the following thought-experiment given Blackburn's and Dworkin's list of values. Given that you love the smiling baby (strictly speaking, Blackburn refers to "the smile of the baby," not to the baby herself, but we shall assume it would be hard to love the smile without loving the baby), which of these two realities would you hope is the case?

> **Reality One:** The smiling baby (let's call her Mary) lives on to adulthood; she become a graceful dancer who sings and plays instruments in a wonderful choir; she has a loving and intimate partner with whom she enjoys climbing mountains, making love, making chairs and other pieces of furniture, and competing in sports (she throws an excellent curve ball); and she also finds time to discover cures for diseases and write poetry. In this reality, naturalism is true. At death, Mary perishes everlastingly, as does her partner and all those who loved and enjoyed her.

Reality Two: The smiling baby Mary grows into adulthood to become a graceful dancer who sings in a wonderful choir; she has a loving, intimate partner, and so on, exactly as before. However, this time, Platonic theism is true. The cosmos has been created and is sustained in being by the maximally excellent God, who calls everyone to a life of compassion, justice, reconciliation, and joyful worship. This living, loving, powerful, transcendent God offers redemption to Mary and all persons through calling them to renounce evil and sin to come into a great, fulfilling, loving union with God in a life beyond this life.

It might be reasoned that one should not believe that Reality Two is the case because the very notion of an afterlife seems metaphysically or conceptually absurd. Even so, if you truly love Mary, would you not *hope* that the notion of a life beyond life is a metaphysical and conceptual possibility and that Reality Two were the case?

By focusing the thought-experiment in terms of what you would do if you truly love another person, we avoid putting the stress on our self-serving or self-centered concern with what death will mean for ourselves. It might be thought that a person's desire for an afterlife rests on a kind of misplaced self-importance (e.g., I am so important, that of course I would wish for myself Reality Two). My desire for eternal life (driven by an inflated view of my importance) seems a bit more like a Promethean desire than, say, the desire of a St Francis of Assisi. But if we turn the tables and we think of St Francis' love for the poor, it would be shocking if the Saint did not pray that the poor be forever important to the loving God whom he worships and follows. And if they are forever important to the most holy, living God (or some similar conception of ultimate reality), there is also a reasonable hope that they may not find death to be the end of their very being.

Three additional points on Blackburn's and Dworkin's immanent alternative are worth making:

First, Blackburn's thesis that "a smile does not need to go on forever in order to mean what it does" is clever, for the task of holding a smile indefinitely conjures up the idea of a forced smile. Forced smiles, like forced laughter, often feel like something faked and disingenuous. But it is another thing altogether to be indifferent about whether the person smiling will live on, whether this is for seconds, days, and years, or beyond that in union with the God of theistic faith. Similarly, Dworkin's prizing of the *smaller* tasks that have *their own value* gives one reason (in my view) to deeply yearn for Mary's achievements not to end. If one truly loves Mary, and one considers which worldview would be better for Mary and more fulfilling of your love, Reality 2 seems immanently preferable because it offers a greater, more extensive meaning concerning Mary. Dworkin refers to Mary's achievements as complete in themselves. Let us allow that her life remains highly valuable, given naturalism, while at the same time offering this challenge: Platonic Theism fosters the view that Mary's achievements and death do not exhaust meaning. Given Platonic Theism, there is a vista of redemption and flourishing for which (I suggest) a true lover of Mary should hope.

Second, Blackburn's comments might suggest that if Theism is true, there is one goal to which all things (should or are made to) tend. While Jewish and Christian faith does identify inseparable common goals in human life (love of God and love of neighbor), this is not a call to homogeneity or a call for us to love God and neighbor in the same ways. Historically, Judaism and Christianity (and other theistic faiths) have always recognized the good in any number of different and meaningful ways of life that are hallowed by God.

Finally, an excellent formulation of the contrast between Blackburn's and Dworkin's concept of meaning and good versus the Jewish and Christian values of faith and hope is found near the end of G.K. Chesterton's 1908 classic, *Orthodoxy* (with apologies about the antiquated use of masculine terms to represent humanity):

> The mass of men has been forced to be gay about the little things, but sad about the big ones. Nevertheless (I offer my last dogma defiantly) it is not native to man to be so. Man is more himself, man is more manlike, when joy is the fundamental thing in him, and grief the superficial. Melancholy should be an innocent interlude, a tender and fugitive frame of mind; praise should be the permanent pulsation of the soul. Pessimism is at best an emotional half-holiday; joy is the uproarious labor by which all things live. Yet, according to the apparent estate of man as seen by the pagan or the agnostic, this primary need of human nature can never be fulfilled. Joy ought to be expansive; but for the agnostic it must be contracted, it must cling to one corner of the world. Grief ought to be a concentration; but for the agnostic its desolation is spread through an unthinkable eternity. This is what I call being born upside down. The sceptic may truly be said to be topsy-turvy; for his feet are dancing upwards in idle ecstasies, while his brain is in the abyss. To the modern man the heavens are actually below the earth. The explanation is simple; he is standing on his head; which is a very weak pedestal to stand on. But when he has found his feet again he knows it. Christianity satisfies suddenly and perfectly man's ancestral instinct for being the right way up; satisfies it supremely in this; that by its creed joy becomes something gigantic and sadness something special and small. The vault above us is not deaf because the universe is an idiot; the silence is not the heartless

silence of an endless and aimless world. Rather the silence around us is a small and pitiful stillness like the prompt stillness in a sick-room. We are perhaps permitted tragedy as a sort of merciful comedy: because the frantic energy of divine things would knock us down like a drunken farce. We can take our own tears more lightly than we could take the tremendous levities of the angels. So we sit perhaps in a starry chamber of silence, while the laughter of the heavens is too loud for us to hear.[7]

While Blackburn and Dworkin put a good face on treasuring what matters to us here and now, consider Bertrand Russell's assessment of life from a secular point of view which (in my view) might have been what he told his taxi driver:

Year by year, comrades die, hopes prove vain, ideals fade; the enchanted land of youth grows more remote, the road of life more wearisome; the burden of the world increases, until the labour and the pain become almost too heavy to be borne; joy fades from the weary nations of the earth, and the tyranny of the future saps men's vital force; all that we love is waning, waning from the dying world. But the past, ever devouring the transient offspring of the present, lives by the universal death; steadily, irresistibly, it adds new trophies to its silent temple, which all the ages build; every great deed, every splendid life, every achievement and every heroic failure is there enshrined. On the banks of the river of Time, the sad procession of human generations is marching slowly to the grave; in the quiet country of the Past, the march is ended, the tired wanderers rest, and all their weeping is hushed.[8]

Let us now consider Kitcher's position which is similar to Blackburn's and Dworkin's, but goes beyond it.

3. Kitcher on meaning and human nature

Kitcher locates the meaning of life in terms of personal relationships; or as he puts it, "Mattering to others is what counts in conferring meaning."[9] Kitcher fully allows that the finitude of life, the inevitability of death from a secular point of view, creates a deep cause for distress and despair. But he believes

---

[7] Gilbert K. Chesterton. "Orthodoxy," in *The Essential Gilbert K. Chesterton, Vol. 1: Non-Fiction* (Radford, VA: Wilder Publications, 2008): 107–108.
[8] Bertrand Russell, "On History," in *The Basic Writings of Bertrand Russell* (London: Routledge, 2009): 505.
[9] Kitcher, *Life After Faith*, 101.

that this despair can and should be muted as we reflect on the ultimately unsatisfactory alternative of life after death and as we take up the long view of history. Kitcher offers the following response when contemplating with genuine grief about how he feels about his own death. Does he lament his (inevitable, eventual) disappearance from the lives of those who matter to him?

> I do. As I imagine the world in the years immediately following my death, I feel a more intense regret about not being part of it than when I project forward a century, or even half a century. Increasing the time interval diminishes my sadness—it fades relatively swiftly to indifference. Not because I'm envious of those who live happily and actively into extreme old age. I don't even yearn for the longevity advances in medicine may someday achieve for future generations. Absence from the period just after my death is poignant because so much of the stuff of my life will be continued in it. Whenever I die, people about whom I care most deeply will live on, and I should like to be there, sustaining them and being sustained by them. Endeavors to which I have committed my energies will remain unfinished. Loose ends will be left, and I should like to tie them up—while knowing that ends are always beginnings and strands will inevitably dangle. By contrast, the connections with the more distant future are dim, and I cannot even be confident of the large contours of the remote world from which I shall be excluded. Were I to survive into that world, there would be a continuously evolving set of relationships and activities that would give me a stake in it, but lacking any experience of the development of my life, the concerns I would come to have are not vivid for me. So, as I look forward sufficiently far, regret declines into indifference.[10]

I believe we should be grateful for Kitcher's candor.

Kitcher offers the following, interesting diagnosis of the state of those who wish for life beyond life: they wind up entertaining and possibly even hoping that human persons might become nonhuman.

> We cannot, I think, fully imagine what it would be like to be the kind of being for which immortality was a condition for joy. If my diagnosis is correct, distress at the prospect of not being is founded in confusion. For absence from any part of the future is only terrible because something has been felt to be lost. If extended sufficiently far, the threat of termination—indeed, cessation—would ultimately appear as a blessing.

---

[10] Ibid., 98.

What lies behind the sense of horror at not being is regret at being human. To my humanist sensibility that species of regret appears one we should try to overcome—just as we should seek to accept, even enjoy, the arc of aging. Our real problem is posed by the prospect of a removal from a web of connections that matter deeply to us.[11]

My preliminary reply to Kitcher is as follows. If Kitcher were right that relationships matter (recall Kitcher's comment "Mattering to others is what counts in conferring meaning"), wouldn't a relationship with God as understood in Platonic Theism itself be a source of unfathomable delight? Because filling out such a proposal here would require more attention than space will allow, I refer readers to another work where this proposal is addressed cogently.[12] Putting to one side the effort to vindicate the view that if you like mattering to others, mattering to a maximally excellent being would be maximally excellent, I focus on Kitcher's view of human nature.

Let's reconsider Kitcher's thought experiment, in which his sense of sadness diminishes the longer he imagines life continuing fifty or a 100 years after his death, by putting it in a second- or third-person point of view. Again, as in the thought experiments in Section 1, imagine you deeply love Mary and you think it is possible for her to flourish for fifty or a 100 years (with no diminishment of the quality of her life). Isn't it clear that there would be something unloving, odd, or even churlish if you hoped she only lived for fifty years? Now imagine you are contemplating two worldviews, naturalism and Platonic Theism: in one worldview Mary is annihilated at fifty or 100 years and in another she lives on with greater and more exquisite varieties of goods. I suggest that as a person who truly loved Mary, you would want the second. Kitcher writes that he would be less and less sad as life continued after his death because he would (or does) relate less and less to future people. He feels less sad as he realizes that he personally has less at stake in what happens; his concern for what happens becomes less vivid for him the more distant in the future he thinks about people. This point is fairly taken, but put in the third person it begins to seem profoundly disturbing. When you love someone else and consider their living on past your death and even without themselves perishing, when would the time come that you would not feel any sadness at their perishing? Perhaps Kitcher is truly reporting his own subjective position that he has no vivid concern with others when he imagines a remote future which he has trouble picturing. But it seems very hard to see

---

[11] Ibid., 100.
[12] See Kai-man Kwan's *The Rainbow of Experiences, Critical Trust, and God: A Defense of Holistic Empiricism* (London and New York: Continuum Press, 2011).

how someone who truly loves Mary would want her to perish when she has lived long enough such that the lover ceases to have a vivid picture of what Mary's life might be like.

At this point, it is crucial to bear in mind that in the context of this reply to Kitcher, I am comparing worldviews and asking which worldview you would hope is true given the meaningful and ultimately good love you have for another person. I am also asking you to assume the evidential even-match between Platonic Theism and naturalism. If naturalism is clearly the more evident worldview, and Platonic Theism clearly unreasonable, then hoping Platonic Theism is true would be mere wish-fulfillment.

Continuing with my reply: Consider Kitcher's worry that desiring unbounded life would involve the horror of wishing that Mary ceased being human. Kitcher writes; "We cannot, I think, fully imagine what it would be like to be the kind of being for which immortality was a condition for joy."[13] Let us grant that one might truly take joy in Mary and in being in relationship with Mary, given naturalism. One can take joy in Mary under the assumption of naturalism and the conviction that Mary, we, and all persons will perish. There remains, however, the point I am pressing: if one truly takes joyful love in Mary, would one properly hope naturalism (rather than Platonic Theism) is true? It is not as though one cannot have joy, given naturalism. It is a question of how high the bar would be longed for in terms of meaning, given a choice between naturalism and Platonic Theism.

What about Kitcher's point that if we did think of human persons surviving death, we would feel horror at their no longer being human? Kitcher thinks that being human is ipso facto to be a being who perishes absolutely at death. Recall that Kitcher writes: "What lies behind the sense of horror at not being is regret at being human. To my humanist sensibility that species of regret appears one we should try to overcome—just as we should seek to accept, even enjoy, the arc of aging."[14] There are a few things amiss here.

First, it is likely that the vast majority of human beings who have lived have believed that there is an afterlife. In some cases, people have believed that in the life after life they would remain human, as in the case of those who believe in the resurrection of the body and those who believe in reincarnation in human bodies. Thus, life after life does not necessarily imply a non-human life. But putting that point to one side and assuming that the desire to have life after life involves a desire to transcend being a *Homo sapien*, it is hard to see this as horrifying. Of course, we can imagine some kind of grotesque transformation, but we can just as easily imagine something awesome.

[13] Kitcher, *Life After Faith*, 100.
[14] Ibid.

Speaking personally, I doubt that I would be horrified to be transformed into a griffon or unicorn.

Finally, as I write this a good friend of 30 years just died. His arc of aging was horrific. As I think of Jim Brandt and contemplate the truth of either naturalism or Platonic Theism, one gives me hope for his continued existence while the other does not. Naturalism misses entirely the point of this hope; that beyond this arena of immanent goods is a life beyond in which Jim might be renewed in another dimension. It seems radically counterintuitive to hope for anything less.[15]

---

[15] I thank Samuel Benson, Stewart Goetz, and Joshua Seachris for their comments and assistance with earlier drafts of this chapter.

8

How God Makes Life a Lot More Meaningful

Richard Swinburne

My concern in this chapter will be with the meaning of the lives of humans on earth before death; if, as I believe, there is life after death, that will be relevant to my discussion only insofar as its character affects the meaning of life before death. The question of what is the meaning of life can be understood in many ways, the most obvious of which are: "What purpose did anyone have in making humans?" "Which states of affairs or actions would give meaning to human lives?" and "Which states of affairs or actions do humans believe would give meaning to their lives?" I shall ignore the third question, as it is clearly one for social psychologists to answer. The first question would take us into the whole issue of whether there is a God who created and sustains us and what he is like; and I shall not seek to answer that question here. But I shall argue here that the answer to it is relevant to the second question which is surely the one being asked by most of those who wonder about whether life has a meaning. And what the question seems to be getting at is: "What would make a life worthwhile, or good to have lived?" I shall understand it thus. I shall answer the question by appealing to intuitions which I believe almost all of us already have. I shall consider initially what would be worthwhile in our life on earth if we ignore the possible existence of God and a life after death; and then proceed to consider what difference would be made to the worthwhileness of our life on earth if there is a God and life after death.

1. Worthwhile life

Many kinds of states of affairs and actions are good, and any enumeration of them must begin with enjoyment. It is good to be in a state of affairs where you desire (or in the modern sense, "want") to be, to have the feelings, desires, and beliefs which you desire to have, and to be doing an action which you desire to be doing—this is equivalent to enjoying being thus situated or doing that action. A person is happy insofar as on balance he is so situated or doing such actions. This may or may not involve sensations of pleasure—thrills or warm feelings—but, if a person has those, they are part of what makes their action or situation enjoyable. But there is an obvious kind of qualification to be put on this. Someone who is getting his enjoyment from having feelings of hatred or other bad feelings, or from false beliefs or from doing what is morally wrong is not having or doing something which contributes to a worthwhile life, whether or not he realizes that he is having bad feelings or doing something objectively morally wrong. Indeed getting enjoyment in these ways is worse than not getting enjoyment at all. But, subject to this kind of qualification, surely all states and actions which are enjoyed are good because they are enjoyed, and so I side with those who think that if Sisyphus were injected with a drug which makes him enjoy endlessly pushing a stone up a hill, then that is a good state of affairs,[1] though of course there are better ones. And more generally, I suggest that (with some exceptions) the better the state of affairs in which one enjoys being or feeling, or the better the action one enjoys doing, the better is the state of enjoying it. Blessed is the person who does not merely help others but enjoys doing so.

Yet as most people recognize, there is more to a worthwhile life than enjoyment. There are states of affairs in which it is good to be whether or not you enjoy them as—despite his professed utilitarianism—Mill recognized in his famous sentence, "It is better to be a human being dissatisfied than a pig satisfied; better to be Socrates dissatisfied than a fool satisfied."[2] These states include both internal and external states. The former are involuntary states of oneself, often involving a relation to something outside oneself; the latter are states outside oneself which affect one. It is good for us to have power to make a difference to ourselves and the world, above all if we have some libertarian freewill, so that it is up to us to choose how to exercise our power independently to some extent of the influences acting on us. It is good if our power includes some power over what happens to others; that is, that we have responsibility for others. It is a blessing for us to need and to have children and friends whose well-being depends on us, and to desire to help them. To be no use to anyone is tragic. It is also good for us to have others such as parents, a spouse, and friends who know about our needs and can forward

---

[1] See Richard Taylor, *Good and Evil* (New York: Macmillan, 1970), chapter 18.
[2] J. S. Mill, *Utilitarianism*, ed. M. Warnock (London: Collins, 1962), chapter 2.

our well-being and desire to do so, for that makes it possible for them to be involved in our life in a deep way.

It is good to have true beliefs and correct feelings. It is good to have true beliefs (which I shall call simply "knowledge") about anything but especially about what is intrinsically good or bad, and about the causes of intrinsically good or bad states, and more generally about deep moral, metaphysical, aesthetic, and scientific matters (which may be obtained by appreciation of literature and other arts, as well as by studying rigorous philosophical arguments). It is good to have good desires—for the well-being of all humans (and animals), and especially of those close to us, and of ourselves—hence the goodness of Mill's human who desires to know more, and so is "dissatisfied." It is good to have correct feelings—of sympathy for those suffering, of affection for those friends who have interacted with us in important ways over a long time (parents and children, among others), of grief at the deaths of such friends, of sorrow at the failure of their projects, of anger at wrongdoers, and of respect for all humans, especially for the good and wise and powerful. It is good to feel respect for all humans for what is good in them, and so especially for the morally good, but also for those who have great power and responsibility—since having these is good in us, it is good in anyone else—so long as they exercise their power wisely. It is good to be well situated externally, to live in a beautiful city, or a law-abiding and prosperous country. For many of us our lives are worthwhile in many of these respects.

But it is a basic intuition that what we do with our powers and especially what we do successfully contributes more to the worthwhileness of our life than what happens to us. All actions as such, so long as they are not for bad goals, are, I suggest, good, for it is good to be the cause of things. But actions are better the more their goals take time and energy to achieve; it is as such good to have and fulfill a project. And it is better, the better the goal; while actions with bad goals are bad. I shall henceforward use the adverb "morally" in a wide sense so as to call any action which is overall good "morally good" and any action which is overall bad "morally bad." The morally good actions will therefore include obligatory actions (i.e., duties), and morally bad actions will include wrong actions, those which are obligatory not to do. Obligatory actions include feeding and educating our children, caring for our parents, keeping promises, telling the truth (possibly subject to qualifications), and expressing our gratitude to our benefactors. Wrong actions include breaking promises, lying, murdering, maiming, raping, and so on. Morally good actions also include the best actions of all, supererogatory actions, actions "beyond the call of duty," actions of doing more than we are obliged to do—caring for our parents and educating the children of others, and sacrificing one's own life (not merely some time and energy) to save the life of someone else. Morally good actions will also include "creative acts"[3]—fulfilling some project in no way obligatory or supererogatory, which involves effort and patience; and such an action is better, the better objectively is the goal of the project. Any acquisition of new knowledge or powers is good, but it is better the more important is the topic of knowledge, or the area of the power. It is better to study the origins of Buddhism than to list different types of beer label; better to learn an ancient language than to invent a new language, for the former saves an ancient culture from oblivion and honors its members. It is very good too to write novels, poems, and plays; play music, paint pictures, and develop one's understanding of the moral, metaphysical, and aesthetic realities, even if solely for our own benefit. But it is surely in general more important to fulfill an obligation than to do a supererogatory good act, and clearly more important than to do a creative act. Morally bad actions include ones which are not wrong, and which I call "infravetatory." It is wrong to rape or steal, yet it is bad but not wrong to watch many low-grade thrillers on television rather than read one or two great works of literature. And surely in general it is more important not to do what is wrong than not to do what is infravetatory. Almost all feelings which it is good to have, and situations in which it is good to be, are such that it is good to share them with others. It is better to get the sensations of sexual pleasure through the development of a personal relationship, not by themselves. Almost all actions which are good to do are better to do in cooperation with others. It is better to drink alcohol in company than alone. It is good for siblings to work together to look after parents, good to work with others to save a decaying waterway or an ancient language.

We have special obligations to those to whom we owe much, and especially to our parents who are to some small degree the cause of our existence, and—if they are also nurturing parents—for all their actions of feeding and nurturing us. We have special obligations to spouses who have promised us their lifelong loyalty; and special obligations to children whom we have caused to exist in an initial condition of total impotence. And we have lesser obligations to those who have benefited us in lesser ways, including simply by cooperating with us at work or having a friendly conversation with us. It is especially good for us and them if we benefit them spontaneously and supererogatorily; and, as many writers have stressed, long lasting personal relationships are central to a worthwhile life.

If we do wrong to others, it is obligatory to make atonement. Making atonement has four parts, not all of which are needed in the case of serious

---

[3] For Susan Wolf such "creative acts," as I call them, are central to what makes a life "meaningful," although she holds that a life being meaningful also involves fulfilling one's "duties" and being "happy." See her *Meaning in Life and Why It Matters* (Princeton: Princeton University Press, 2010).

wrongs. We must repent, apologize, make reparation, and do something extra to "make up" for the wrongdoing, which I call a "penance."[4] And it is good, if we make atonement, for the person wronged by us to forgive us (i.e., to resolve to treat us in the future as though we had not wronged them), though in my view not obligatory to do so.

The goodness of all these actions is an objective goodness, which exists whether or not the agent realizes that they are good, and objectively our lives would be much more worthwhile insofar as we do these actions. It is good in the case of many of these actions if we do them spontaneously, helping those in need for example because they are in need. But it is also good if we force ourselves to do the action despite a contrary desire, just because it is morally good to do—good for us, though not as good for those we seek to help. Yet of course no one action can be both spontaneous, and also done with difficulty for moral reasons. Not all our attempts to do good actions succeed, but it is good to have tried—good for those we tried to benefit, and good that someone tried to benefit them. It is good too if we tried to benefit ourselves, and so good that we tried to learn a foreign language, even if we failed. This is because trying is itself an action, and it is good that such an action should be directed toward a good end. We are exercising our powers in pursuit of the good. "Better to have loved and lost than never to have loved." But of course even better to have loved and won; successful actions contribute much more to the worthwhileness of a life than unsuccessful actions.

So in summary, a life of enjoyment, enriched by acquisition of knowledge, right feelings and deep friendships, is worthwhile, and we can make it much more worthwhile by helping others to enjoy themselves, acquire knowledge, right feelings, and abilities.

2. The difference God makes

So far in considering what makes a worthwhile life, for humans on earth before death, I have not taken into account the difference which would be made by our relation to anything transcendent. There is only space to consider the difference which would be made by one possibility, that there is a God who has the properties and has done the actions described in the Christian creeds. In this section I shall ignore the claim that God will give us a life after death, and consider that only in the following section. My conclusion will be that if there is a God of the kind described in the Christian creeds our situation would be far better than it would be otherwise, but that we have

---

[4] See my *Responsibility and Atonement* (Oxford: Oxford University Press, 1989) for full treatment of the concepts of atonements and forgiveness.

the power to make it both a lot better still or very much worse than it would be otherwise. Our life has a cosmic significance, good or bad, instead of a significance very limited in time and space. As before, I am describing the objective situation which would exist if there is a God, whether or not we realize it.

The Christian religion teaches that the whole universe and all its inhabitants including ourselves were created and are sustained by God who loves each one of us. I claimed in the previous section that it is a great good to have some understanding of the nature of things. The existence of God and his interaction with us makes available to us a deeper understanding of the ultimate nature of things than we would have otherwise. For even if we cannot understand why there is a God, at least we can understand why there are laws of nature and why humans exist—because God made and sustains them because he seeks to bring about good states of affairs. I claimed in the previous section that it is good for us to have others who know all about our needs and can forward our well-being. If there is a God, he knows all our needs and seeks to meet them in the best way. For so many humans, there is no other human who knows very much at all about their pains and pleasures; I suspect there is no human whose pains and pleasures are fully known by any other human. Anyway human friends die, but if there is a God, he keeps in his memory all the details of our significant and insignificant private and public lives. And we have the power to ask him (in prayer) to do good things for us and for others; if it is good that he should grant our requests he will do so. I noted earlier that it is good to feel reverence for the great who are also good, and to feel gratitude to benefactors. If there is a good God who made us, it is therefore very good to have the right feelings of enormous reverence for the supremely good and ultimate source of things and great gratitude for our own existence and all the good things our life contains. If there were no God, there would be no one to whom to be grateful for our existence, for although your parents may have chosen to have a child, they could not have chosen to have you. While it is good for us to have some good thing, it is always better if the good thing is given in an act of love for us. So it is very good for us if our whole life does not come to us by chance but by the act of a loving creator.

The very existence of God makes new actions obligatory or otherwise good, and we can make our life much more worthwhile by doing these actions. Whether or not we feel gratitude and reverence, we have an obligation to show the proper attitude toward God in grateful worship, and to cultivate those proper feelings. And it is supererogatorily good to do these things to a greater extent than we are obliged to do. Further, the mere existence of God makes acting morally always more important and sometimes very much more important than it would otherwise be. For we owe it to God not to waste the life he has given us, but to use it in good ways, as (to a much smaller degree) we owe it to our parents (if they are nurturing as well as biological parents) not to waste our life. So it is obligatory to fulfill our human obligations for a reason additional to the reason that we owe it to others to do so; and good too to benefit them in supererogatory ways, for a reason additional to the reason that it is good for them that we should do so. Further, other humans (and indeed animals) are, like ourselves, God's creatures, and so in a sense our brothers and sisters; therefore, our obligations to them are much stronger than they would be otherwise. And if we harm them we harm their creator, God, just as if I hurt your child, I wrong not merely the child but also you who have languished your love on her. And since each of us is God's creature, we have an obligation to God (although not to ourselves—an obligation is a debt; and one cannot have a debt to oneself) to care for ourselves. So, even without any commands issued by God, our scope for doing good or bad becomes much greater if there is a God, and so too therefore does the meaningfulness of our life if we choose the good.

But Christianity also teaches that God has issued particular commands, and that these impose new obligations on us. Benefactors often lay down a condition for the use of their gift. I may give a sum of money to one of my children on condition that they use it to buy a house. They are not obliged to accept the gift on that condition, but if they do accept it they have an obligation to fulfill the condition. Sometimes, however, the recipient of a gift subject to a condition is not able to understand the condition. Parents who are not just biological parents, but are nurturing and educating parents, give a lot to their children. And although they would not think of themselves as giving nurture and education to their children subject to a condition, they do expect and society expects them to expect that in return the children will do certain things for them, both when the children are young and when the parents are old. When children are young, parents command them to do certain things (e.g., to do the family shopping), and the command creates an obligation which would not otherwise exist. And when the parents are old, the children have an obligation to care for them. Since the children who receive so many good things from their parents were in no position to accept or reject them, they are rightly, in virtue of the goodness of the gifts, presumed to have accepted them, and to have accepted the obligations which accompany acceptance of the gift.

Parents are our greatest earthly benefactors. But God, for the reasons I have just discussed, is an incomparably greater benefactor. Hence our obligations to him are incomparably greater. Although he is never in the position of aged parents, we are in effect for all our life in the position of young children, totally dependent on him, having from him the good gift of life itself while originally being in no position to choose whether or not to accept that gift (yet, I hesitate to mention it, normally able subsequently to reject the gift by committing suicide). Hence God's commands, like the commands of a parent, impose upon us obligations to do what he commands, obligations which would not otherwise exist. The Book of Genesis pictures God as creating man and telling him how to use his life—"Be fruitful and multiply," "Fill the earth and subdue it," but do not eat of the tree of the knowledge of good and evil.[5] And all Western religions claim that God has issued in the course of time more specific commands, among them the "Ten Commandments." That we should obey God's commands is the condition under which he gives us life, and we who have used the life he gave us for many years must accept the condition under which we have been given it. God's commands make it contingently the case that some action which would otherwise be only supererogatorily good or morally indifferent is now obligatory, and his forbidding it makes an action morally wrong, when previously it was only infravetatorily bad or morally indifferent. And the teaching of Jesus has filled out for us how God commands us to live. While endorsing the obligations captured in the "Ten Commandments" and other obligations which secular morality recognizes (e.g., "render into Caesar the things which are Caesar's" which in the context of its utterance implies "pay your taxes"), he clearly regarded God as having commanded all humans to do more and more demanding actions of kinds which, but for God's command, would be merely supererogatory—giving food to the hungry and drink to the thirsty, welcoming the stranger, clothing the naked, and visiting the sick and those in prison.[6] And he commands particular individuals to fulfill their own often difficult vocations, such as spreading the Gospel in particular places (such as his command to Jonah to preach to the people of Nineveh the need for repentance). In issuing commands of these kinds to particular individuals God entrusts the fulfillment of his purposes to them, and thus, not merely do we need God, but God has put himself in a position where he needs us. I argued earlier that it is a good thing to be needed; it is a very good thing to be needed by the creator of the universe in the fulfillment of his greatly good purposes for humans. The new obligations which I acquire if there is a God are obligations to do greatly worthwhile actions, and the existence of God and his commendations providesgreat scope for further supererogatory good acts. It is good to render praise in supererogatory ways to God for creating and sustaining us, and good to visit the sick and those in prison more than we are obliged to do. These acts are not merely good for the sick and those in prison, but good

---

[5] See Genesis 1:27–28 and 2:17.
[6] See Matthew 25:31–46.

for God who created us to do such good acts and thereby forward Christ's Kingdom of love on earth, and also good for us.

In all these ways, the existence and commands of God make it possible for us not merely to do more and more important good acts, but thereby to form a good character. For each time we do a good act, it becomes easier to do a good act next time. As Aristotle remarked, "we become just by doing just acts, prudent by doing prudent acts, brave by doing brave acts."[7] So by doing such acts, we may make it natural to do them, and so come to enjoy doing them.

But of course we may fail and waste our lives, and then we must apologize not merely to any wronged humans but also to God, who made us to be good and whose children the wronged humans are. While it is bad for me if my life is wasted, it is worse if I am the cause of the waste, but not so bad if compensation is available for the waste of the life or my wasting it. If there is no God, there is no compensation available either for the waste of my life or for my wasting it. Christianity, however, teaches that Jesus Christ, God incarnate, died on the cross to provide a reparation (and penance) which we can offer back to God with our repentant apology in atonement for our sins, that is, our wrongs against him; and if we do, he will forgive us, subject to the condition that we forgive those who have wronged us. And for that atoning act of Jesus we owe immense further gratitude to God. Forgiving someone who has wronged you involves treating them as though they had not wronged you, and so you compensate the wrongdoer for the badness of their action (though not its consequences). Many of us have wasted our lives in many ways. If my life is a gift from God and I have wasted it, then I owe God repentance for having done so and he can forgive me and so treat me as though I have not wasted my life. My wasted life was not mine to waste—I owed it to God to lead a good life, and so by my wasting my life, it is God, not I, who has lost something. By forgiving me, God will remove the badness of my wasting my life. Only a religion with a creator God offers the possibility of compensation for the badness of my wasting my life. And God can also remove the bad consequences of my wasting my life.

I owe my life in small part to my parents. I also owe it to them as well as to other humans whom I have harmed to repent and apologize, and also to make reparation. If I do repent, apologize, and make such reparation as I am able to make, to those other humans, God provides a considerable incentive to them to forgive me, even without adequate reparation on my part—since God's forgiveness of them is conditional on their forgiveness of me. Nevertheless, even if others forgive me for having wronged them, the bad consequences of my action may remain; if I have maimed them or even killed them, I cannot undo

---

[7] Aristotle, *Nichomachaean Ethics* 1103b.

this damage, but God can. In most cases God has given them so much good anyway that the harm they have suffered at my hands is already compensated by the good life which he has provided for them so far; but sometimes the harm which I have caused them may outweigh the good aspects of their lives, and God can help here too. I will come to this point shortly.

So the existence and actions of God, on the Christian account of these, makes our situation on earth more worthwhile than it would be otherwise, and gives us enormous scope to make it yet far more worthwhile by doing morally good actions which have a deeper importance than they would have otherwise. But a God who creates morally free agents would surely not think it right to impose on them obligations which cover every moment of their lives. So I endorse the Catholic view in opposition to classical Protestantism,[8] that there is a limit to the obligations which God imposes on humans. There is scope for "works of supererogation" and also—I suggest—for "creative acts," though we certainly would not need to do these in order to give meaning to our lives.

But, just as the existence of God opens up enormous possibilities for good not available otherwise, it also opens up enormous possibilities for evil. If we fail to worship, fail to fulfill God's commands, and fail to fulfill our ordinary secular obligations (which are now doubly obligatory), we do great wrong to our creator. And if we go on doing this, we become naturally bad people, and so people motivated to do actions less and less by the goodness of those actions, until eventually we become insensitive to moral considerations. We "lose our souls," and become merely a theater of competing desires. To lose the possibility of so much good would be a great evil.

3. The difference afterlife makes

Good as life on earth could be for all humans, especially if there is a God, even if he did not provide an afterlife, it could be even better if, as Christianity claims, God provides an afterlife for us. As in both the previous sections, I am describing the objective situation which would exist in this case if there is a God and an afterlife, whether or not we realize that.

I begin with one aspect of the teaching of Jesus about the afterlife which has been given little consideration in the subsequent tradition—the

---

[8] The line between the obligatory good acts (stated in "precepts") and the supererogatory (stated in "counsels") has been drawn in different places by different theologians. Aquinas, for example, saw the instructions about "true love for enemies and the like" as precepts telling us that "we should be ready to do good to enemies and so on when necessity demands"; but also as counsels to do this "when no special necessity arises"— *Summa Theologiae* Ia2ae 108.4 ad 4.

possibility of a good (maybe temporary) afterlife in compensation for suffering on earth. Some humans on earth are so racked with pain and ignorant of the possibilities of good action that their earthly life is on balance barely good, and maybe even bad. Although their suffering may provide opportunities for others to help them, God as our benefactor must compensate those who suffer in this way. And God has it also in his power to compensate after death those whom I have hurt for the hurt which I have done to them when I cannot repair this and when he has not already compensated for it on earth. The parable of the rich man and Lazarus suggests that Jesus taught that a good state in the afterlife is sometimes a compensation for a life of suffering on earth, rather than always being a reward for a life of virtue.[9] On earth the rich man "feasted sumptuously every day" while Lazarus "longed to satisfy his hunger with what fell from the rich man's table," but after death Lazarus "is comforted," but the rich man is "in agony." There is no suggestion in the parable that Lazarus lived a particularly saintly life; what gained him the good afterlife was simply his suffering on earth. The possibility of a good afterlife as compensation for those who suffer too much on earth adds much to the worthwhileness of life on earth. That an afterlife at least on balance good is available for reasons other than that they have lived a saintly life on earth was suggested also by the medieval theory of Limbo, the place between Hell and Heaven which would be occupied by unbaptized babies.

However that may be, the central Christian doctrine of the afterlife concerns the final separation of those who have lived good lives on earth from those who have lived bad lives. The former are promised heaven. The second Vatican Council declared that while "salvation" and so Heaven was not open to those who had without justification rejected the Christian message, it was open to non-Christians (including atheists) so long as they have "striven to live a good life."[10] In declaring this, the Council repeated the view of some of the most important Christian theologians of past centuries.[11] It is open, that is, to those who have got into the habit of living a good life, and so would be ready to avail themselves of the atonement provided by Christ when they learn about it. The New Testament (apart from its last book, *The Book of Revelation*) has relatively little to say about what Heaven would be like, but some patristic and medieval theologians developed what it had to say,[12] and I suggest the following as a reasonable account of the Christian view of this.

---

[9] Luke 16:19–31.
[10] Vatican II. *Dogmatic Constitution on the Church: Lumen Gentium* (Chicago: Pauline Books, 1965), §16.
[11] For example, see my *Faith and Reason*, 2nd edn (Oxford: Oxford University Press, 2005), 208, note 5.
[12] See B. E. Daley, *The Hope of the Early Church* (Cambridge: Cambridge University Press, 1991). I am indebted to Daley for his very full description of the understanding of the

Christian theology emphasizes that the life of Heaven is something which begins on earth for the person who pursues the Christian way. This is because the pursuit of that way on earth involves starting to do the tasks of Heaven—which are the good actions described in the previous sections—for a short time under difficult conditions. The Christian on earth has begun to understand the divine nature (by Bible reading, receiving religious instruction, etc.), to worship (in the Eucharist with music, poetry, art, etc.), and to show the divine love to others. But his tools are poor, his mind and his instructors provide weak understanding of the divine nature, his organs and choirs are poor things, and so often neither in worship nor private prayer does he feel in contact with God; other humans are hostile to his religion, his attempts to help others fail, and he often has strong desires to do bad actions. These obstacles to the full pursuit and enjoyment of the Christian way would be removed in Heaven. Those who have shown serious dedication to the good by persistently doing good actions on earth would have no inclination to do evil when the obstacles to doing good are removed.

More precisely, the removal of earthly obstacles will mean growth in unclouded awareness of the nature of God himself, traditionally called the "Beatific Vision" of God,[13] and responding to it in grateful adoration and service. The *Book of Revelation* represents God as making his home among humans, and declaring "I will be their God and they will be my children."[14] Since God is a being of infinite wonder, it can take beings of finite power an eternity to comprehend him. Those who "follow the way of God's wisdom," wrote Origen, should think of themselves as living in tents, "with which they always walk and always move on, and the further they go, so much more does the road still to walk grow long and stretch out endlessly ... [The mind] is always called to move on, from the good to the better, and from the better to still higher things."[15] Heaven will also involve friendship with good finite beings, including those who have been our companions on earth. The task of comprehending and worshipping God will be a cooperative one. Augustine wrote that the description of Heaven as "the city of God" would have no meaning "if the life of the saints were not social."[16] Christian theology has

---

afterlife by Christian theologians of the first 500 years of Christianity. He brings out how there is virtually total agreement among those theologians about the nature of Heaven, although there is much less agreement about whether there is a purgatorial state through which some have to pass on the way to Heaven, and about the fate of those (if any) who do not get to Heaven.

[13] Apostle Paul: "Now we see in a mirror, dimly, but then we will see face to face" (1 Cor. 13:12).
[14] Revelation 21:7.
[15] Origen, Homily 17 on Numbers, cited in Daley, *The Hope of the Early Church*, 50.
[16] St. Augustine, *City of God*, 19.5.

always stressed both that Heaven will involve a renewal of earthly acquaintance, and that the enjoyment of such acquaintance will not be its main point. And of course one always enjoys acquaintance better if it serves some further point—if one and one's fellows are working together in a worthwhile task. The saints reign with Christ in glory,[17] and so have other work to do—interceding before God for humans on earth or elsewhere, and executing God's purposes in other ways, and thus bringing others into the sphere of God's love. So the occupations of Heaven are simply the occupations which, I argued in the previous section, are the occupations which would be good on earth if the Christian doctrine of God is correct, but the occupant of Heaven will be able to pursue them in a far fuller way without impediment. The inhabitant of Heaven would inevitably be greatly happy, for happiness consists in doing and have happen to you what you want to be doing and have happen to you. Aquinas taught that man's ultimate goal is *beatitudo*,[18] which is not merely supreme "happiness" but supreme happiness derived from doing successfully what is supremely worthwhile. And that is what the life of Heaven would be, when the obstacles to living the Christian life are removed, and so the blessed are successful in securing the vision of God so difficult to obtain on earth. The person who has the wrong character does not want to pursue the occupations of Heaven, and so, even if he got to Heaven, he would clearly not be happy there and so not have the well-being possessed by those who want to be there. So if there is a Christian God who also provides life after death, there is available to us on earth a meaningful life on earth, which has, among other goals, the goal of attaining that heavenly life, and which would make life on earth even more meaningful than it would be otherwise.

But of course the greater the goal, the greater the loss if we fail to secure it. And, given the availability of Heaven (which may for many of us, on Orthodox or Catholic views, require an intermediate and perhaps purgatorial period, in which we can make ourselves more fully dedicated to the good), we have the power on earth to deprive ourselves of an enormous good by finally rejecting it. Majority Christian tradition has emphasized that this can happen only by our own (what I reasonably construe as) "libertarian" free choice (i.e., a choice not fully caused by anything else, be it God, nature, or nurture). And, in rejecting "universalism" (the view that necessarily all humans will be saved, that is, go to Heaven), it allows the possibility that someone will so frequently and seriously

---

[17] See Christ's words to his disciples: "Truly, I tell you, at the renewal of all things, when the Son of Man is seated on the throne of his glory, you who have followed me will also sit upon twelve thrones, judging the twelve tribes of Israel" (Matt. 19:28). "Judging" may mean here "ruling over."

[18] "By a single, uninterrupted and everlasting act the mind of a human being will be united with God in that state of beatitude." *Summa Theologiae*, 1a 2ae. 3. 2 ad.4.

reject good choices that they lose all sense of moral goodness and so all inclination to do the good, and thus they will not be saved. Hell is the "place" for such persons. There is, I suggest, no need to take talk of "fiery" torture (*poena sensus*) too literally, but it will certainly—on Christian tradition—involve *poena damni*, the penalty of the loss of God, which Augustine, a firm advocate of everlasting sensory "punishment" for the wicked, acknowledged as by far the most important part of the "punishment" of Hell.[19] But if God is really to give humans a choice of the kind of people they are to be, he must offer them the choice of rejecting him permanently, and allow them, if they really insist on making that choice, to have what they choose.[20] If there is a God and an afterlife, we do indeed have the power to make our life very much better and also very much worse than it would be otherwise.

4. A practical argument for living the Christian life

What I have been describing in the previous sections is what I regard as the features of human life, both those features for which we are not responsible, and the actions which we can choose to do, which make it meaningful. In the first section I appealed to common intuitions about this; but in the two subsequent sections, I applied the results of the first section to show that life could be very greatly meaningful if we choose to do certain kinds of action, on the assumption that there is a God of the kind which Christianity postulates who will provide us with an afterlife. I have not given arguments here for the latter assumptions, although I have given them at length elsewhere.[21] But each of us can only do our subjective best—live the life which would be the best to live, given our own beliefs about what this is. If you believe my assumptions, then your subjectively best life would be what I have claimed to be the objectively best life. But suppose you are agnostic about these matters.

---

[19] See his *Enchiridion*, chapters 112 and 113.
[20] Aquinas wrote: "There would be no everlasting punishment of the souls of the damned if they were able to change their will for a better will ... The souls of the wicked will cleave unchangeably to the end which they themselves have chosen." *Summa Contra Gentiles*, 4.93.2 and 5.
[21] See my *Existence of God*, 2nd edn (Oxford: Oxford University Press, 2004), and the much shorter "popular" version of this, *Is There a God?* revised edn (Oxford: Oxford University Press, 2010) for arguments for the existence of God. See my "popular" book *Was Jesus God?* (Oxford: Oxford University Press, 2008) summarizing arguments contained in several of my other books, in favor of the detailed Christian doctrines about the nature and actions of God and the doctrine that he will provide an afterlife. See my book *Responsibility and Atonement* (Oxford: Oxford University Press, 1989), especially chapters 11 and 12, for a fuller account of the doctrine of the afterlife in Christian tradition.

Suppose you believe perhaps that it is as likely as not that there is a God and an afterlife of the kind which Christian tradition claims, but suppose that you also believe that if any theistic religion is true, it is most probable that the Christian religion is true. What in that situation is the point of trying to live a Christian life? My answer is that living the Christian life could still be the subjectively best life for you to lead, because although it would consist in trying to reach goals which might well not be attainable, yet because those goals are such great ones, the attempt to attain them would give significant meaning to your life.

I begin by considering the part of that life which involves prayer and worship. Consider this analogy to your situation: suppose that you are poor and badly need money, and then you learn that some anonymous person has put a large sum of money into your bank account which will enable you to satisfy your needs. You do not know who the donor is, but you think that it is as probable as not that it is a certain person, Smith. Surely, you would think it good (even if not obligatory) to thank Smith profusely, even though he refuses to acknowledge being the donor. You would think very badly of yourself if you had not made some serious attempt at gratitude, not merely saying words of gratitude but doing some minor favor for Smith. If you are in the same position in relation to God, it would surely be good to make a similar attempt at expressing gratitude and trying to do the things which, if he exists, he would want you to do.

Second, while only the obligations toward your fellow humans would be subjectively obligatory for you, all the obligations toward your fellows which result from the existence of God and from the commands of God to do even more and more demanding actions of the same kind of thing (give more to the poor, help to educate those in more distant countries, and so on) are ones which even secular morality recognizes as supererogatorily good. To live the best possible life involves doing much good beyond obligation.

So even as an agnostic, in order to live the subjectively best earthly life, you have good reason to try to live the Christian life. But for agnostics, even more than for theists, it's not easy to live that life on earth, and it would be good for you to live that life in a Heaven where there are no obstacles to its fulfillment. Yet you would only enjoy that life in Heaven if you desire to live it, and the only way to get to desire to live there is to try to get into the habit of living that life on earth when it is difficult. So, if you think that there is, say, a probability of 1/2 that the Christian doctrinal system is true, and you want what it offers (i.e., Heaven) a lot more than you want other things (and if my arguments so far are correct, it is good to want this), it would be good to live the Christian life on earth, especially since it is good anyway to live most parts of that life. So for an agnostic, as for a Christian believer, the subjectively best life to live would be the Christian life. (But of course that conclusion does not follow if you believe that it is very improbable that Christian doctrines are true.) It gives great meaning to life to seek a greatly worthwhile goal, even if there is a significant probability that you will not achieve it.[22]

---

[22] This paper overlaps to a considerable extent a paper "Why the Life of Heaven is Supremely Worth Living," in *Paradise Understood: New Philosophical Essays About Heaven*, eds. T. Ryan Byerly and Eric J. Silvermann (Oxford University Press), forthcoming.

Part Four

The Purpose(s) of Life

9

Affective Gethsemane Meaning for Life

Paul K. Moser

Philosophical debates about "the meaning of life" or, less ambitiously, "the meaning in life" include questions about whether there is an overarching, all-inclusive purpose for human life. The debate does not concern whether everyone *knowingly* has such a purpose, because it is obvious that not everyone does. Instead, the debate concerns whether such a purpose is available to be known by humans and thereby to guide human lives. This chapter explores this topic, contending that philosophers have overlooked an important option for resolving the matter: the *affective Gethsemane option* that directly involves a human's will and affections relative to God's will and affections. Meaning from God may be sensitive to a human's will and affections in a manner that makes the recognition of such meaning variable and elusive. In this regard, such meaning would fit with the elusiveness of God.

1. Meaning and purpose

Most philosophers have no objection to ordinary talk of the meaning "in life," given that humans typically have various purposes (or intentions) in life. Those purposes can yield meaning in life, at least for the people with the purposes. I can intend to become the world's best photographer of abandoned American farms, for example, and that can give meaning in my life, at least for me. The plot thickens regarding "the meaning of life," however, because it is unclear to many people that there is any such thing as "the purpose of life." In particular, it is unclear that there is any source for such a singular, overarching purpose.

A key question is: *Whose* intention or will is to yield "the purpose of life"? No merely human intention will serve, because such an intention will not automatically be normative for all others. Merely human intentions, in addition, are transient in that they do not endure without end, and thus they can fail to bear on some humans. They also can be distorted and misguided relative to what is genuinely good for humans, and hence can be harmful. We shall ask whether something that transcends merely human purposes could provide "the purpose," and hence "the meaning," of human life.

If God is perfectly good and thus compassionately redemptive toward humans, the will of God could underwrite an enduring purpose for humans, even if humans are unaware of this will and their own purposes conflict with it. Perhaps God allows human wills to obstruct God's perfect will to some extent. In that case, God could hide his will from some humans when such hiding is best for them, such as when they would only deride it or otherwise diminish its significance. As a result, the meaning for human life, as represented in God's will, could be hidden from them, at least for a time. So, humans may need to seek for this meaning and discern it in some way.

We shall consider that a certain kind of *affective Gethsemane resolution* is needed not only to bring human wills, purposes, and affections in line with God's will, purposes, and affections, but also to reveal, in a well-founded manner, God's will and affections to humans and hence any overarching meaning for human life. In this perspective, well-founded human discernment of God's will and affections requires a Gethsemane resolution that includes human agreement with the attitude of Jesus toward God in Gethsemane: "Not what I will, but what You, God, will" (see Mk. 14:36). The Gethsemane resolution demands that humans die to what they will apart from God's will, in order to live by what God wills. In this regard, humans must die into God's purpose, meaning, and life for the sake of lasting life with God.

Because God's will would include compassion for people, including enemies, it would be irreducibly affective.[1] The meaning of life, then, could be hidden from humans, but would be available to them in a Gethsemane resolution relative to God's will and affections. Just as God would hide for redemptive purposes, so also the meaning of life depending on God's will and affections would be elusive and even hidden from some humans for redemptive purposes.

Although a purely *de dicto* statement representing the meaning of life could be made to people in general, it would lack, for many people, the distinctive kind of *de re* evidential base available only from a first-person affective Gethsemane perspective. We shall consider a first-person *de re* component that is crucial to the needed supporting evidence, but this component

---

[1] On God's having passions, see Abraham Heschel, *The Prophets* (New York: Jewish Publication Society of America, 1962); and Paul S. Fiddes, *The Creative Suffering of God* (Oxford: Clarendon Press, 1988).

allows for a purely *de dicto* statement that represents the meaning without the needed first-person evidence. The merely stated meaning will lack an evidential motivation for people in the absence of the supporting first-person evidence, and therefore it will be evidentially hidden from many people, in the way that God is hidden.

Many defenders of Christian belief assume that God's purpose for human life can be identified simply on intellectual grounds, on the basis of the historical evidence now available to everyone. They look to the history of Jesus in the New Testament, and infer that this history reveals God's purpose for human life for all humans. The rough idea is that this history indicates that God's purpose for human life is for humans to trust, obey, and love God in Christ and thereby to love all other persons, even enemies. This rough idea may be correct, but it lacks something from the standpoint of meaning that moves, or motivates, a person. It can strike a person as just another objective truth that fails to prompt one to act, to live one's life accordingly. In that regard, it seems abstract and devoid of motivating significance. If it offers the meaning of human life, it does not offer *lived* or *experienced* meaning, at least for many people. Something is missing, and we need to identify the missing piece.

Somehow a human must be motivationally connected to any objective meaning or purpose for the latter to become lived meaning for that human. Otherwise, the meaning will float free of what moves the person to live one kind of life rather than another. In that case, the meaning will be life-indifferent for that person, in the way that an abstract truth of mathematics (say, the Pythagorean theorem) can be motivationally irrelevant to my life. We can distinguish between a lived meaning *in life* and a lived meaning *of life*, the latter being broader in scope than the former, and more controversial too.

A lived meaning in life for me will depend on an actual intention or purpose I have in my life. For instance, my intention to revive an abandoned farm town in North Dakota could give me a lived meaning in my life, complete with bracingly cold winters. This meaning would be limited to considerations regarding my reviving the abandoned town. In contrast, a lived meaning of life for me would bear on the meaning of my life as a whole; it would not be limited to considerations regarding a particular project in my life. This meaning of life for me would ideally guide all of the particular purposes in life for me in a way that makes them subsidiary to it; it thus would function as an umbrella norm for meaning in life for me. Even so, a lived meaning of life for me would have a basis in what I intend for the meaning of life for me. In that regard, it would be motivating for me and hence would be a lived meaning for me.

2. Meaning and will

Although many philosophers refrain from acknowledging an overarching meaning of life for a person, we should give the idea of such meaning our careful attention. One problem is that the idea is often tied up with a notion of God, and many philosophers doubt, for various reasons, that the latter notion picks out an actual personal agent with causal powers. Nonetheless, we need to give the idea of such meaning a cautious hearing, because it suggests something that would be important for human life: a kind of overarching meaning that integrates, at least ideally, the various meanings in human life. That kind of integration would unify a human life in important ways, and perhaps even add to its resilience in the face of obstacles and failures.

If a meaning of human life depends on an agent's will that is normative for humans, we face a question about the relevance of God's will. Here we may think of the term "God" as a maximally exalted title (and not a name) for a being who is worthy of worship and hence morally perfect. Being thus perfect, God would want what is best, all things considered, for all agents, even enemies of God, and God's affections, particularly God's compassion, would follow suit. God would be perfectly compassionate in a way that seeks the redemption of all humans in reconciliation to himself. This sets a high standard for God, but that kind of standard should be expected of God. The use of the term "God" as a title allows us to speak of God even if God does not exist.

If God wants what is best for humans, we have to consider the following result noted by Blaise Pascal:

> God wants to motivate the will more than the mind. Absolute clarity would be more use to the mind and would not help the will. Humble their pride.[2]

The key point is that God would want to move human wills toward eager cooperation with God's perfect will. This would include a challenge to human pride, or presumed self-sufficiency, because God's perfect will would have priority over human wills. In addition, God would want to move human wills in a manner that does not coerce them and thereby extinguish human agency. The divine redemption of human persons would fail if it destroyed the persons needing redemption by removing their volitional agency. As a result, God would seek to woo people by a manifestation of divine love

---

[2] Blaise Pascal, *Pensées*, Trans. Honor Levi (Oxford: Oxford University Press, 1657/1995), sec. 266.

without coercion. The aim would be to encourage human wills to yield to, and cooperate with, God's perfect will, for the good of humans.

John's Gospel identifies an important role for a human will relative to God's will, as follows: "Anyone who resolves [=wills] to do the will of God will know whether the teaching is from God or whether I [Jesus] am speaking on my own" (Jn. 7:17, NRSV, here and in subsequent Biblical translations). Resolving to do the will of God goes beyond reflection on God's will. It includes an exercise of the will to cooperate with God's will, in a manner that involves obedient action. Thinking about God's will need not include, or even lead to, obeying God's will. In fact, a person can think about God's will but hate it and resolutely disobey it. In that case, one will be, in effect, an enemy of God. One then will not be reconciled to God. Such a volitional problem would be central to God's dealings with humans, because God would want to include all humans in eager cooperation with the divine will, for their own good.

The divine redemption of humans, I have proposed, would seek the reconciliation of all humans to God.[3] God would first pursue humans in various ways (before humans pursued God) to offer them reconciliation to God as the center of a renewed life. We have no singular way for God to pursue humans throughout history; nor should we expect one, given significant human differences across time and cultures. We do have, however, some striking cases that arguably include God's pursuit of humans. Perhaps the most striking is the life of Jesus the Jew from Nazareth. Our best evidence indicates that Jesus regarded his life as a call from God to humans to receive the Good News of God's offer of reconciliation (see, for a sample, Mk. 1:14-15, Lk. 11:20, Mk. 14:22-24, Lk. 15:3-7). This call includes a call to faith, or trust, in God, and it extends to anyone who would sincerely listen to God, regardless of social or religious affiliation. It is thus the kind of call one would expect of a God who perfectly loves all people, and not just a select group.

A distinctive feature of the call from the life of Jesus is its emphasis on God's offer of forgiveness to humans. In one context, Jesus asks the following: "Which is easier, to say to the paralytic, 'Your sins are forgiven,' or to say, 'Stand up and take your mat and walk?' But so that you may know that the Son of Man has authority on earth to forgive sins—he said to the paralytic—'I say to you, stand up, take your mat and go to your home'" (Mk. 2:9-11). Jesus uses the example of physical healing to lend credibility to what he deems more important: his authority from God to offer forgiveness to humans. Similarly, he presents himself as a physician for human problems

---

[3] For discussion, see Ralph P. Martin, *Reconciliation: A Study of Paul's Theology* (Atlanta: John Knox, 1981).

that concern sin and righteousness: "Jesus … said to them, 'Those who are well have no need of a physician, but those who are sick; I have come to call not the righteous but sinners'" (Mk. 2:17). He offers a divine cure for spiritual illness, and it includes forgiveness from God. Of course, he does not think that some humans are actually righteous on their own; instead, he acknowledges that some humans presume to be self-sufficiently righteous and hence in no need of God's cure. One might say that, in his perspective, they are in serious denial.

The Gospel of Luke offers a concluding summary by Jesus that puts forgiveness at the center of his mission: "[Jesus] said to them, 'Thus it is written, that the Messiah is to suffer and to rise from the dead on the third day, and that repentance and forgiveness of sins is to be proclaimed in his name to all nations'" (Lk. 24:46–47). Luke portrays Jesus as having come to offer God's forgiveness to humans, even at the cost of his own life. So, Luke is aware that people do not universally receive the forgiveness on offer, and that some people oppose the offer vigorously and even violently. In one passage of conflict over forgiveness, he represents Jesus as commenting thus: "I tell you, her sins, which were many, have been forgiven; hence she has shown great love. But the one to whom little is forgiven, loves little" (Lk. 7:47). "The one to whom little is forgiven" is the one who does not receive the forgiveness on offer and perhaps even denies his or her need of it. So, the divine offer of forgiveness can generate conflict and controversy among humans.[4]

The divine offer of forgiveness would not be an end in itself. It would be an intended means to an end, that is, the reconciliation of humans to God and to other humans. God would offer reconciliation, including forgiveness, to humans, who may or may not receive what is being offered. Forgiveness, at its core, is a release from condemnation, hostility, and ill will from the one who forgives. When it is received, the person forgiven is (ideally) released from fear of condemnation, hostility, and ill will from the one who forgives. This kind of release can enhance the prospect of reconciliation, because it removes the fear that hinders reconciliation.

Divine reconciliation would include interpersonal relations that are peaceful, friendly, and good for the person reconciled to God and to other persons. Ideally, it would remove enmity, avoidance, and resistance from humans in relating to God and to other humans. It would replace those obstacles with eager and harmonious cooperation with God by the reconciled humans. God would seek and empower a good, peaceful community of all cooperative persons, and therefore reconciliation to God, as one whose goodness is

---

[4] For discussion, see Paul S. Fiddes, *Past Event and Present Salvation* (London: Darton, Longman, and Todd, 1989), 171–189.

authoritative for all persons, would be a priority for God relative to humans. As a priority, it would figure centrally in the divine effort to restore humans to a cooperative relationship with God.

Humans would be able to opt out of divine forgiveness and reconciliation, as we see from the resolute opponents of Jesus in the New Testament. This would amount to choosing death over life, if life is sustained by God. The human will, then, is crucial to the reception of divine forgiveness and reconciliation, even if God's will is in favor of this reception. So, this reception is not a matter of divine coercion. Instead, it depends on the cooperation of humans with God's will. Such cooperation depends on the human experience of God's will.

3. Experiencing God's will

The human recognition of God or God's will in experience would not be a casual, spectator sport. God would be too morally profound and serious for that kind of superficiality. Humans would need to discern the reality of God or God's will in their experience, with due attentiveness, given God's morally robust purpose of reconciliation. God's will would include a divine intention or purpose of reconciliation, and humans would need to discern this purpose in their experience. As a result, they would need to avoid being "out of focus" with God's reality and will. Herbert H. Farmer has remarked in this connection: "Many questions are answered wrongly, not because the evidence is contradictory or inadequate, but because the mind through its fundamental dispositions and presuppositions is out of focus with the only kind of evidence which is really available."[5] Humans can overlook the reality of God's will in their experience if they are out of focus with it, for instance, in a situation where they focus only on their own will. In that case, they may settle for agnosticism or atheism, and deny any role to God in life's meaning.

God's morally perfect will would not be fully continuous with an imperfect human will. In experiencing God's will, with due attention, an imperfect human would notice a disconnect, a fracture, in conscience at some point between one's own will and God's will. One's own will would not line up fully with God's will. God's will would involve a demand in human conscience, to conform to God's will, and this demand at some point would manifest the shortcoming of an imperfect human will relative to God's perfect will. A human can experience such a demand in conscience without acknowledging or recognizing that it is a demand from God. One might attribute it to

[5] Herbert H. Farmer, *Things Not Seen* (London: Nisbet, 1927), 5.

such an influence as one's parents, one's peers, or even one's reflective self. So, the role of God in conscience would not bind a person to acknowledge God. Alternative interpretations are typically live options for a person.

Why should one suppose that there is a divine will at all? Maybe one should not, if one lacks the needed evidence. We would need, in any case, to discern God via God's will and God's character revealed in that will. We could not apprehend God as if God were a scientific object (e.g., an electron), a household object (e.g., a sink), or an office object (e.g., a book). We could not approach God as if the attitude of the inquirers, including our own attitude, did not matter, because God would have a redemptive aim for humans even in their knowing God. Just as God's reality and will could be hidden from a person, perhaps owing to that person's uncooperative attitude toward God, so also the meaning of human life, anchored in God's will, could be similarly hidden. The elusive meaning would be the purpose of God for human life found in God's will.

Given God's unique character and its evidential significance, God would seek for one to know God directly, or person-to-person, at least at times. Otherwise, one would lack direct acquaintance or encounter with God's character. We humans have a hard time, and even resist, depending on or holding onto God and God's will only or even primarily. We find substitutes more convenient, if only because they are less challenging to us. In presenting us with a new standard in God's character, direct interaction with God can upset our lives, including our personal agendas, our peer networks, our social climbing, and our self-indulgent ways. So, we tend to neglect, avoid, and shy away from direct interaction with God, including any power in our experience that offers such interaction.[6]

A familiar alternative to direct interaction with God occurs in natural theology that relies on versions of the traditional arguments for God's existence: including ontological, cosmological, design, fine-tuning, and moral arguments. People using those arguments typically assume that direct interaction with God is cognitively inadequate, at least for many people, and that therefore an argument from natural theology is needed. The arguments offered are rarely compelling for people without an antecedent commitment to God's existence, and, bracketing ontological arguments, the arguments fail to yield a God who is worthy of worship and hence self-sufficiently morally perfect. The latter defect raises the difficult question of how one reasonably can proceed further, to a God worthy of worship. If one appeals at some point to direct experience of such a God, the question will arise as to whether the

---

[6] For discussion, in connection with New Testament interpretation, see David Crump, *Encountering Jesus, Encountering Scripture* (Grand Rapids, MI: Eerdmans, 2013).

arguments of natural theology then become dispensable. If direct experience is ultimately doing the work for access to God, the arguments in question will seem superfluous, especially if they fail to yield a God worthy of worship.[7]

Another common alternative to direct interaction with God emerges from religious rituals of various sorts. I can attend religious services every week or even everyday and participate in all of the rituals offered, such as a communion ceremony, a candlelight event, or a sacred procession. Even so, I could fail to have a direct experience of God, and even acknowledge this failure. Indeed, I might come to prefer the religious rituals to a direct experience of God, because the rituals do not require me to change my life toward cooperating with God's will. I could use the rituals to replace the hard redemptive work of cooperating with God's will, including the demand to forgive and love others, even my enemies. In addition, I could use the rituals to divert my attention from a direct interaction or encounter with God. This may be a misuse of the rituals, but many people have confessed to such a misuse.

We have a kind of control over arguments and rituals that we would not have over God's will. In particular, I cannot control what God wills, including when God wills to offer self-manifestation to a person, although I can do things that obstruct my discernment of God's will and self-manifestation. I can divert my attention from God, perhaps out of either fear of divine challenge to me or a desire to maintain control for myself. The resulting lack of direct interaction with God would entail a lack of direct evidence of both God and meaning from God. One is reminded of the human demand for a human king in the Old Testament, as an alternative to God as king (see 1 Sam. 8:1-22).

In diverting my attention from God, I would look away from any experience in my conscience of my will's being challenged by God. The latter experience would include an event of attention-attraction from God that makes me aware of an alternative to my will, that is, an alternative in God's will. For instance, I could be convicted in conscience to forgive and to love my enemies, including those who are currently harming me. I could not give this experience of attention-attraction and conviction to others, but I could report it to others. The key point, however, is that I would need to decide how to respond to the volitional challenge at hand: I could ignore it, reject it, or yield to it.

---

[7] For detailed argument, see Paul K. Moser, *The Evidence for God* (Cambridge: Cambridge University Press, 2010), 142-184; *The Severity of God* (Cambridge: Cambridge University Press, 2013), 120-137; "God without Argument," in *Is Faith in God Reasonable?*, eds. Corey Miller and Paul Gould (London: Routledge, 2014), 69-83.

I could live in sympathetic cooperation with the alternative will in question, and, in doing so, I could become indirect evidence for others of God's unique will. This would be human personifying evidence of God, owing to God's will being reflected in a cooperative human life.[8] A distinctive feature of God's will would be its demand for forgiveness and love of one's enemies, even toward those who are now harming oneself. A god who failed to make this demand would fall short of moral perfection and hence worthiness of worship. We have, then, a way to identify false gods. We also have a way to let God be Lord and God, in our yielding to the divine will self-manifested to us.

One's experience of God's will in conscience should prompt one to ask: What is the meaning of this? (see Acts 2:12). Perhaps such an experience would be dismissed by many, just as the distinctive experience of Acts 2 was in its original setting. Some people, however, would discern something important in an experience of God's will in conscience, and make themselves available to God by way of response. Accordingly, they might ask: What is this? A new teaching? (see Mk. 1:27).

In making themselves cooperatively available to God, people would be willing to be apprehended and known by God, and not just to apprehend and know God (see Gal. 4:9). As a result, they would defer to God by allowing God to have authority over themselves and their lives. They would sincerely resolve to let God alone be God relative to who they are and what they do. Such resolve would be irreducible to factual knowledge (that something is the case), because it would put one in a relation of submission toward God. One's sincere resolve to submit to God may be imperfect, but it would not be empty; it would have definite implications how one responds to God. We need to link such resolve to faith in God and meaning from God.

4. Faith and felt meaning

People do not ordinarily acknowledge that one's apprehending meaning from God depends on one's having faith in God. Perhaps this fact results from widespread misunderstanding of what faith in God is. One common misunderstanding is that faith in God is the same as belief that God exists. One can believe, however, that God exists, but refrain from trusting God at all. Because faith in God requires trust in God, belief that God exists falls short of faith in God. Faith in God is to have a directness toward God that removes the need for substitutes for God. It is prompted by a direct acquaintance with God's will, to which one responds with a resolve to trust and cooperate with

---

[8] For discussion, see Moser, *The Evidence for God*, 209–230.

God. Faith in God, then, is a response to an experience of God, perhaps in conscience, and therefore it is irreducible to wishful thinking or guesswork about God.[9]

Faith in God is anchored in experiential evidence, because it is a response to a direct experience of God and God's will. A direct experience of God that is pertinent to meaning would be a direct experience of God's will, and a direct experience of God's will that is pertinent to meaning would be a direct experience of God. Meaning for human life requires purpose for human life, and God's purpose for human life would be in God's will. God would be the ultimate source of God's purpose, and this purpose would cohere with God's morally perfect character, a character worthy of worship.

Faith in God would be the avenue to God's purpose, because faith in God is positively responsive and sympathetic toward God in a way that makes one available to understand God's purpose to some extent. Faith in God excludes the kind of resistance to God that impedes one's understanding of God's purpose. The understanding (or meaning) in question is *felt*, affective understanding (or meaning), not merely intellectual understanding (or meaning). It depends on the feelings of an agent. Likewise, God's purpose would not be merely intellectual, but would be a felt purpose, given its including perfect compassion, even toward enemies. The same holds for God's will: It would be affective owing to its inclusion of felt compassion, and not just a notion of compassion. We no longer have God's will if we divorce it from felt compassion for others.

God's purpose would be subtle, elusive, and affective in a way that calls for an affectively sympathetic response from humans if they are to understand it adequately, that is, in the manner intended by God. God would intend that humans have this kind of sympathetic response, and could reasonably hide from humans in the absence of it, for the sake of preserving the redemptive value of his purpose or meaning for human life. The intended response would include one's feeling something with God, or better, sharing in God's feeling in God's purpose. In the absence of such a response, humans will be left with vague glimmers at best, because they will not be available to understand adequately the kind of purpose God would offer. Their understanding would be intellectual at most, and, in any case, would fall short of what God intends in affective and volitional understanding.

God's purpose would encompass affective enemy-love, including enemy-compassion, as part of its content. So, a human failure to apprehend such love and compassion affectively would inhibit adequate understanding of them

---

[9] For details, see Moser, *The Evidence for God*, 90–125, and Moser, *The Severity of God*, 115–120, 144–159.

and the corresponding divine purpose. It also would obstruct one's knowing God. As the writer of 1 John suggests: "Whoever does not love does not know God, for God is love" (1 Jn. 4:8). I take this to imply that whoever does not receive and exemplify God's kind of love does not know God, because God is inherently loving. The love in question is affective and volitional, not just intellectual.

Without receiving God's kind of compassion (knowingly or unknowingly), even for enemies, humans will lack a source and model for such felt compassion. It is doubtful that humans can create it by themselves in a manner that captures what would be God's perfect compassion. Here, again, the writer of 1 John points in the right direction: "love is from God" (1 Jn. 4:7). I lack the evidence to hold that humans on their own can produce and sustain the kind of affective volitional love that would be characteristic of God, even though they can share in that love. We see a kind of enemy-love in memorable cases where a person forgives with compassion another person who has intentionally brought great harm to the former person. These are arguably cases of sharing in God's unique love, even if one is unaware of doing so. When humans take credit for such love, they exaggerate what they produce on their own and take the risk of dishonoring the divine source of this love.

We should highlight the idea of understanding God's purpose or meaning of human life *to some extent*. One can have faith in God that includes volitional and affective sympathy with God's will, but still have meaning from God that is incomplete and puzzling. Gaps in God's revealed will would leave humans with incomplete meaning and understanding. The book of Job offers a powerful illustration of this lesson; Job is left with many unanswered questions about God's purposes in allowing evil and in creating the world. We overreach if we expect a perfectly complete system of meaning from God, especially a complete theodicy that explains all of God's purposes in allowing evil. If the meaning of life for humans depends on God's purpose for human life, and God has not revealed the latter purpose fully to humans, then we will not fully comprehend the meaning of life. We are, I suggest, in that situation of incomplete meaning, for better or worse. This should be no surprise, because humans seem not to be in a position now to understand God's redemptive purpose fully.

The incompleteness of the meaning we apprehend does not challenge the reality of that meaning. It does call, however, for modesty regarding how much we understand about the meaning of life. We might come to know that God wants us to learn to love as God loves, but this lesson can leave unanswered many of our questions about God's purposes. In this regard, we live with fragmentary meaning at best. Perhaps this limitation helps to save us from unbridled arrogance about our explanatory resources in connection with life's meaning. Perhaps, too, this is part of God's purpose for human life. In any case, it is doubtful that our having an incomplete understanding of the meaning of life would interfere with God's purpose to have us learn to love as God does. We still could grow in the kind of affective and volitional love characteristic of a God worthy of worship. Such love does not require that we fully understand God's purpose for human life. As one sympathetically cooperates with divine love more deeply, however, one can understand God's redemptive purpose more deeply.

If meaning from God is apprehended by faith in God, we will face considerable variability in human perception of the meaning of life. We have similar variability in human recognition of the reality of God; hence the existence of theists, atheists, and agnostics. Just as the reality of God appears to be hidden from some people, so also does the meaning from God for human life. (We might say the same for grounded hope in lasting meaning.) As a result, we should not expect to have a cogent argument for the meaning of life that convinces all inquirers, just as we should not expect to have such an argument for God's reality that is acknowledged by all inquirers (all special pleading from natural theology aside).

Arguably, many agnostics about divine meaning for human life, like many agnostics about God's existence, can reasonably be agnostics, given the evidence they have. So, if I am a theist, I should not expect to silence all dissenters with an argument. The relevant evidence is too variable among persons for such an expectation. Perhaps this fact will discourage us from misplaced arrogance about the scope of our evidence for God and the meaning of life. Perhaps it also is part of God's purpose for cognitive modesty in human life, especially for those who presume to have knowledge of God or even good evidence of God's reality and character. In any case, apologetic purposes can lead one to be overconfident, if not dogmatic, about the reach and the cogency of the evidence for God's reality.

Perhaps the meaning from God for human life has normative value, in that it would be good for all people to embrace. Even if it has such value, it does not follow that all people are in an evidential or psychological position to embrace it now. Many people may not be prepared now to embrace the meaning from God, for one reason or another. This consideration does not challenge the normative value of meaning from God. Instead, it challenges a claim that all people are now motivated, or otherwise ready, to recognize such meaning. As a result, God may hide such meaning from some people, to protect its value for a future redemptive purpose, that is, to avoid having them detest, trivialize, or finally reject it now and thereby block a future redemptive opportunity.

God would reveal meaning to humans in ways that suit God's redemptive purposes, and God would know that some people are not ready now to satisfy, or even to take seriously, those purposes. God thus would be able to delay self-manifesting and the corresponding revelation of divine meaning for human life until an opportune time for such people. It does not follow, however, that we have a complete account of the purposes for divine hiding at times. I doubt that a complete account is now available to us.[10] Proponents of Theism sometimes overreach by disregarding the kinds of variability just outlined, and this makes their Theism appear to depend on special pleading in a way that disregards evidence. Such neglect also can repel people from Theism as a well-founded option.

5. Death and meaning

If God truly wants to build a good community among humans for the sake of their redemption, a painful obstacle emerges: death. Death interrupts such a community and development toward it. Would a redemptive God who seeks to give meaning to human life allow for such an obstacle? If so, why? These are big questions that confront any account of meaning from God, and I doubt that we have complete answers. As I suggested, we humans should not expect to have now a complete understanding of God's purposes in allowing the difficulties of human life. If the book of Job is right, God has not seen fit to reveal all of those purposes, and we have no reason to think that we can identify them on our own. So, cognitive modesty is in order, as is usual with explanations regarding God's ways toward human life.

We sometimes portray a divine redemption of humans as a continuous development from the life we now have. In other words, it is more of the same, but better. This, however, may be an uncritical portrayal. Perhaps divine redemption is not, at its core, a development from this life, but is instead a break from it, with a new beginning. Some of the New Testament writers suggest as much, and we should not ignore this possibility. For instance, the apostle Paul remarks as follows: "if anyone is in Christ, there is a new creation: everything old has passed away; see, everything has become new" (2 Cor. 5:17). Similarly, in John's Gospel, Jesus suggests that redemption in God's kingdom is a matter of being "born again, from above" (see Jn. 3:3,7). In this portrayal of divine redemption, we have something other than a continuous development from the life we now live. Instead, we have a new

---

[10] See Paul K. Moser, *The Elusive God* (Cambridge: Cambridge University Press, 2008), 105–113, 140–143; and Moser, *The Evidence for God*, 254–262.

beginning, a new "creation." The theme of new creation looms large in the New Testament story of divine redemption,[11] and it bears on the problem of death and meaning for humans.

We can understand death in the New Testament in terms of its symbolic value, namely as signifying the need for a new beginning with God as supremely authoritative. This new beginning is not life as usual, because it includes a new center of authority, power, and meaning: namely, God.[12] Even our knowing other people becomes new, in Paul's thought. He remarks: "From now on, therefore, we regard no one from a human point of view; even though we once knew Christ from a human point of view, we know him no longer in that way" (2 Cor. 5:16).[13] Paul thought of this new way of knowing as guided by what God has done for humans in the death of Christ; that is: "God proves his love for us in that while we still were sinners Christ died for us" (Rom. 5:8). The death of Christ, as God's beloved Son, becomes the demonstration of God's self-giving love for humans. It shows that God gives his very best to call humans out of alienation from God into reconciliation with God.

In Paul's story of Good News, God raises Christ from death, thereby validating the latter's self-giving love on behalf of God for humans. So, God's demonstration of self-giving love in the death of Christ is not made futile by death, because God overcomes death in the resurrection of Christ. This act of God can open the door to lasting meaning from God for human life. We humans cannot by ourselves supply lasting meaning, in contrast with temporary meaning, because we do not, and cannot, last by ourselves. Lasting meaning for us requires that we cooperate with, and share in, the power of one who does last. Otherwise, the death of humans will be the end of meaning for humans.[14]

Some humans claim to have no objection to being without lasting meaning, on the assumption that this life is enough. Others, however, hope for

---

[11] See Paul Minear, *Christians and the New Creation: Genesis Motifs in the New Testament* (Philadelphia: Westminster, 1994); and Moyer V. Hubbard, *New Creation in Paul's Letters and Thought* (Cambridge: Cambridge University Press, 1998).

[12] See Roy A. Harrisville, *Fracture: The Cross as Irreconcilable in the Language and Thought of the Biblical Writers* (Grand Rapids, MI: Eerdmans, 2006), 98–102.

[13] See also J. L. Martyn, "Epistemology at the Turn of the Ages: 2 Corinthians 5.16," in *Christian History and Interpretation: Studies Presented to John Knox*, ed. W. R. Farmer et al. (Cambridge: Cambridge University Press, 1967), 269–287; and Thomas E. Boomershine, "Epistemology at the Turn of the Ages in Paul, Jesus, and Mark: Rhetoric and Dialectic in Apocalyptic and the New Testament," in *Apocalyptic and the New Testament: Essays in Honor of J. Louis Martyn*, ed. Joel Marcus and Marion L. Soards (Sheffield, Eng.: Journal for the Study of the Old Testament Press, 1989), 147–167.

[14] See Bertrand Russell, "A Free Man's Worship," in *Mysticism and Logic* (New York: Doubleday, 1903), 44–54.

lasting life and lasting meaning from God. I suggest that we not lower the bar for desired meaning and life in advance of a search for meaning, including meaning from God, that is not only intellectual but also affective and volitional. Philosophers often assume that the search is simply intellectual, relative to the evidence one now has, but this assumption is too narrow.[15]

The search in question would be open to finding a meaningful life that is lasting. In Matthew's Gospel, Jesus remarks: "Those who find their life will lose it, and those who lose their life for my sake will find it" (Mt. 10:39; cf. Lk. 9:24). This claim seems enigmatic at best. We can make some sense of it, however, if we relate it to the self-giving life of Jesus himself. The relevant idea is: Those humans who seek to find a lasting meaningful life on their own terms and power will fail, owing at least to the impending demise of their lives, but those who rely on God, volitionally and affectively, for the meaning of their lives can enjoy lasting meaning for their lives, courtesy of God's power and purpose. The contrast, then, is between a human life limited to human power and purposes and a human life that cooperates with God's power and purposes for human life. The merely human power and purposes will not last, because humans will not last on their own, but the divine power and purposes offer viable candidates for lasting meaning for human life.

Perhaps death is to serve as a wake-up call for humans who tend to overlook that the value, purpose, and meaning of human life are fragile and at risk. If human life has a final demise, its value, purpose, and meaning will go with it. Everything human will then be lost. Death may be a signal that something beyond human power is needed to avoid a final demise. Paul suggests as much, as follows: "we have this treasure [of God's Good News] in clay jars [subject to physical destruction], so that it may be made clear that this extraordinary power [of new, lasting life] belongs to God and does not come from us" (2 Cor. 4:7). Paul holds that only God's power can solve the human predicament of death, and that this power must not be confused with human power. A lasting good life, in his perspective, cannot make do with human power, but must rest on God's unique power.

Death may be the suggested signal even if some humans have no desire to avoid a final demise for human life. This lack of desire is a bit disconcerting if it bears on people generally. Even if one has no concern for lasting life in one's own case, one might consider that some other people do prefer lasting good life in a good community. It would be puzzling for one to desire that the lives of these other people also have a final demise. It seems more charitable and

---

[15] For an analogous lesson regarding evidence, see Paul K. Moser, "God and Evidence: A Cooperative Approach," *European Journal for the Philosophy of Religion* 5 (2013): 91–105.

less grudging to endorse their desire for them at least, even if one excludes oneself from it. In any case, a lasting human life under the power and purpose of a morally perfect God seems to be a plausible candidate for a good life. We should not dismiss it as a bad thing, even if one thinks that the supporting evidence for its reality is thin.

In suggesting that death may be a wake-up call, I am suggesting that it could have existential value. It could prompt people to evaluate the direction of their lives and their options for redirecting their lives if appropriate. The undertaking of such an evaluation is no small project. In fact, it may be hard work, and it may take a lifetime. Some people may not want to be bothered by it, but that omission could result in a missed opportunity that is important and meaningful for human life. I see no reason to exclude the opportunity in question.

I have suggested that the undertaking should not be merely intellectual, but should attend to affective and volitional considerations about the inquirers in relation to God. In particular, the inquirers should be prepared to share in God's affective and volitional states. They should be open to feeling and willing what God feels and wills, as a way to be in a position to receive salient evidence of God's reality and will. Perhaps the best way to know God is to share in God's affections and will. That sharing also may be the best way to receive meaning from God; indeed, that may be the locus of meaning from God, in one's sharing in God's affective and volitional character.

A big problem is that we humans fail to love as God would love, and this failure would alienate us from God, at least to some degree. If God's compassionate love is inherent to, and characteristic of, who God is, one's being out of step with it will entail one's being out of step with God. Humans often are out of step with God in that regard, as human interactions with other humans show. Arguably, our affective and volitional set strays from God's, and this obstructs our receiving good things from God, such as evidence, purpose, and meaning. The practical issue for us becomes: Are we willing to redirect our affections and wills toward God's?

The issue has us face this difficult matter: Are we willing to forgive and love with compassion our enemies, even enemies now harmful to us, in the way that God would? The track record of humans is not encouraging on this front. As a result, we are familiar with harmful conflicts with others that seem not to go away. It is rare when such conflicts end in forgiveness and reconciliation. When they do end thus, they often end up in stories of exceptional, rather than normal, human behavior.

The problem here is not merely intellectual, and hence is not solved just by thinking harder or more clearly. Instead, it concerns how we feel and will toward others, in particular, our enemies. We often refrain from willing what is best for them, and will that they suffer punishment or condemnation, often on the assumption that they deserve it. In addition, we often harbor negative feelings toward our enemies and do nothing to counter those feelings. Compassion is not among those feelings, but animosity often is. We end up, then, out of step with what God would will and feel toward the people in question. We thus become out of step with God.

Is there a solution in our cooperating with God? Evidence from my experience suggests an affirmative answer. Even so, I cannot presume that all others have the same evidence. So, I have not assumed that God's existence or redemptive power is indicated by the experience or evidence of all others. I have talked of what God *would* do or *would* be like, to avoid begging key questions. I can recommend, however, that inquirers make the effort to inquire properly about God, and thereby put themselves in a position to receive evidence of God's reality and meaning from God. That effort can change the direction of a person's life, for the better, if the relevant evidence and meaning are found. In that case, lasting meaning will eclipse despair, and one's will and affections will be renewed by the unique character of God. Life then can begin again, for the better, with new purposes and meaning.

10

St. Isaac's Dictum

Terence Cuneo

For nearly fifteen years, I have had on my office wall an icon of St. Isaac the Syrian.[1] Like many icons, this one includes both an image—in this case, one of Isaac himself—and words attributed to him. The words are these: "This life has been given to you for repentance. Do not waste it on vain pursuits." St. Isaac's dictum, as I'll call it, is both severe and striking. Literally rendered, it appears to say that the point of this life is to repent (and that much else is vain pursuit). When set against the rest of Isaac's thought, it is clear that the person to whom we are to repent is God. So, what the dictum tells us is that the point of this life is to repent to God. Given the additional assumption that, if one's life has a point or purpose, then one ought to pursue it, St. Isaac's dictum implies that we should dedicate our lives to repenting to God.

St. Isaac's dictum is a hard saying, even by the standards of traditional Christianity. Although those of us who locate ourselves within the Christian tradition recognize the importance of repentance in the Christian life, few of us savor the activity. It is often difficult to do. In addition to being a hard saying, St. Isaac's dictum is puzzling. Repentance, after all, does not appear to be a good candidate for being the point or end of our lives. At most, it seems to be an activity whose value lies wholly in whatever valuable end it brings about, such as enabling reconciliation. How, then, could Isaac intelligibly maintain otherwise? Moreover, even if we could make sense of the idea that repentance is the point of this life, why would Isaac say that it is? There seem to be many other candidates that are better suited for this role. The Western medieval tradition, for example, nearly unanimously held that beatitude is the point of this life (and, given their theological commitments, it is easy to see why). Finally, supposing that we could answer these first two questions

---

[1] St. Isaac the Syrian (or St. Isaac of Ninevah) (c. 613–c. 700) was a monastic and, for a short period, bishop of the Syriac Orthodox Church in Ninevah. The best introduction to his thought is Hilarion Alfeyev, *The Spiritual World of Isaac the Syrian* (Kalamazoo, MI: Cisterian Publications, 2000).

satisfactorily, what would a life dedicated to repentance look like? As noted above, repentance is not a peripheral activity in the Christian life. But it does not appear to enjoy anything like the prominence that Isaac wishes to give it. When one looks at the texts that the Christian tradition provides for both private devotion and corporate worship, for example, these texts typically include prayers of repentance; but these prayers are hardly their focal point. As a practical matter, it is difficult to envision the ideal that Isaac has in mind.

My project in this essay is to address these three questions. Although I am going to contend that each admits of a satisfactory answer, it is the third question that most interests me; I am particularly interested in describing how pursuing the ideal that St. Isaac's dictum articulates takes shape in the liturgical life of the church. So, my discussion divides into two main sections: the first is dedicated to interpreting the ideal that Isaac articulates, while the second discusses the extent to which the ideal is realized in the liturgical life of the church.

But before I turn my attention to these matters, I need to address a pair of questions that might be on the mind of the reader. St. Isaac does not belong to the canon of figures with whom philosophers regularly engage. Indeed, he has at best a limited presence in the Western Christian tradition. One might rightly ask, then, why we should pay attention to what he says. The brief answer is that while Isaac is largely unknown in the west, he is a towering figure within Eastern Christianity whose writings have shaped its thinking and approaches to various theological and practical issues. For those who identify with or have interests in this tradition, his reputation warrants taking very seriously what he says, however puzzling it may appear initially. For those who do not have such interests, it may prove instructive to engage with a figure whose approach to issues such as what the point or end of this life might be diverges in interesting ways from approaches standardly offered in the Western canon.

The answer I have just offered to the question why it makes sense to engage with Isaac's writings presupposes that Isaac's audience includes non-monastics such as you and me. The second question to address is whether this assumption is correct. Like many monastic theologians, Isaac primarily wrote for his fellow monastics, providing guidance from his own experience (and that of others) regarding the monastic life. And, in fact, a good deal of what Isaac recommends to his fellow monastics—such as how to cope with the rigors of a strict rule of prayer—is largely inapplicable to you and me.[2] It

---

[2] As Isaac himself acknowledges. See *The Ascetical Homilies of Saint Isaac the Syrian*, translated by Dana Miller (Boston, MA. Monastery of the Holy Transfiguration, 1984), 339. When citing this work hereafter, I will abbreviate its title as "I" and cite the sermon number, placing the page number in parentheses. So, the reference above would be given as I/69 (339). I'll refer to Isaac of Nineveh [Isaac the Syrian], *"The Second Part,"* Chapters

is natural to ask, then, whether St. Isaac's dictum should be viewed as advice given only to his fellow monastics and, hence, of limited relevance to the rest of us.

I think we cannot decisively rule out this possibility. But I doubt that it is the best interpretation of St. Isaac's dictum. My primary reason for thinking this is not simply the suspicion that Isaac has put his finger on something very fundamental to the Christian life. It is also because Isaac himself probably did not view his audience so narrowly. Commenting on a related issue in the introduction to the collection of writings known as *The Philokalia*, G. E. H. Palmer, Philip Sherard, and Kallistos Ware note that the monastics of the Eastern Church tended to hold that the activities on which the monastics were commenting, such as prayer and inner stillness, are for everyone to pursue "to the best of his or her ability and whatever the circumstances under which he or she lives."[3] In this respect, they continue, the distinction between "the monastic life and life 'in the world' is but relative: every human being, by virtue of the fact that he or she is created in the image of God, is summoned to be perfect, is summoned to love God with all his or her heart, soul and mind. In this sense all have the same vocation and all must follow the same spiritual path."[4] Later, I'll be returning to this theme of perfection and how it helps to make sense of what St. Isaac says. For now, I'll simply note that if what Palmer, Sherard, and Ware write is correct, St. Isaac's dictum is intended to apply to each of us—or at least to each of us who has committed himself or herself to the Christian way of life.

What should now be evident is that my project in this essay is not to offer a defense of the claim that the Christian tradition provides a rationally compelling account of what the end or meaning of life might be. Rather, it is to explore and make sense of one such account, unusual by the standards of the broadly Western Christian tradition, offered by a prominent figure within the Eastern Christian tradition.

1. The ideal

St. Isaac was not a systematic theologian or even a theologian with systematic tendencies. Kallistos Ware describes Isaac's writings as "full of repetitions,

---

IV-XLI, ed. Sebastian Brock (Corpus Scriptorum Christianonorum Orientalium 554, Scriptores syro 224. Louvain 1991) as "II."

[3] "Introduction," in *The Philokalia*, vol. 1 (London: Faber and Faber, 1979), 16. See also Mother Mary and Kallistos Ware, *The Lenten Triodion* (South Canaan, PA: St. Tikhon's Seminary Press, 2002), 21. I'll refer to this work as *LT*.

[4] "Introduction," 16.

of unexpected transitions, of epigrammatic sayings not fully explained."[5] St. Isaac's dictum belongs to the last category: it is an epigrammatic saying not fully explained. While Isaac might not fully and explicitly explain what he means when he says that this life has been given to us for repentance, it is not difficult to piece together his thinking on the topic of repentance, since it belongs to a short list of topics about which he has much to say.

Repentance, according to Isaac, consists in the "abandoning of former deeds and grieving for them." Building upon this initial characterization, Isaac proposes that:

> the meaning of the word *repentance* (*tyabuta*) … is this: continual and mournful supplication which by means of prayer filled with compunction draws nigh to God in order to seek forgiveness of past offenses, and entreaty for preservation from future [offenses].[6]

Here Isaac describes repentance in its full-fledged form as it pertains to God. So understood, repentance is both complex and demanding. When repenting to God, one must at once own one's own wrongdoing and yet set oneself against it: one must resolve not to engage in such wrongdoing again. In addition, when owning one's own wrongdoing, one must not simply acknowledge or state that one has done what is wrong; one must request to be forgiven of it, and to ask for assistance in not performing such actions again. Finally, Isaac intimates, repentance is not supposed to be an emotionally colorless activity: it is to be performed in such a way that one expresses remorse or grieves over one's wrongdoing. Elsewhere, Isaac writes that feeling such compunction often involves the shedding of "abundant tears."[7] It is in the "sweetness" of such tears, says Isaac, that a person can "see the Lord at all times."[8] Repentance, apparently, is a way that we experience God. I'll touch upon this theme again.

This is to describe what full-fledged repentance is. It is not yet to describe its role in the Christian life. Isaac is forthright regarding this matter:

> Because God, with that compassionate knowledge of his, knew that if genuine righteousness were required of human beings, then only one in

---

[5] "Forward" to Alfeyev, *The Spiritual World*, 12. Of course Isaac's writings would in this regard be similar to the work of Nietzsche and Wittgenstein, which philosophers take very seriously. Here and elsewhere I use the term "theologian" in a more relaxed fashion than does the Christian East, which recognizes only a small number of figures as theologians.
[6] I/70 (340).
[7] I/37 (174).
[8] I/37 (178–179).

ten thousand would be found who could enter the kingdom of heaven, he accordingly provided them instead with a medicine suitable for everyone, namely repentance, so that on every day and at every moment there would be available to them an opportunity easily to be put in the right by means of the strength of this medicine.[9]

In a moment, I am going to consider Isaac's comparison of repentance to medicine, but for now let me point out that Isaac is clearly working with an understanding of repentance and forgiveness according to which the former is a precondition of the latter. Speaking of God, Isaac writes:

Seeing that his face is set all the time towards forgiveness ... he pours over us his immense grace that, like the ocean, knows no measure. To anyone who shows just a little suffering and the will to compunction for what has occurred, to such a person immediately, at once, without any delay, he will grant forgiveness of their sins.[10]

I take Isaac's thought to be this: God has a standing intention to forgive those who have wronged God (and not, say, a standing intention to look past such wrongdoing as if it doesn't matter). But the intention is one that can be exercised only when wrongdoers repent of their wrongdoing. While Isaac is sensitive to the therapeutic dimensions of repentance—recall that he likens it to medicine—the point of the activity is not primarily to relieve oneself of a painful psychological burden; rather, its point is to "be put in the right" with God.

At the outset of our discussion, I asked how Isaac could claim that repentance is the point of this life and what would drive him to say such a thing. The passage just quoted holds the beginnings of answers to these questions. Admittedly, at first glance, it doesn't look that way. The parallel that Isaac draws between repentance and medicine seems only to exacerbate the challenge that his position faces. Those of us who have had the opportunity to introduce students to the distinction between final goods and instrumental goods, often offer medicine (or the taking thereof) as a paradigm example of the latter. Someone who understands what medicine is would never say that the point of this life is to take medicine; it is a purely instrumental or contributory good. The same seems true of repentance.

The key to making sense of what Isaac says is to mark an ambiguity in our talk about the "end" or "point" of a life. Understood in one way, the

[9] II/40, 8–9. Quoted in Alfeyev, *The Spiritual World*, 130.
[10] II/40, 13. Quoted in Alfeyev, *The Spiritual World*, 133.

phrase refers to the ultimate end of one's life: roughly, that end for the sake of which all an agent's actions are (or ought to be) ultimately performed. As intimated earlier, the ancients and medievals were more or less united in their conviction that the ultimate end of a life is eudaemonia, beatitude, or happiness—Aquinas claiming, for example, that such happiness consists in the contemplation of the divine essence. But understood in another way, the point of one's life is some ideal or activity around which one can (or ought to) order one's life. Important for our purposes is the observation that an activity or ideal can function as that around which one orders one's life without being an ultimate end. You might, for example, order your activities around the ideal of becoming an expert musician. But it wouldn't follow that your ultimate end consists in achieving this ideal. It might simply be that you achieve your ultimate end *by* ordering your life around this ideal. At any rate, once we mark this distinction, we can begin to see how Isaac could say that the point of this life is to repent. Under a charitable reading, he is not claiming that repentance is the ultimate end of one's life. Rather, he is claiming that it is an ideal or activity around which we are to order our lives.

Of course the activities or ideals around which we order our lives can bear different relations to one another and have different properties. Some lie close to the center of who we are and what we care about; others lie nearer to the periphery. All such ideals and activities demand time when pursued; many require sacrifice. Most importantly, some activities and ideals warrant ordering our lives around them; others do not. Those that do warrant such ordering enjoy a privileged place, for they can not only justify or make sense of the sacrifices we make to achieve them, but can also render a life ordered around them significant or meaningful. For ease of reference, let's call these *meaningfulness-conferring* activities and ideals. To advert to the example above, being an expert musician is for many a meaningfulness-conferring ideal. Charitably interpreted, Isaac is telling us that the same is true of repentance. It is also a meaningfulness-conferring ideal.

Under a natural understanding, a meaningful life just is one ordered around ideals or activities that warrant such ordering. If we avoid some of the more misleading connotations of the phrase "the meaning of life," we can take a further step and affirm that St. Isaac's dictum tells something about the meaning of life. For, under what we might call a "meaningfulness first" conception, the meaning of life consists in leading a meaningful life. If it does, then St. Isaac's dictum tells us something substantial about the meaning of life.

Suitably interpreted, then, St. Isaac's dictum is perfectly intelligible. It instructs us to order our lives around the activity of repenting. That is why St. Isaac can say that we have been given this life for repentance. Note that St.

Isaac does not say that we have been given this life *only* for repentance; that would make no sense. But it does make sense to say that it is an activity and ideal such that by ordering our lives around it, we would thereby order our lives around something that is fitted to give our lives meaning. Indeed, not only is St. Isaac's dictum intelligible, there is also a sense in which repentance is a good candidate for being that around which a person can order her life: it is not a "one-off" activity but one in which an agent can continually engage.

The question that we need to address is why St. Isaac would give repentance this sort of role in the meaningful life—why he holds that "no virtue is more pre-eminent than repentance."[11] Part of the answer, I believe, is implicit in a passage quoted earlier from Palmer, Sherard, and Ware in which they write that "every human being, by virtue of the fact that he or she is created in the image of God, is summoned to be perfect, is summoned to love God with all his or her heart, soul and mind. In this sense all have the same vocation and all must follow the same spiritual path."[12]

In what is arguably the best known passage in his corpus, Isaac articulates in striking language the ideal of perfection to which we are called. The saints, Isaac writes, "seek for themselves the sign of complete likeness to God: to be perfect in the love of the neighbour."[13] And that, he continues, consists in being merciful "in the likeness of God":

> And what is a merciful heart? It is the heart burning for the sake of all creation, for men, for birds, for animals, for demons, and for every created thing; and by the recollection of them the eyes of a merciful man pour forth abundant tears. By the strong and vehement mercy which grips his heart and by his great compassion, his heart is humbled and he cannot bear to hear or to see any injury or slight sorrow in creation. For this reason he offers up tearful prayer continually even for irrational beasts, for the enemies of the truth, and for those who harm him, that they be protected and receive mercy. And in like manner he even prays for the family of reptiles because of the great compassion that burns without measure in his heart in the likeness of God.[14]

This passage is remarkable not simply in its depiction of what God is like but also in how it expands our ordinary categories of concern, including things such as birds, animals, and demons. Since Isaac includes the latter among our

---

[11] I/32 (153).
[12] Palmer, Sherard, and Ware, "Introduction," 16.
[13] I/71 (346).
[14] I/71 (344–345).

enemies, he draws the conclusion that Christ's commandment to love our enemies implies that we are to pray even for the demons.

Like many in the monastic tradition, then, Isaac takes very seriously the claim that the aim of the Christian life is perfection. And like many in the tradition, he takes a close approximation of what we might call the Christian ideal to be attainable. That this is so is evident in his reflections on the incarnation and death of Christ:

> God the Lord surrendered his own Son to death on the cross for the fervent love of creation ... Yet this was not because he could not redeem us in another way, but so that his surpassing love, manifested hereby, might be a teacher unto us. And by the death of his Only-begotten Son he made us near to himself. Yea, if he had anything more precious, he would have given it to us, so that by it our race might be his own. Because of his great love for us it was his pleasure not to do violence to our freedom, although he is able to do so, but he chose that we should draw near to him by the love of our understanding. For the sake of his love for us and obedience to his Father, Christ joyfully took upon himself insult and sorrow ... In like manner, when the saints become perfect, they all attain to this perfection, and by the superabundant outpouring of their love and compassion on all men, they resemble God.[15]

Fascinating and radical as it is (at least by the standards of dominant strands in Western Christianity), Isaac's soteriology is not what interests me most here. Rather, what interests me is Isaac's affirmation that some saints achieve something approximating the perfection of Christ, thereby resembling God. Satisfaction of the Christian ideal, in Isaac's view, is such that we can genuinely approximate it.[16]

When we couple this fact with the further observation that the Christian way of life consists in committing oneself to approximating the ideal of becoming Christ-like, Isaac's rationale for ordering one's life around repentance emerges: repentance—indeed, continual repentance—is (at least in part) an emotionally engaged recognition that one regularly fails to approximate the Christian ideal to which one has committed oneself. The commitment, it should be added, is not to some abstract ideal "the Christian ideal." Rather, it is (in the first instance) a commitment to God: committing oneself

---

[15] I/71 (345–346).

[16] Elsewhere Isaac draws back from the claim that the saints achieve perfection, writing: "The limit of this journey [to perfection] is so truly unattainable that even the saints are found wanting with respect to the perfection of wisdom, because there is no end to wisdom's journey" I/37 (163).

to the Christian ideal is (in the first instance) to commit to God that one order one's life around the activity of becoming like Christ. Of course the commitment is more than this; it is also a commitment to the Christian community that one order one's life around the activity of becoming like Christ. And it is probably more than this; it is probably also a vow to oneself that one order one's life around the activity of becoming like Christ. At any rate, it follows that the badness of violating this commitment does not lie in the mere fact that one has violated a commitment—even a commitment to God. We can after all, commit to God, each other, and ourselves to doing things that are trivial or evil. Rather, the badness consists in the fact that, in violating this commitment, we fail to order our lives around something that is of supreme importance. So, Isaac suggests, repentance is called for. Paradoxically, the continual recognition that we continually fail to approximate the Christian ideal is what enables us to more closely approximate the ideal.

In the next section, I am going to touch again on the role that commitment plays in making sense of what Isaac says about repentance. For now, I want to note that Isaac's thought that we more closely approximate the Christian ideal by repentance is not simply that such repentance allows us to repair damaged relationships that we have with God or the Christian community but also to *experience* God. When offering a gloss on the beatitudes, Isaac connects his thinking on repentance with the experience of tears:

> Blessed, therefore, are the pure in heart, for there is no time when they do not enjoy the sweetness of tears, and in this sweetness they see the Lord at all times. While tears are still wet in their eyes, they are deemed worthy of beholding his revelations at the height of their prayer; and they make no prayer without tears.[17]

Isaac continues that "even in sleep" the one who sheds tears of repentance "converses with God," for "love is wont to cause such things."[18] In repentance and the shedding of tears, a person becomes "aware of the taste of the love of God."[19] This, in Isaac's view, is crucial, for without "actually direct experience of God's providence, the heart is not able to confide in God. And unless the soul tastes suffering for the sake of Christ, it will not share in knowledge with Him."[20]

What emerges from passages such as these is that Isaac assumes there to be significant asymmetries between repentance as it pertains to other

---

[17] I/37 (178–179).
[18] I/37 (183).
[19] II 18,7. Quoted in Alfeyev, *The Spiritual World*, 141.
[20] *On Ascetical Life* (Crestwood, NY: St. Vladimir's Seminary Press, 1989), 87.

humans and as it pertains to God. As it pertains to fellow humans, repentance is fraught with risk and pain: when repenting, we are aware that people sometimes rebuff the requests for forgiveness that accompany repentance, or accept them but do so in a way in which they attempt to exercise power over the person who repents. When it comes to God, things are different: there are no risks of this sort. Repentance is, as Isaac writes elsewhere, an occasion for God to pour forth "immense grace" that "knows no measure" on the person who repents and, hence, for that person to intimately experience such grace. Isaac, then, is thinking of repentance as medicine of a special sort; it doesn't simply heal fractured relationships, it also allows one to taste the goodness of the One who heals. Given the further assumption that experiencing God in this way can be an important component of coming to more nearly resemble God, we can better see why repentance is an activity that Isaac urges us to order our lives around.

There is more to Isaac's thinking about the connections between repentance and approximating the ideal of perfection than just this, however. Isaac is also keen to emphasize that ordering one's life around repentance alters one's orientation to God and others. The alteration consists in clothing oneself in what Isaac calls the "raiment of the Godhead," namely, humility. Throughout his writings, Isaac continually returns to this theme, singling out humility as a primary way in which we resemble God:

> Humility is the raiment of the Godhead. The Word who became human clothed himself in it, and he spoke to us in our body. Everyone who has been clothed with humility has truly been made like Him who came down from his own exaltedness and hid the splendour of his majesty and concealed his glory with humility, lest creation be utterly consumed by the contemplation of him ... Blessed is he that has gained it, because at every moment he kisses and embraces the bosom of Jesus.[21]

Humility, Isaac goes on to say, "makes man god on earth."[22]

Isaac's thought seems to be that humility can take several forms. In one form, the trait consists in lowering oneself in such a way that one underemphasizes or even "conceals" one's own excellence or accomplishments for the purpose of being able to relate to others in ways that would otherwise be impossible. A parent, for example, might exhibit such humility when entering into imaginary play with a child, voluntarily not employing her own advanced abilities in order to build bonds of trust with the child. In another

---

[21] I/77 (381–382), (384–385).
[22] I/6 (60).

form, humility consists in lowering oneself in such a way that acknowledges and emphasizes one's own lack of excellence or accomplishments for the purpose of relating to oneself and to others in ways that might otherwise be impossible. If our relationship is fractured, you might set aside whatever excellences or accomplishments you have, acknowledging ways in which you have failed, and do this for the sake of reconciling.

In its first form, Isaac says that God is the paradigm of humility. In its second form, Isaac indicates that the saints are the paradigm of humility. While these forms of humility are importantly different, Isaac seems to think that they are species of a common genus, since both involve a type of "lowering," where this is a matter of distancing oneself from, underplaying, or not attending to one's excellences or accomplishments for the sake of obtaining some interpersonal good, such as building bonds of trust or reconciling. If Isaac is right about this, the acquisition of humility in either of its forms is a way in which we can resemble God. Moreover, acquiring it in its second form is both the fruit of and motivation for ordering one's life around repentance. It is the fruit of such an ordering because we come to acquire this trait by engaging in full-fledged repentance. The acquisition of humility is the motivation for ordering one's life around repentance, since it is by acquiring this trait that we can more nearly approximate the Christian ideal.

Let me now summarize the interpretation of St. Isaac's dictum that I've offered. The dictum states that the point or end of this life is repentance. I've suggested that we interpret this to mean that we are to order our lives around the activity of repenting. The reason for doing so is that those who have committed themselves to the Christian ideal have committed themselves to an ideal whose achievement is extremely demanding. Each of us will repeatedly fail to approximate it. The remedy or "medicine" for this failure, Isaac says, is to order one's life around the activity of repenting. Yet repentance is, according to Isaac, an unusual sort of "medicine": in the very activity of acknowledging that one has failed God, one thereby can experience and resemble God. Paradoxically, the acknowledgment of failure to approximate the Christian ideal is that which allows someone committed to the Christian ideal to more closely approximate it.

Let me now add a layer of nuance that may help Isaac's view come into sharper focus. According to the interpretation that I've developed, repentance is the activity that Isaac recommends in the face of our failure to achieve the Christian ideal. That can make it sound as if repentance is something external to the Christian ideal and only contingently and instrumentally related to it. Recall, though, that Isaac advocates an ideal such that those committed to it "seek for themselves the sign of complete likeness to God: to be perfect in the love of the neighbor," God, and creation.[23] Keeping this in mind can help us to see that, for Isaac, repentance is not an activity external to or merely contingently related to the Christian ideal. Rather Isaac's idea is that to fully commit oneself to pursuing this ideal is to commit oneself to the activity of repenting. Given our nature and God's, there is no other way genuinely to pursue it.

2. Implementing the ideal: Liturgy

I dedicated the last section to addressing the questions of whether we could make sense of St. Isaac's dictum and, if so, why Isaac would say that the end of this life is repentance. There is, however, a third question I raised that concerns what, as a practical matter, a life ordered around repentance would look like. The question seems worth raising because, while the texts that the Christian tradition provides for both private devotion and corporate worship typically include prayers of repentance, these prayers are hardly their focal point. In light of this, it is tempting to conclude that if one attempted to implement Isaac's advice, one would have to significantly supplement what the tradition offers. Perhaps one would have to become a monastic.

Although there is something to this generalization regarding the place of repentance in the Christian tradition, much depends on where you look within the tradition to ascertain the role that repentance plays in the life of the church. Given Isaac's location within and influence on the Eastern Christian tradition, one would expect that it is within this tradition that one might find something that approximates the ideal that Isaac articulates. These expectations are not disappointed; if anything, they are exceeded. The extent to which the Eastern Church implements the ideal in both its personal and corporate prayers and rites is considerable.

On this occasion, I shall mention only in passing that the activity of repenting figures heavily in the daily rule of prayer as it is understood within the Eastern tradition. (The paradigm Psalm of repentance—namely, Psalm 50—is included in the daily rule of prayer.)[24] And I'll have nothing to say about the role that the sacrament or mystery of confession plays in the life of the Eastern Church, which is considerable. Instead, I want to focus on the role that repentance plays in the Eastern Church's corporate worship services. My rationale for doing so is not simply that one might suspect that it plays a lesser role in these services than in the prayers employed in personal

---

[23] I/71 (346).
[24] Psalm 51 in the Christian west's numbering of the Psalms.

devotion. It is also because repentance takes on a unique character in the church's liturgies. (When I say this, I don't mean simply to draw attention to the fact that repentance is performed in a public setting.) The corporate services that I have in mind, however, are not the various versions of the Divine Liturgy—although it should be noted that, for a type of service whose central event is the celebration of the Eucharist, the *mood* of this service is strikingly penitential.[25] Rather, the services on which I want to focus are those that compose the period known as the Great Fast, which is a ten-week period of daily services that includes (but is not limited to) the forty-day period known as Great Lent, in which the church prepares itself for the celebration of Pascha or Easter. Alexander Schmemann calls this period the church's "school of repentance."[26] It is worth noting that many texts used in these services are from the fifth through the eighth century, having their provenance in the Syriac and Palestinian Christian tradition to which Isaac belonged.[27]

Unless you hail from the broadly Pentecostal tradition, the corporate prayers of repentance and their mode of expression with which you are familiar are probably succinct and staid (albeit sincere). That is not, however, how the prayers of repentance and their expression take form during the services of the Lenten Fast. These prayers are not succinct or staid; they are elaborate and effusive, even turbulent.

Let me illustrate. Having declared that the "season of repentance is at hand,"[28] the prayers during the first week of Great Lent, which are in the first-person, begin with the acknowledgment that our need is dire:

> The multitude of my transgression is like the deep waters of the sea, and I drown in my iniquities. Give me Your hand, O God my Saviour; save me as You saved Peter, and have mercy on me ... rouse my thoughts to repentance, and make me a tried labourer in Your vineyard ... Grant me the firm intent to turn back to You, for You alone love humankind, and have mercy on me.[29]

Lest one be under the impression that repentance is something that we can accomplish under our own power, the liturgical text offers a corrective: it is not

---

[25] To be more exact, its mood is a complex admixture of reverence, celebration, and repentance. The "kyrie liasons" that the congregation repeatedly offers in response to the litanies that compose the Divine Liturgy have multiple layers of meaning, but they are prayers of repentance at the very least. I address this issue at more length in section III of "Love and Liturgy," *The Journal of Religious Ethics* 43 (2015): 587–605.

[26] *Great Lent* (Crestwood, NY: St. Vladimir's Seminary Press, 1969), 9.

[27] See Ware, "The Meaning of the Great Fast," in *LT*, 40–42.

[28] *LT*, 210.

[29] *LT*, 184. Mary and Ware use King James English in their translation. I have modernized it.

something that we can perform under our own power. Nor, for that matter, are the actions that are the "worthy fruits" of repentance, such as the acquisition and practice of the virtues: "Do not demand from me worthy fruits of repentance, for my strength has failed within me. Give an ever-contrite heart and poverty of spirit, that I may offer these to You an acceptable sacrifice."[30] These expressions of distress and pleas for resolve and strength are coupled with the acknowledgment that deep compunction is absent when the effort to repent is made: "When I try to repent, I have no tears to shed ... I have no tears, no repentance, no compunction."[31] These acknowledgments are followed by still more petitions: "Grant me tears falling as the rain from heaven, O Christ ... Give me tears, O God, as once You gave them to the woman who had sinned, and count me worthy to wash Your feet that have delivered me from the way of error."[32] Variations on this last theme are repeated again and again.

These are only a very small sample of the many prayers included in the liturgical text used during the Lenten Fast. But they are representative of the character of the text: the prayers consist in petitions for the resolve or strength to repent, acknowledgments that one lacks this resolve and proper compunction, and still more petitions to have such compunction. A moment ago, I referred to these as "prayers of repentance." But that is probably not the best description of them. For, strictly speaking, these prayers do not express repentance. Rather, they are acknowledgments of distress, petitions that one be given the strength to repent, and exhortations to emulate figures who repent, such as the woman who washed Jesus's feet with her tears. These elements of the liturgical text are better categorized as *repentance-oriented* prayers.

Interestingly enough, the Eastern Church's paradigm prayer of repentance, the Prayer of St. Ephraim the Syrian, also appears to be not a prayer of repentance but a repentance-oriented prayer. This prayer, which is said at least once at each weekday office during the services of Great Lent, runs as follows:

> O Lord and Master of my life, give me not a spirit of sloth, despair, lust for power, and idle talk.
>
> But give to me your servant a spirit of sobriety, humility, patience, and love.
>
> O Lord and King, grant me to see my own faults and not to condemn my brother: for blessed are you to the ages of ages. Amen.[33]

---

[30] *LT*, 414. This passage, I take it, is supposed to stand in contrast to ones such as this: "Let all of us set forth eagerly on the course of the Fast, offering our virtues as gifts to the Lord" (*LT*, 191).

[31] *LT*, 184, 238; cf. 272.

[32] *LT*, 188.

[33] I cite the prayer as it is translated in *LT*, 69.

Like the prayers cited above, this prayer is not a confession or expression of repentance in any straightforward sense; were one sincerely to recite this prayer, one wouldn't thereby confess that one has wronged God or one's fellow human beings. That one has seems to be taken for granted. Instead, the prayer takes the form of a petition, asking God that one not have certain characteristics, such as lust for power and despair, but that one exhibit others, such as patience and humility.

I say that the Prayer of St. Ephraim *appears* to be a repentance-oriented prayer. But there is more to the Prayer of St. Ephraim than the text I have cited indicates. This becomes evident when we mark the distinction between a *liturgical text*, on the one hand, and a *liturgical script*, on the other.[34] A liturgical text is roughly a collection of sentences that would be uttered by the assembly in the enactment of a liturgy; in the Eastern Christian tradition, the liturgical text is nearly always given in written form. In contrast, while a liturgical script often includes a liturgical text, it also includes instructions for when a liturgy is to be performed, by whom, what actions are to be performed during a liturgy, and in what manner and when. For example, the liturgical script for the Stichera of Repentance offers instructions that this service only be performed on the first Sunday of Great Lent by the assembled, that they are to utter the sentences that compose the liturgical text, and are to do so by employing whatever musical tones that are used for that week. (The Eastern Church alternates between eight "tones" that it uses to sing or chant the liturgical text.) Most importantly for our purposes, the liturgical script for the weekday services of Great Lent instructs the assembled to fully prostrate themselves when reciting the Prayer of St. Ephraim: after each verse, one falls to the ground, touching the ground with one's forehead.

The Greek term used to refer to these prostrations is *metanoia*, which means *repentance*. Once one appreciates that the scripted performance of the Prayer of St. Ephraim involves not just the recitation of a liturgical text but also the performance of bodily actions of this sort, we are better able to see that to liturgically perform this prayer is to perform (at least) two distinct speech acts: it is both to petition and to repent.[35] When all goes well, the linguistic act of uttering the text of the prayer counts as petitioning God; the bodily act of fully prostrating oneself counts as repenting.

---

[34] What I am calling the "liturgical script" corresponds to what Schmemann calls the ordo in his *Introduction to Liturgical Theology* (Crestwood, NY: St. Vladimir's Seminary Press, 1966).

[35] Of course it may be more than this; it could also express humility and reverence, for example. I am helping myself here to the somewhat controversial assumption that there is the speech act type *repenting*.

The linguistic act of reciting the Prayer of St. Ephraim and the performance of a full prostration, I've said, count as petitioning and repenting to God when all goes well. The qualification is necessary because the liturgical performance of these linguistic and bodily actions is not perforce to petition or repent. One can, after all, perform a speech act insincerely, as when one says "I'm sorry" when one is really not. In such a case, one would perform the speech act of repenting but not repent. More importantly, given the tradition's robust understanding of repentance (*metanoia*) in which it is the enactment of a resolution to transform one's mind, one could perform the speech act of repenting and even express the resolve to repent, but fall short of *enacting* the resolution and, hence, genuinely repenting. As Isaac emphasizes, whether one enacts this commitment by genuinely turning away from what one resolves to leave behind is something that happens over time to different degrees, taking place not simply in the performance of speech acts but also in one's day-to-day activities. When sincerely and competently performed, then, a liturgical action such as performing the speech act of repenting may have limited implications for the actual process of repenting and, hence, making progress toward approximating the Christian ideal.

The texts of the services that compose the Lenten Fast are sensitive to this last point. Indeed, it is because they are sensitive to this point that we can make sense of what might appear to be a puzzling feature of the services of the Lenten Fast. The texts of these services, I've pointed out, are composed in large measure of repentance-oriented prayers. But if the aim of these services is to enable people to repent, why would so many prayers be of this sort? Why wouldn't these texts simply—or at least primarily—contain prayers of repentance? Answering these questions, I want to suggest, helps us to identify the unique character of repentance as it takes shape in the liturgies of the Eastern Church.

This coupling of prayers of repentance with these repentance-oriented prayers makes sense, I want to suggest, when we reflect on what it is to perform the speech act of repenting. According to the account of speech acts that I take to be correct, the performance of this type of speech act consists in committing oneself to the world being a certain way and to one's being in mental states of certain kinds.[36] In the case of repenting, for example, one commits oneself to (i) the fact that one has engaged in wrongdoing and to one's believing or acknowledging that one has engaged in such wrongdoing; (ii) one's being against what one has done; (iii) one's being sorry or remorseful for what one has done; and (iv) one's being committed to not performing

---

[36] I defend this position in *Speech and Morality* (Oxford: Oxford University Press, 2014).

such an action again.[37] Call these the *commitment conditions* of repentance. (When Isaac describes what it is to repent, he includes each of these conditions.) In taking on these commitments, one alters one's normative position with regard to God, the fellow members of the assembly with whom one performs these actions, and oneself. For, in the performance of the speech act of repenting, one puts oneself "on the hook," laying oneself open to correction, admonition, or even blame if the conditions just cited are not satisfied. (Unless I indicate otherwise, in what follows, I'll use the term "repent" to mean the *speech act* of repenting.)

As I read them, the liturgical texts are keyed into the ways in which we often fail to satisfy these conditions upon (or subsequent to) repenting. It is because we so regularly fail these conditions, I want to further suggest, that repentance-oriented prayers figure so prominently in the liturgical texts.

Consider, to begin with, passages such as the following:

> I have rivalled in transgression Adam the first-formed man, and I have found myself stripped naked of God, of the eternal Kingdom and its joy, because of my sins.
>
> David, the forefather of God, once sinned doubly, pierced with the arrow of adultery and the spear of murder. But you, my soul, are more gravely sick than he, for worse than any acts are the impulses of your will.
>
> I fall before You, and as tears I offer You my words. I have sinned as the Harlot never sinned ... but take pity on your creature, O Master, and call me back.[38]

Interpreted from one angle, these passages appear to engage in moral self-abasement, even if one allows for hyperbole in expression. Relatively few of us are inclined to hold that the "impulses" of the will are worse than actually murdering someone.[39] Interpreted from another angle, however, these passages function as correctives to the tendency, which many of us exhibit, to think of the wrongdoing in which we engage as not particularly serious. Under this reading, the point of these passages is to sensitize or alert us to the tendency to assume that the actions that we perform do not put us at

---

[37] I use the phrase "things that we do" capaciously so that it also refers to acts of omission.

[38] *LT*, 199, 205, 262. Similar claims are made in every Divine Liturgy in the pre-communion prayers.

[39] There is an interesting issue to address here, and that is whether in denying that you are worse than other sinners commits you to the claim that you are better (in this respect) than they are. I take there to be no such commitment. One could hold—very plausibly, to my mind—that while few are in a morally good state, the moral differences between us are largely incommensurable: your moral standing is neither worse than, better than, or identical with mine.

variance with God or tend not to matter that much. For, when we exhibit this tendency, we fail the first of the commitment conditions of repentance, the satisfaction of which implies that one believe or acknowledge that one has engaged in wrongdoing—where the assumption is that in having such a belief, one presupposes that what one has done matters.

Other passages of the liturgical text voice similar themes but address other ways in which our acts of repentance can be defective:

> When I examine my actions, O Saviour, I see that I have gone beyond all men in sin; for I knew and understood what I did; I was not sinning in ignorance.... With full knowledge and by my own free choice, I have eagerly desired a shameful and prodigal life.[40]
>
> Alas! What will become of me? What shall I do? I feel no pang of conscience when I sin, nor do I fear the Master. Because of this ... I stand condemned. O just and loving Judge, turn me back and save me.[41]
>
> When I try to repent, I have no tears to shed ... I have no tears, no repentance, no compunction.[42]

To satisfy the second and third commitment conditions of repentance, one must not only be against one's wrongdoing but also be remorseful for it. The texts of the repentance-oriented prayers call our attention to the fact that we often fail to satisfy these conditions, voicing a plea for help in avoiding these failures.

And then there are passages that address the last of the commitment conditions of repentance in which the prayers of the liturgies use the technique of a narrator addressing his own soul:

> The Law is powerless, the Gospel of no effect, and the whole of Scripture is ignored by you; the prophets and all the words of the righteous are useless. Your wounds, my soul, have been multiplied, and there is no physician to heal you ... You have heard, O my soul, of Job justified on a dung-hill, but you have not imitated his fortitude. In all your experiences and trials and temptations, you have not kept firmly to your purpose but have proved inconstant.[43]

Once again, the idea seems to be that, when repenting, we need to be aware of the ways in which we can and often fail in satisfying that to which we commit

---

[40] *LT*, 242, 319.
[41] *LT*, 212.
[42] *LT*, 184, 238; cf. 272.
[43] *LT*, 207–208, 222.

ourselves. Repentance begets repentance at this point. Failure to satisfy the conditions of repentance generates still another reason to repent. One begins to get a sense for why Isaac claims that the activity must be continual!

My aim in this section has been to address the question of what, as a practical matter, it might look like to order one's life around repentance. With an eye on the liturgical practices of the Christian East, I've noted that repentance figures prominently in these practices, more so than in any other tradition within Christendom of which I am aware. In this way, the Christian East implements the ideal stated in St. Isaac's dictum. I've also pointed out that, when one examines the prayers and practices of the Great Fast, it becomes evident that many of the prayers included in the church's liturgical texts are not prayers of repentance but repentance-oriented prayers. Although this orientation can initially appeal puzzling, I've suggested that when we specify the commitment conditions of repenting, we can see why these liturgical texts include these repentance-oriented prayers. In one or another way, they address the fact that we frequently fail to satisfy these conditions, and that we need to be aware of this when repenting. The reason we need to be aware of these tendencies, I take it, is not simply that we need to have an acute awareness of the fact that we are likely to fail in our endeavors to genuinely repent. It is also that we should repent with a clear-eyed recognition that the activity ought not to be an episodic event in the life of the Christian. Given its character and ours, repentance is an activity in which someone committed to the Christian ideal must continually engage. When read against the rest of his thought, I take this to be exactly what St. Isaac's dictum says. And it is something made manifest in the liturgical texts of the Great Fast.

3. Universal but not corporate

As Alexander Schmemann tells the narrative, the liturgies of the Christian East are the product of three main influences: the influence of the synagogue, the Byzantine court, and the monasteries.[44] The liturgies of the Great Fast are the product of the last influence. One telltale sign of this is that their prayers of repentance and repentance-oriented prayers wholly concern themselves with and intensely scrutinize the inner spiritual life of the believer. We've seen that both the prayers of repentance and the repentance-oriented prayers are typically cast in the first-person—although it should be noted that the

---

[44] *Introduction to Liturgical Theology.*

voice employed in these prayers is often that of a biblical character such as the Prodigal Son or the Publican with whom the assembled are to identify.[45]

To my knowledge, there are no prayers of repentance or repentance-oriented prayers in these liturgies that deviate from this pattern. There are, for example, no collective prayers of repentance or repentance-oriented prayers in which a congregation confesses its shortcomings.[46] In one sense, this is not surprising, given the monastic provenance of these texts. But in another sense, it is surprising. The Eastern Church thinks of itself not as a group of individuals organized around common ideals and activities but as a tightly unified collective: a person is baptized into the church and it is the church that is "actualized" in the celebration of the Eucharist.[47] The church's unity, Ware writes, "is not maintained from without by the authority of a Supreme Pontiff, but created from within by the celebration of the Eucharist" by various congregations.[48] This strong sense of unity is true not only of the church, but also of the individual congregations that (partially) constitute it: they too are united around the celebration of the Eucharist.[49] Under the plausible assumption that congregations no less than individuals have obligations and responsibilities that they can fulfill or fail to fulfill, it is surprising that the Eastern Church's liturgies of repentance do not appear to recognize this dimension of repentance. If it did, it might recommend that we would have to expand our understanding of St. Isaac's dictum: those committed to the Christian ideal are to order their lives around repenting not only of their own individual wrongdoings but also those of the congregations and groups, which constitute the church, to which they belong.

In recent years, there has been a flurry of work done on the topic of group agency.[50] This work raises the question of whether communities can have lives and whether they also can be meaningful. If they can lead such lives by ordering their activity around meaningfulness-conferring activities, it might

---

[45] I explore the liturgical practice of identifying with characters in the liturgical script in "Liturgy and the Moral Life," *Character:New Directions from Philosophy, Psychology, and Theology*, ed. Christian Miller (Oxford: Oxford University Press, 2015: 572–589).

[46] For an explanation of why the Eastern Church would not talk of the *church* repenting, see Timothy (Kallistos) Ware, *The Orthodox Church*. New Edition (New York: Penguin, 1997, ch. 12). Here I speak of the liturgies of the Great Fast. The Eucharistic liturgies, I believe, are plausibly interpreted to include corporate prayers of repentance.

[47] A theme that Schmemann, *Introduction to Liturgical Theology* emphasizes.

[48] *The Orthodox Church*, 246.

[49] In his book *The Orthodox Church*, John Meyendorff writes: "Now the *fullness* of this reality ... is present in every local church, in every Christian community gathered around the Eucharistic Table and having a bishop at its head" (New York: Pantheon Books, 1962, 212).

[50] See, for example, Christian List and Philip Pettit, *Group Agency: The Possibility, Design and Status of Corporate Agents* (Oxford: Oxford University Press, 2011).

be that we can intelligibly speak of what it is for those congregations that constitute the church to lead meaningful lives. Given an expanded understanding of St. Isaac's dictum, such a life would also consist in being ordered around repentance.[51]

---

[51] Thanks to Jon Jacobs, Rico Vitz, Nick Wolterstorff, the editors of this volume, and an audience at the Theistic Ethics Workshop at Wake Forest University for their comments on a version of this chapter. Work on this chapter was made possible through the support of a grant from the John Templeton Foundation. The opinions expressed in this publication are those of the author and do not necessarily reflect the views of the John Templeton Foundation.

Part Five

Meaning in Ecclesiastes

11

Wisdom and Meaning: Philosophy and the Theology of the Meaning of Life in Ecclesiastes

Craig G. Bartholomew

*"Truly, light is sweet
and it is good for the eyes to observe the sun."*

Ecclesiastes 11:1

1. Introduction

Analytical philosophy has tended to ignore or to be hostile toward the question of the meaning of life. On my desk I keep as a handy reference Peter Angeles' *Dictionary of Philosophy*,[1] which, although somewhat dated, is invariably helpful as a first port of call. It has 23 entries under "meaning" but none dealing with the meaning of life. Indeed, it is only in the last 25 years that analytical philosophy has begun to wrestle seriously with the question of life's meaningfulness.[2]

Within analytical philosophy debate continues about whether or not "the meaning of life" is even a legitimate, meaningful question to address. Doubtless there is value in clarifying the question and its components but, in my view, taken too far this is an example of an unhelpful detachment of philosophy from the concerns of "ordinary people," that is, nonphilosophers. The twentieth century opened amidst great hubris that reason and science would lead us forward on a grand path of progress. In retrospect it turned out to be what many consider the most brutal century in history. Technologically

---

[1] Peter Angeles, *Dictionary of Philosophy* (NY: Barnes and Noble, 1981).
[2] Two recent collections on the topic are E. D. Klemke, ed. *The Meaning of Life*, 2nd edn (New York: Oxford University Press, 2000); Joshua W. Seachris, ed. *Exploring the Meaning of Life: An Anthology and Guide* (Malden, MA: Wiley-Blackwell, 2012).

we have made great advances but this serves upon reflection only to frame more acutely the question a cabdriver once addressed to Bertrand Russell, "So what's it all about?"

It is ironic that analytic philosophers have avoided this question since modernity has unintentionally forced it to the surface again and again. In his preface to Michael Polanyi's *Meaning*, Harry Prosch notes that Polanyi's lectures are intended to "show the reader how the modern mind has destroyed meaning"[3] and how Polanyi's own work hoped to indicate how to restore meaning through his philosophy of personal knowledge.

Max Weber (1864–1920), one of the greatest modern sociologists, while embracing post-Enlightenment thought, remained obsessed with the question of meaning in the modern world. He was deeply in touch with the shadow side of modernity and prophetically told German students after World War 1 in his famous lecture on politics as a vocation, "It is not 'summer's front' which lies before us, but first of all a Polar night of icy darkness and severity."[4] Weber saw that the scientism of modernity makes "the belief that there is such a thing as the 'meaning' of the universe die out at its very roots."[5] In exchange for this loss of meaning we receive individual autonomy, a bargain that Weber thought worth it!

It is important to note that Weber did not think that modern reason was natural or inherent:

> Intellectualization, he believed, rested upon the most unnatural motivation, led to the most abstracted orientation, and inspired the most desiccated organization the world had ever known.... Weber holds that only if the irrational basis of rationality is accepted can the tortuous development of rationality properly be understood and the precarious condition of individual autonomy be appreciated.[6]

Autonomy grants us mastery but ironically it also allows us to be mastered by others and by modern structures, a condition Weber evocatively refers to as the "iron cage" of modernity. Intriguingly, in his later years Weber developed his doctrine of *vocation* as the means whereby moderns can escape this iron

---

[3] Harry Prosch, "Preface," in Michael Polanyi and Harry Prosch, *Meaning* (Chicago and London: University of Chicago Press, 1975), ix–x.
[4] Max Weber, *Selections in Translation*. Edited by W. G. Runciman (Cambridge: CUP, 1978), 224.
[5] Max Weber, *From Max Weber*. Edited by H. Gerth and C. Wright Mills. (New York: OUP, 1946), 142.
[6] Jeffrey C. Alexander, *The Dark Side of Modernity* (Cambridge: Polity, 2013), 33.

cage. One needs a sense of inner calling and a moral cause, of "some kind of faith," an ethics of responsibility.[7]

Analytic philosophy is one branch of learning that has avoided succumbing to postmodernism. Until recently both, however, shared the view that asking about the meaning of life is a nonstarter as a philosophical question. Whereas prior to the advent of postmodernism one might expect the realization that life is meaningless to drive one to despair or suicide, postmodernism, as Gertrude Himmelfarb points out,[8] has sought to tame such beasts of the abyss and to encourage us to embrace them in a type of *cheerful nihilism*. An example of such a view is articulated by Brassier:

> The disenchantment of the world deserves to be celebrated as an achievement of intellectual maturity, not bewailed as a debilitating impoverishment.... . Nature is not our or anyone's "home," nor a particularly beneficent progenitor. Philosophers would do well to desist from issuing any further injunctions about the need to re-establish the meaningfulness of existence, the purposefulness of life, or mend the shattered concord between man and nature.... . Nihilism is not an existential quandary but a speculative opportunity.[9]

As we move deeper into the twenty-first century, it should be difficult—if not impossible—to attend to the question of the meaning of life as a—if not *the*—question of our day.

2. Introducing Qohelet

While this question is accentuated in our day, it is no new issue. The Old Testament/Hebrew Bible contains *Ecclesiastes*, a quite extraordinary text wrestling throughout with the issue of the meaning of life. Its ascription to Solomon is a fictional device designed to engage the reader's imagination so as to envisage the central character "Qohelet" as one of the wisest and most

---

[7] Ibid., 49.
[8] Gertrude Himmelfarb, *On Looking Into the Abyss: Untimely Thoughts on Culture and Society* (New York: Vintage, 1994).
[9] Ray Brassier, *Nihil Unbound: Enlightenment and Extinction* (Basingstoke, UK: Palgrave Macmillan, 2007), xi. For comparable quotes from Jacques Monod and Steven Weinberg see Jonathan Sacks, *The Great Partnership: Science, Religion, and the Search for Meaning* (New York: Schocken, 2011), 25. Sacks, ibid., 25–26, refers to Ecclesiastes for similar sentiments in the Hebrew Bible.

powerful men of his day.[10] Qohelet has at his behest all that is required to engage in the most rigorous research project about the meaning of life.

A crisis of meaning is not unique to Ecclesiastes in the OT or among the literature of the Ancient Near East.[11] Job, Jonah, Habakkuk, many of the Psalms, Jeremiah's "Confessions," etc., bear eloquent witness to the fact that a crisis of meaning was not at all unknown among the ancient Israelites. However, of all such texts, Ecclesiastes is the most philosophical. Unlike Job, we have no idea what launched Qohelet into his crisis, and while, like Job, his crisis is existential, Qohelet's struggle is more intellectual than existential.

Qohelet deliberately and consciously sets out to explore the question of the meaning of life: "I set my heart to seek and to explore by wisdom all that is done under the heavens" (1:13). He articulates his research question not as "the meaning of life" but through the refrain: "What is the benefit for humankind in all one's labor at which one labors under the sun?"[12] (1:3; etc.). Using the typical vocabulary of OT wisdom he describes his methodology as to seek and to explore "by wisdom" all that is done under the heavens. The Hebrew *hokmah* is the common word for wisdom in the OT, and it receives its normative exposition in Proverbs.[13]

Thus far most contemporary commentators on Ecclesiastes are in agreement. However, interpretation of this enigmatic book divides over whether it is one of despair or finally one of joy and hope. The majority see Ecclesiastes as a book of despair with the epilogue as a later addition/s. In my published work I defend the view that Ecclesiastes is finally a book of hope and one that affirms meaning, but *only* at the end of a long struggle. Ecclesiastes, as befits the struggle for meaning, is complex, and below I will unpack the main contours of my reading of this challenging book.

For now, let me make my own position clear. In my view Ecclesiastes overall *affirms life as meaningful* and locates the ground for this view in starting with God as creator, in profound reverence for God (the fear of God), and in living a life under his reign (obedience). Ecclesiastes never suggests that this solves the many mysteries of life, the most profound of which is death, but does argue that life is, and can be experienced as, meaningful in the context of living life *coram deo*. In this way Ecclesiastes offers *both* a substantive view of the meaning of life *and*, through the narrative of Qohelet's tortuous

---

[10] On this and other interpretive issues see Craig G. Bartholomew, *Reading Ecclesiastes: Old Testament Exegesis and Hermeneutical Theory*. Analecta Biblica 139. (Rome: Pontifical Biblical Institute, 1998); *Ecclesiastes*. BCOTWP. (Grand Rapids: Baker Academic, 2009).

[11] See, for example, "Harper's Songs" in William W. Hallo, ed. *The Context of Scripture. Volume 1. Canonical Compositions from the Biblical World* (Leiden: Brill, 1997), 30–31.

[12] Translations are by the author. See Bartholomew, *Ecclesiastes*.

[13] Craig G. Bartholomew, *Reading Proverbs with Integrity* (Cambridge: Groves 2001).

struggle, immensely practical advice for how to live such meaning amidst the challenges of life.

Qohelet's articulation of his method as "by wisdom" evokes for the reader the sort of wisdom we find in Proverbs, rooted in the fear of YHWH. A body of work has now appeared on the epistemology of wisdom and as one examines Qohelet's epistemology more closely it becomes clear that it is in fact very different to that advocated by Proverbs. Proverbs advocates an epistemology that begins with the fear of YHWH and embarks on a journey of discovery of the world through this lens. By contrast Qohelet's epistemology can be characterized as follows:

- *Autonomous and Individualist.* A significant characteristic of Ecclesiastes is the continual use of the first-person singular. His search is grounded in himself rather than starting with the fear of YHWH. The repetitive "I" alerts us to the solitariness, the individualism of his search.
- *Empirical.* Michael Fox has rightly pointed out that the epistemology of Proverbs is not empirical,[14] but Qohelet's is! As he explores area after area of life in his quest for meaning it becomes clear that his search is based on observation, reason, and experience alone.

It is the application of this epistemology that leads him again and again, no matter what areas of life he attends to, to his famous *hebel* (enigmatic) conclusion. *Hebel* functions as a multivocal symbol in Ecclesiastes and there has been endless debate about how to translate it. "Meaningless"[15] or "useless"[16] is an inadequate translation since Qohelet is not denying that there might be meaning but asserting that if there is he cannot find it; hence my translation of *hebel* as "enigma" or "enigmatic."

Qohelet's negative conclusions are undoubtedly full of despair but surprisingly we find juxtaposed next to them throughout the book his so-called joy or *carpe diem* passages. In my view these are not an expression of a despairing hedonism but an expression of *the goodness of created life* which Qohelet has learned from his Israelite tradition and personal experience. Indeed the juxtaposition of the *hebel* conclusions with the *carpe diem* passages brings us to the heart of Qohelet's struggle. As a believer he cannot deny the goodness of life but his epistemology drives him again and again to the conclusion that all is enigmatic. This creates an unbearable tension, a tangible angst, and the

---

[14] Michael Fox, "Qohelet's Epistemology," *Hebrew Union College Annual* 58 (1987): 137–155.
[15] New International Version.
[16] Good News Bible.

book as a whole deals with how to find one's way back to firm ground when caught on the horns of such a dilemma.

In my reading Qohelet does indeed find resolution to his dilemma. Landmarks in his journey are found in 5:1–7 [4:17–5:6 in the Hebrew] and in 7:23–29. Lohfink thinks that 5:1–7 is at the center of the structure of Ecclesiastes,[17] and it serves as an intriguing counterpart to Qohelet's epistemology with its emphasis on approaching the Temple reverently to listen in order to be taught. 7:23–29 is akin to 1:12–18, except that in 7:23–29 Qohelet pauses to reflect on where he has arrived in his journey "by wisdom" (7:23). His insight is that what he thought was wisdom has led him right into the arms of Dame Folly.

Qohelet's journey is intellectual and existential and his move toward resolution is flagged by a deeply existential proverb in 11:1:

"Truly, light is sweet and it is good for the eyes to observe the sun."

Resolution comes for Qohelet, not by denying the data that seem to point to despair but by recontextualizing the data within the framework of "Remember your creator ... " (12:1). The narrator sums up Qohelet's journey in the epilogue (12:9–14) and particularly in v. 13: "The end of the matter, all has been heard. Fear God and keep his commandments, for this is the whole duty of humankind." This is indeed where Qohelet arrives but only through a great struggle as witnessed by the main body of Ecclesiastes. Importantly the epilogue affirms such a struggle with its affirmation of Qohelet as a teacher of wisdom. What is often not noted by commentators is that if Qohelet does indeed find resolution to his struggle, then, in retrospect *all the areas of life* that he has examined become meaningful. As Gordon Spykman eloquently comments, "Nothing matters but the kingdom, but, because of the kingdom everything matters."[18]

3. Defining our terms

Ecclesiastes is the most philosophical book in the Bible but it is not a philosophical treatise. Qohelet backs into the question of the meaning of life through his rhetorical refrain about the value of work under the sun. Thus, as

---

[17] Norbert Lohfink, *Qoheleth*. Translated by S. E. McEvenue. Continental Commentary. (Minneapolis: Fortress. 2003).

[18] Gordon J. Spykman, *Reformational Theology: A New Paradigm for Doing Dogmatics* (Grand Rapids: Eerdmans, 1992), 478.

we connect Ecclesiastes to the contemporary debate about the meaning of life we need to pause to define our terms. This is particularly important because of the alleged vagueness of the expression "meaning of life."[19]

In terms of the current debate and in relation to Ecclesiastes I find Seachris's case for a nonlinguistic usage of "meaning" insightful. He points out that in relation to the meaning of life we are after the worldview or metanarrative in which the relevant elements and questions of life fit. The themes associated with the quest for life's meaning include:[20]

1. Why does anything or we or I exist at all?
2. Does life have a purpose and, if so, what is its nature and source?
3. Do the worth and value of the projects and pursuits we engage in so passionately need grounding in something else, and, if so, what?
4. Why are pain and suffering part of the universe?
5. Is death final and is there an eschatological remedy to the ills of the world?

4. Worldview, Qohelet, and the amalgam hypothesis

In comparison to the "worldview" approach above, the favored view nowadays is to discard the word "meaning" and to reformulate the question of meaning into a cluster of other, apparently less vague questions. This approach is known as *the amalgam thesis*,[21] which views the question of life's meaning as a "long disjunctive question or an amalgam of related yet distinct requests about existence, purpose, value, worth, significance, death, and futility, among others."[22] Two sets of questions can be discerned within the amalgam thesis: cosmic questions and individualist or local questions. The latter set would include questions like: "What purposes should order my life?" "What gives value to my life? and "What makes my life worthwhile?" The majority of philosophers attend to the latter set of questions.

Qohelet is intriguing in that he evidences *a strong individualism*, as noted above. In Nagel's language he conducts his investigation primarily from an *internal viewpoint*,[23] exploring area after area of life to see if it can solve his problem.

---

[19] See Seachris, ed. *Exploring the Meaning of Life: An Anthology and Guide*, for a useful anthology introducing the reader to the current debate.
[20] Joshua W. Seachris, "General Introduction," in *Exploring the Meaning of Life*, ed. Seachris, 1–20, 9.
[21] See R. W. Hepburn, "Questions About the Meaning of Life," in *Exploring the Meaning of Life*, ed. Seachris, 48–61.
[22] Seachris, "General Introduction," 4.
[23] Thomas Nagel, "The Absurd," in *Exploring the Meaning of Life*, ed. Seachris, 236–244.

For Nagel a tension arises because of the discrepancy between an external and an internal viewpoint. In the midst of daily life—the internal viewpoint—we are fully engaged and serious about what we are up to. When problems arise within the internal viewpoint we can try to adjust the world to fit with our expectations or we can try to alter our expectations to fit with the world. However, when we step back—a uniquely human capacity—we see that we are only a speck in a vast universe, here today and gone tomorrow, so that what we are engaged with and passionate about appears arbitrary, indeed, absurd, even if we succeed in finding a match between the world and our expectations. The struggle with absurdity thus stems from our capacity to transcend ourselves and to ask the big questions. Nagel argues that this is in fact not a problem; it is part of our being human and should be handled ironically rather than lead to despair or heroism in the face of absurdity.

Qohelet, one suspects, would not let Nagel off the hook so easily! It is precisely *through his internal viewpoint* that Qohelet keeps running into problems with the meaning of life, the big question.

Qohelet would not have been helped in his struggle by being told that life would still be absurd even if he was successful in his effort to adjust the world to fit his expectations or his expectations to fit the world. Qohelet's situation is like that of Job as Buber describes it: "Job cannot forego either his own truth or God,"[24] and his perspective on life pushes him to find a resolution between the two.

In one sense Ecclesiastes is itself a long disjunctive question exploring diverse areas of life as possible ways of conferring meaning and value on his life. For a whole variety of reasons he finds all such areas unsatisfactory. Furthermore Qohelet insists on linking the different areas of life back into the cosmic, worldviewish questions, performatively insisting that they are inseparably linked and again he would not have been helped by being told that this is just part of being human and he should approach the problem ironically.

Irony does indeed play an important role in Ecclesiastes but in a very different way to Nagel. Especially in Ecclesiastes 7:23–29 Qohelet's autonomous epistemology, which he describes earlier as "wisdom," is exposed as "folly." Resolution comes for Qohelet by making an internal adjustment but one that *includes* the big questions. Qohelet moves from an epistemology based on observation, reason, and experience alone to one that starts with reverence for God, as discussed in more detail below.

---

[24] Quoted by Harold Bloom, ed. *The Book of Job* (New York: Chelsea House, 1988), 2.

5. Qohelet, time, and (meta)narrative

An example of the way in which Qohelet backs into the big questions through his internal viewpoint is found in Eccl 3: 1–15. In his famous poem on time Qohelet recognizes that time and a sense of universal order are fundamental to human existence. "When we look at life, says Qohelet, it seems like a rich tapestry of contrasting colours; with every thread in place and everything seems to fit."[25] The crunch for Qohelet comes in v. 11:

> He [God] has made everything fitting in its time. Furthermore, he has placed eternity in their heart, but still one is unable to discern what God has done from the beginning to the end.

There is considerable discussion about this verse and not least the meaning of "eternity" (ha'olam). In my view it refers to the human need for a sense of beginning and ending at the metanarrative level, without which one is unable, according to Qohelet, to discern what is fitting in the present. One is left, as it were, with a sense of purpose and order, but without the key to access such purpose. For Qohelet it is precisely the internal viewpoint that creates the tension and not just a discrepancy between internal and external viewpoints.

Qohelet's reflections on time, "eternity," and being human raise the issue of narrative and the meaning of life. Qohelet suggests that a sense of origin and ending—a metanarrative—is essential if life is to be meaningful. Recent decades have seen a veritable explosion of interest in narrative, and in philosophy Paul Ricoeur, Alasdair MacIntyre, Charles Taylor, and others have taken up the theme of narrative with vigor. MacIntyre addresses the way in which all human life and thought is traditioned and argues that our life decisions are shaped and ordered by our sense of how they fit within a larger story or tradition[26] and insists that, "I can only answer the question, 'What am I to do?' if I can answer the prior question, 'Of what story or stories do I find myself a part?'"[27] "What am I to do?" is an ethical question, which is related to, but distinct from, the question of the meaning of life. The ethical question arises from an internal viewpoint. However, according to MacIntyre it can only be answered in relation to a larger story of which I am part, and, Mark Wallace notes that for Ricoeur,

> Everyone needs a story to live by in order to make sense of the pastiche of one's life. Without a narrative a person's life is merely a random sequence

---

[25] Robert Davidson, *Courage to Doubt: Exploring an Old Testament Theme* (London: SCM, 1989), 198.
[26] See Alasdair MacIntyre, *After Virtue: A Study in Moral Theory*, 3rd ed. (Notre Dame: University of Notre Dame Press, 2007), 237–262.
[27] Ibid., 250.

of unrelated events: birth and death are inscrutable, temporality is a terror and a burden, and suffering and loss remain mute and unintelligible.[28]

Ricoeur, in line with Qohelet, recognizes the need for a macro narrative to make sense of a person's life, of events like birth and death, of temporality, of suffering and death, all major themes in Ecclesiastes. The million dollar question is *Whose Story? Which Metanarrative?* Does such a story need to take God into account or can a naturalist worldview yield an adequate metanarrative, as Goodenough argues?

> And so, I profess my Faith. For me, the existence of all this complexity and awareness and intent and beauty, and my ability to apprehend it, serves as the ultimate meaning and the ultimate value. The continuation of life reaches around, grabs its own tail, and forms a sacred circle that requires no further justification, no Creator, no superordinate meaning of meaning, no purpose other than that the continuation continue until the sun collapses or the final meteor collides. I confess a credo of continuation.[29]

6. Qohelet, God, and the meaning of life

There is far more than one metanarrative within which humans can find meaning. Four major philosophical views of the meaning of life have emerged in current discussions: supernaturalism, objective naturalism, subjective naturalism, and pessimistic naturalism or nihilism. And, of course, within each of these views many different variants are located. A central question is whether or not "God" is needed for a metanarrative to provide adequate meaning for life. Both forms of naturalism deny that God is necessary for life to be meaningful.

In attending to this question it is worth distinguishing between *objective meaning* and *subjective meaning*. It is undoubtedly true that many naturalists and nihilists experience life as fulfilling and meaningful; their life is meaningful *subjectively*. Similarly there are doubtless theists who experience life as meaningless. However, it is another question altogether as to whether or not such experience fits with the way the world actually is, that is, whether or not life is *objectively* meaningful, that is, that we are made to find life meaningful.

---

[28] Mark I. Wallace, "Introduction," in *Figuring the Sacred: Religion, Narrative, and Imagination*, ed. Paul Ricoeur, 1–34. (Minneapolis: Fortress, 1995), 1–34, 11.
[29] Ursula Goodenough, "Emergent Religious Principles," in *Exploring the Meaning of Life*, ed. Seachris, 367–370, 375.

These two versions of meaning should be distinguished but the boundary between them is porous. It is often only when the subjective experience is shaken that the objective question moves to the foreground, and, as we noted in our introduction, there is more than enough at work in our world to shake a subjective sense of meaningfulness. Once again Qohelet is instructive in this regard.

From the *carpe diem* passages we can conclude that Qohelet knew well the subjective experience of life as meaningful. However, something—we know not what—had shaken this experience and challenged it to its core. The result is that he embarks on a journey to discern whether or not life really is, that is, objectively, meaningful. What this reveals is that the subjective experience is inadequate in and of itself; it needs to be grounded in a sense of the world as objectively meaningful. Similarly an objective sense of life as meaningful is inadequate without a subjective correlate. The two are distinguishable but ultimately inseparable.

Unlike naturalists Qohelet never moves God out of the picture in his quest for meaning. However, like the naturalists Qohelet embraces an autonomous epistemology rooted in himself, and dependent on observation, reason, and experience alone. This raises a number of important issues.

First, Ecclesiastes through its narrative of Qohelet's journey foregrounds the issue of how we can know if life is meaningful, that is, *the epistemological question*. Central to modernity and all three brands of naturalism is a strong version of human autonomy. Ecclesiastes attempts to show through Qohelet's quest that an epistemology grounded in human autonomy can never overcome the enigma of life, that is, it cannot solve the question of the meaning of life. It is hard not to think that there is validity in this perspective since humans live and die in relatively short lifespans and are imbedded in history without ever being able to gain a view of life by themselves *sub specie aeternitatis*. One might expect, therefore, that naturalists would be *agnostic* about the question of the meaning of life but, as the literature shows, this is not the case.

Second, the issue thus emerges of what difference the question of God makes to the question of the meaning of life. Some philosophers have argued that typical attributes of God indicate that he makes no difference.[30] In this respect Qohelet's journey is once again instructive. Ecclesiastes never uses the typical, personal Israelite name for God, viz., YHWH. Instead he uses the more generic Elohim. However, it is clear from Ecclesiastes as a whole that by "Elohim" the author has YHWH in view. This is clear, for example,

---

[30] John Cottingham, "Introduction," in Pages 115–120 in Seachris, ed., *Exploring the Meaning of Life*, 115–120, 118; Thaddeus Metz, "Introduction" in Seachris, ed., *Exploring the Meaning of Life*, 23–28.

from his advice about going to the Temple to listen, his knowledge of Israelite cultic law, the references to Torah, etc. As is typical of the Bible, Ecclesiastes never engages in philosophical analysis of the nature of God of the sort that the philosophers above refer to. However, Qohelet's journey does draw our attention to one major characteristic of God, namely *God as Creator*. This is at the heart of the resolution of his journey and of fundamental importance for the question of the meaning of life. Viewing our world *as creation* evokes a radically different view to that which is agnostic at this point or views our world as the random product of an arbitrary evolutionary process. Humans are created from an OT perspective and find their purpose and thus meaning in relation to God's purposes for his creation and for humans as the *imago dei* in the creation. There is clear intertextuality between Ecclesiastes and the opening chapters of Genesis, in which it is clear that humans are creatures, made for relationship with God and with each other, and appointed to exercise royal stewardship over God's good creation so that it is developed such that it resounds more and more to his glory. That one word in the Hebrew of Eccl 12:1, "your Creator," makes all the difference in the world and provides for a thick understanding of the meaning of life. From such a perspective it would be absurd to suggest that "God" makes no difference to the question of the meaning of life. He is its origin and goal and humans find meaning above all else in relationship with him.

Third, Qohelet's attention to God as Creator of all takes us back to the *amalgam thesis*. Ecclesiastes is an OT wisdom book and OT wisdom is grounded in a theology of creation. Proverbs emphasizes that it is by wisdom that YHWH created the world (Prov 3; 8) so that the world is awash with wisdom. Proverbs evokes this through the figure of Lady Wisdom who is portrayed as calling out in the public spheres of life to all who will listen. Thus there is some truth in the view advocated by Julian Baggini, for example, who offers "a deflationary account of life's meaning"[31] so that, "To understand life's meaning therefore does not require rare wisdom."[32] Baggini asserts that,

> It is straightforward enough to say that life can be worthwhile in itself, particularly if it is a life with a balance of authenticity, happiness and concern for others; one where time is not wasted; one which engages in the ongoing work of becoming who we want to be and being successful in those terms. But putting this all into practice is difficult.[33]

---

[31] Julian Baggini, *What's It All About?: Philosophy and the Meaning of Life* (Oxford: OUP, 2005), Kindle Location 1896.
[32] Ibid., 1897.
[33] Ibid., 1902–1904.

Baggini argues for a democratic and egalitarian view of the meaning of life which returns to each one of us the ability and responsibility to discover and in part to determine meaning for ourselves.

Much of this accords with OT wisdom. We are immersed in wisdom according to Proverbs and it is altogether in line with our humanity so that we should not think of the meaning of life as some esoteric entity unrelated to who we already are.[34] Wisdom in this respect is to be located in "the ordinary," which surrounds us at every step and includes the squirrels that Wielenberg writes about.[35]

Few authors have drawn such clear attention to this in relation to the Bible than Eric Auerbach. A fascinating aspect of Auerbach's reading of the Bible is that its literary nature forges a vision in which the sublime (divine) and the everyday are inseparable.[36] In chapter 2 of *Mimesis* Auerbach compares chapter 37 and part of 38 of Peronius's *Fortunata*, the ancient view of the instability of fortune, and part of Tacitus's *Annals*, Book 1, with the story of Peter's denial of Jesus in Mark's Gospel. In contrast with this ancient literature Peter "is the image of man in the highest and deepest and most tragic sense"[37] and the scene of his denial "fits into no antique genre."[38] Auerbach asks why this narrative arouses in us the most serious sympathy.

> Because it portrays something which neither the poets nor the historians of antiquity ever set out to portray: the birth of a spiritual movement in the depths of the common people, from within the everyday occurrences of contemporary life, which thus assumes an importance it could never have assumed in antique literature. What we witness is the awakening of "a new heart and a new spirit." All this applies not only to Peter's denial but also to every other occurrence which is related in the New Testament.... Peter and the other characters in the New Testament are caught in a universal movement of the depths which at first remains almost entirely below the surface and only very gradually ... emerges into the foreground of history ... What we see here is a world which on the one hand is entirely real, average, identifiable as to place, time and circumstances, but which on the other hand is shaken in its very foundations, is transforming and renewing itself before our eyes. For the New Testament authors who are their contemporaries, these

---

[34] Cf. Dietrich Bonhoeffer, *Ethics*. Edited by E. Bethge. (London: SCM, 1955), 101–122.
[35] Erik J. Wielenberg, "Introduction," in *Exploring the Meaning of Life*, ed. Seachris, 277–281, 278.
[36] Erich Auerbach, *Mimesis* (Princeton: Princeton University Press, 1953, 2003), 22–23.
[37] Ibid., 41.
[38] Ibid., 45.

occurrences on the plane of everyday life assume the importance of world-revolutionary events, as later on they will for everyone.[39]

Remarkably, as a Jew, Auerbach connects this vision with the incarnation. It is a material, earthly vision which takes life in its rich, creational viscerality seriously, a vision that the church has not always sustained. In his *Sources of the Self* Charles Taylor has a delightful chapter entitled "God Loveth Adverbs" on the way in which the Reformers and Puritans recovered an emphasis on the ordinary.[40] Such an emphasis finds ample biblical support in OT wisdom and in the NT Jesus is depicted inter alia as wisdom incarnate.

Thus, we should expect humans to be stumbling across facets of the meaning of life every day. The Christian art historian Hans Rookmaker expresses a view close to that of Baggini in the title of his book *Art Needs No Justification*. What Rookmaker means by this is that art is a possibility built into the creation and, as such, needs no justification. The Dutch philosopher Herman Dooyeweerd expresses a similar insight in his view of *creation as meaning*. Creation, including human life, is inherently good and worthwhile.

Where OT wisdom differs from Baggini is in his espousal of the autonomous self: he refers to "one which engages in the ongoing work of becoming *who we want to be* and being successful in those terms."[41] Rather than asking who we are created to be and to become, we decide who we want to be and plan accordingly. Built into such an anthropology is the view of ourselves as our own creators. Of such a view Cottingham rightly notes that,

> By supposing the unaided human will can create meaning, that it can merely by its own resolute affirmation bypass the search for objectively sourced truth and value, he [Nietzsche] seems to risk coming close to the Protagorean fallacy. For meaning and worth cannot reside in raw will alone: they have to involve a fit between our decisions and beliefs and what grounds those decisions and beliefs.[42]

By contrast OT wisdom's poignant insight, according to Gerhard von Rad,[43] is the recognition that if one goes wrong at the start of the quest for knowledge the whole is irretrievably skewed. Furthermore, Proverbs' picture of Lady

---

[39] Ibid., 43.
[40] Charles Taylor, *Sources of the Self: The Making of the Modern Identity* (Cambridge: Harvard University Press, 1989).
[41] Emphasis added.
[42] John Cottingham, *On the Meaning of Life*. Thinking in Action. (London and NY: Routledge. 2003), 17.
[43] Gerhard Von Rad, *Wisdom in Israel* (Nashville: Abingdon, 1972).

Wisdom calling out needs to be balanced with Job 28, an extraordinary poem in which Job acknowledges the great abilities of humankind but foregrounds their inability to find *the source* of wisdom, namely YHWH. For the OT wisdom and thus meaning is like a multifaceted diamond, the whole of which is held together and correctly grasped in proportion by a right relationship with God. Disavowal of this relationship OT wisdom describes as folly.

This view allows us to affirm with Baggini that wisdom is to be found all over the place, while insisting that unless the piece of the puzzle we find is fitted correctly into the larger picture it will become distorted and be unable to bear the weight we assign to it.[44]

There are philosophers who argue—with Qohelet—that meaning in life depends upon God. Wittgenstein is one such, and he states his view uncompromisingly:

To believe in God means to understand the question about the meaning of life.
To believe in God means to see that the facts of the world are not the end of the matter.
To believe in God means to see that life has a meaning.[45]

7. A broken world: Qohelet, the meaning of life, and folly

An emphasis of the Dutch theologian and polymath Abraham Kuyper was that scholarship needs to address the question of whether or not the world as we experience it is *normal or abnormal*. Kuyper rightly noted that most modern scholars proceed on the assumption that it is normal, but he disagreed. Theologically Kuyper insisted that the world as we now experience it has been deeply affected by sin, the fall, and God's judgment.

Qohelet similarly recognizes that there is something profoundly wrong with the world which inhibits the search for meaning. In parts of his struggle he blames God for the brokenness of the world: "It is an evil task that God has given to human beings with which to be afflicted.... What is crooked cannot be made straight, and what is lacking cannot be counted" (1:13, 15). In 7:13 Qohelet asserts, "Observe the work of God, for who can straighten what he has made crooked?" However by 7:29 we find a different perspective

---

[44] The best articulation of the epistemology at work here that I know of is that articulated by Oliver O'Donovan, *Resurrection and Moral Order: An Outline for Evangelical Ethics*, 2nd ed. (Leicester: Apollos; Grand Rapids: Eerdmans, 1986, 1994), 76–100.
[45] Ludwig Wittgenstein, *Notebooks, 1914–16*, 2nd ed. Translated by G.E.M. Anscombe. (Chicago: University of Chicago Press, 1979), 74.

expressed, coming at the end of one of the landmark passages in Qohelet's journey as noted above: "Only observe this: I have found that God made the human being straight, but they have sought out many schemes." Here Qohelet foregrounds the effect of *sin* on the search for meaning in life.

There is one quote from Ecclesiastes in the NT in Romans 3:10, in which Paul is thought to quote Eccl 7:20[46]—"For there is not a righteous person on the earth who does good and does not sin."—as part of his argument that all have sinned and fallen short of the glory of God. This verse fits with Paul's "use" of it in Romans 3 as is confirmed by an examination of Eccl 7:20 in the context of Ecclesiastes as a whole. 7:20 occurs shortly before 7:23–29, a section that marks major progress in Qohelet's journey toward self-understanding. 7:13 with its exhortation to observe the work of God who has made the world crooked is a link verse between 7:1–13 and 7:14–22. In vv. 14–22 Qohelet reflects on how to approach wisdom and folly if this is the state of the world. His advice boils down to, be moderate in both and excessive in neither! Amidst his struggle, and lying between 7:13 and 7:29, 7:20 marks the movement in Qohelet's journey toward insight into *human responsibility before God*. This, of course, fits with how Paul uses 7:20 in Rom 3, amidst a collection of quotes to show that all are under the power of sin. The vocabulary of *sin* is not alien to Qohelet as 7:20 indicates, and Ecclesiastes provides us with a deep insight into what Paul calls "the power of sin" (Rom 3:9).

Scholars also discern a connection with Ecclesiastes in Rom 8:20 in which "futility" ($\mu\alpha\tau\alpha\iota\acute{o}\tau\eta\varsigma$) is the same word the LXX (Septuagint, Greek Translation of the OT) uses to translate *hebel* in Ecclesiastes. "For the creation was placed in subjection to *futility*, not by its own will, but through the one who subjected it, in hope that the creation itself will be liberated from the servitude of corruption into the freedom of the glory of the children of God."

Sin; futility; judgment; these are not words that one finds in much of the renascent literature on the meaning of life! An exception is John Cottingham who observes that,

> It is reasonable, as John Hare has argued, to think that the idea of a moral gap between how we humans are and what we aspire to be, is central to the religious impulse. In theological terms, this may be expressed in terms of the concept of original sin, or the Fall; more prosaically, we are

---

[46] Richard B. Hays, *The Conversion of Imagination: Paul as Interpreter of Israel's Scripture* (Grand Rapids: Eerdmans, 2005), 90, notes that Paul prefaces his five citations from the Psalms "with a universal indictment of human unrighteousness from Eccles 7:20 and interspersed a powerful passage from Isa 59:7–8 that prophetically decries Israel's unfaithfulness." As a perusal of commentaries on Romans shows, not all are as sure that Rom 3:10 does contain a quote from Ecclesiastes.

all aware (to paraphrase a point made by Aristotle, though in a different context) that the very best life we could live would be one that is superior to the ordinary human level.[47]

How might such insights bear on the search for meaning in life? Qohelet is revealing in this respect, especially in 7:23–29, in which he comes to the realization that his epistemology of "wisdom" has led him right into the arms of Dame Folly, that is, what he thought was wisdom was in fact folly! There is, in this respect, a fascinating parallel between Qohelet's journey and that of Augustine in his *Confessions*. Augustine says of his search for the truth in relation to the origin of evil that, "My ignorance was so great that these questions troubled me, and while I thought I was approaching the truth, I was only departing the further from it."[48] Later in the *Confessions*, Augustine comments that, "I was trying to find the origin of evil, but *I was quite blind to the evil in my own method of research*."[49] Like Ecclesiastes, Augustine's *Confessions* is autobiographical,[50] and like Qohelet, Augustine, while thinking he was wisely engaged in a quest for wisdom, "blundered upon that woman in Solomon's parable who, ignorant and unabashed, sat at her door and said *Stolen waters are sweetest, and bread is better eating when there is none to see*. She inveigled me because she found me living in the outer world that lay before my eyes, the eyes of the flesh, and dwelling upon the food which they provided for my mind."[51]

Ecclesiastes thus puts firmly on the agenda of contemporary thought the issue of what's wrong with the world and how this impacts the search for meaning in life. Qohelet and Augustine would agree with G.K. Chesterton who famously commented, "What's wrong with the world? I am." Clearly if there is something wrong with the world and with us this has radical implications for the meaning of life! Indeed one of the insights flowing from such a perspective is that our folly shows itself again and again in taking a real good in the creation and absolutizing it. An example of this in Ecclesiastes is found in 10:1–20 and v. 20 in particular: "One makes bread for laughter, and wine gladdens the living, but *money answers everything*!" Prosperity and money are creational goods, but once we locate ultimate meaning in them—"money

---

[47] John Cottingham, *The Spiritual Dimension: Religion, Philosophy and Human Value* (Cambridge: Cambridge University Press, 2005), 74.
[48] Augustine, *Confessions* (London: Penguin, 1961), III, 7.
[49] Ibid., VII, 5. Italics mine.
[50] See Tremper Longman III's, *Fictional Akkadian Autobiography: A Generic and Comparative Study* (Winona Lake, IN: Eisenbrauns, 1990), important comparative work in this respect.
[51] Augustine, *Confessions*, III, 6.

answers everything"—they turn sour and distort our experience of life as meaningful. Humans are indeed surrounded by wisdom but we have a tendency to take creational goods and absolutize them. The common biblical word for this is idolatry. Qohelet's word is folly.

8. Qohelet and the end: Death, immortality, and eschatology

It is true in my view that continental philosophy never lost an interest in the meaning of life.[52] This is not to say it has come up with better answers. Heidegger analyzed human life in terms of *Dasein* (being thrown into existence) and characterizes it as *being-toward-death*. Death casts an ultimate shadow over life and raises a host of questions in relation to life's meaningfulness. For Qohelet death *is* a major problem. It results in humans and their achievements being forgotten (2:16); it means that we have no control over what is done with our labors by those who follow us (2:18–19); humans share the same fate of death with animals (3:19–20); we have no idea what, if anything, follows death (3:21); death is the common fate of both righteous and wicked (9:1–3).

Here again we see how, to use Nagel's categories, Qohelet insists on holding an inward perspective together with an external or cosmic one. Human life is transient and one thing we all know is that we will die. Qohelet correctly sees that death places a major question mark against any affirmation of the meaningfulness of life.

Seachris develops his thought in this area in relation to narrative endings.[53] Along with Ricoeur, Girard, and others Seachris argues that the ending is vital to a meaningful narrative since it brings closure. Girard speaks evocatively of the endings of narratives as the "temple of truth."[54] We have seen above how Qohelet in his reflection on time recognizes the need for a sense of origins and telos if human life is to have meaning. In Eccl 3: 20–21 Qohelet despairs of knowing what happens at death:

---

[52] At the same time we are witnessing what has been described as the theological turn in phenomenology in the works of Jean-Luc Marion, Michel Henry, Jean-Yves Lacoste, and Jean-Louis Chrétien, works which take religion (Christianity) as constitutive of meaning. The work of these authors is by far the most creative work being done in continental philosophy at present.

[53] Joshua W. Seachris, "Death, Futility, and the Proleptic Power of Narrative Ending," in *Exploring the Meaning of Life*, ed. Seachris, 461–480.

[54] René Girard, *Deceit, Desire, and the Novel: Self and Other in Literary Structure*. Translated by Y. Freccero. (Baltimore: Johns Hopkins University Press, 1965), 307.

> "All go to the same place. All came from dust and will return to dust. Who knows whether the spirit of humankind ascends upward and spirit of animals ascends downward to the earth?"

However this is not Qohelet's last word on the subject. In 12:7 he asserts that,

> "and the dust returns
> to the earth as it was,
> and the spirit returns
> to God, who gave it."

Here there is a far more positive view of death with the human spirit returning to its giver. In the OT the perspective on what follows death is limited compared to the NT. Jesus's resurrection is the formative event demonstrating that death has been conquered once and for all, and it is the sign that at the culmination of history a new heaven and a new earth will be ushered in, a world without sin and death; one characterized by *shalom*.

This returns us to the question of what difference belief in God makes to the question of life's meaning. "Eternal life" does involve immortality but it refers to far more than that. Against a Jewish background "eternal life" means the life of the age to come, life as God intended it to be. This involves many things: a setting of wrongs right; an erasure of sin and evil from the creation; an entry into embodied life in all its fullness and richness that God intended for it; profound relationship with God; etc. From this perspective the "ending" of the Christian metanarrative does indeed frame the question of the meaning of life, not least in relation to evil and injustice.

9. Qohelet, evil, and the meaning of life

The problem of evil is seen as one of the great defeaters against belief in a good, sovereign God. What is not always noticed is that evil remains a problem—in my view a bigger one—once God is removed from the picture. This returns us once again to Nagel's internalist vs. externalist viewpoint. Qohelet works largely from an *internalist* viewpoint and it confronts him again and again with the problem of evil: the evil of oppression (4:1–3), the evil of injustice (3:16); the failure to hold wickedness to account (8:10); unhealthy rivalry in the workplace (4:4); etc. Qohelet is surely right in this respect that it is not just the tension between an internalist and an externalist viewpoint that creates a discrepancy; there is more than enough pain and horror in the world to raise the most acute questions about the meaning of life apart from an externalist viewpoint. Indeed, at points in his journey

Qohelet would have agreed with Benatar that coming into existence is always a harm (cf. Eccl 4:2–3).[55]

Leonardo Boff, the Brazilian theologian, evokes the experience of far too many in our world when he writes, "There is a suffering humanity whose way of the cross has as many stations as that of the Lord when he suffered among us in Palestine."[56] It is surely not necessary to document the immense variety of suffering and injustice that is prevalent in our world today. One example will suffice. In 4:4 Qohelet notes, "Then I observed all the labor and the skill involved in work—it results from one person's jealousy of his neighbor. This too is enigmatic and a striving after wind."

René Girard has developed an insightful and influential theory of mimetic desire as central to human development and interpersonal relations. Girard alerts us to how mimetic desire can morph into mimetic rivalry which can, if uncontained, eventually explode in violence. Girard is more positive than I am about our globalized consumer culture, which, in my view, is a recipe for a conflagration of mimetic rivalry. Indeed, even Girard speaks of our day as awash in a hurricane of desire in a recent interview.[57]

There are certainly no signs that the twenty-first century will be peaceful. We witnessed our first genocide in Sudan and the specter of violence in the West is an ever-present reality, courtesy of Islamic terrorism. At the same time there is a town in Pakistan that is the drone capital of the world, having experienced more drone attacks than anywhere else!

Many commentators now see the West as in crisis and it is not difficult to see how Qohelet's struggle with evil, injustice, oppression, and rivalry is as—or more—real today as it was in his own context. Philosophically this brings us onto the terrain of *theodicy* with the variety of views proposed in order to account philosophically for evil. Personally I find the sort of theodicy expounded in Seachris's narrative-endings approach most convincing.[58] Qohelet, of course, does not have anything like a developed eschatology. He does embrace a doctrine of judgment (11:9) and as we noted above, he does move to the view that at death the spirit returns to God who gave it (12:7). 12:1–8 is read by scholars in a variety of ways. For example, some read it as an allegory of old age. I have argued that Qohelet here appropriates cosmic prophetic language for the coming judgment. Whether this is true or not, it is the case that Qohelet lacks a developed eschatology as does most of the OT.

---

[55] David Benatar, "Why Coming into Existence is Always a Harm," in *Exploring the Meaning of Life*, ed. Seachris, 245–261.

[56] Leonardo Boff, *Passion of Christ, Passion of the Word*, 2nd ed. (Maryknoll, NY: Orbis, 2001), ix.

[57] Referred to by Bob Goudzwaard, http://www.cpj.ca/part-iii-%E2%80%93-rapidly-changing-world-christian-response.

[58] Seachris, "Death, Futility, and the Proleptic Power of Narrative Ending."

What is remarkable, about Proverbs and OT wisdom, is that without a sure sense of the future, the OT wisdom authors keep open a hopeful attitude toward the future. Thus, in relation to Seachris's narrative-ending approach it is interesting that such authors could find a way toward hope and meaningful life apart from a clear eschatology. Clearly, however, the rich eschatology of the NT looking toward a new heavens and a new earth strengthens this hope immeasurably.

10. Conclusion

As I have read the emerging literature in analytic philosophy on the meaning of life I have been struck time and again how closely it connects with Ecclesiastes and Old Testament wisdom. Ecclesiastes remains a fertile source from which to engage this vital issue. It depicts the struggle both existentially and intellectually that this question can generate, as well as pointing a way toward resolution. Resolution of this question is found in the deeper waters where logic and rationality can no longer wade but in which faith can swim. The limits of logic and thus analytic philosophy are particularly clear in Job, where resolution comes not through a clear answer as to why he suffered but through a deep encounter with God as creator (Job 38–42).

Ecclesiastes, as we have noted, has more of a philosophical character than Proverbs or Job.[59] But even with Qohelet, the return to remembering God as creator is, at least, more than logical. It implies the need for an external perspective to provide a context within which to live, even if not fully to understand, one's internal wrestling with this issue. Qohelet would resonate with Tolstoy's comment that, "By appealing only to reason I could not get myself out of the quagmire of finitude, and thus life was meaningless. But by faith I could find an answer to life's meaning."[60]

The epilogue of Ecclesiastes is thought by most scholars to be an addition to the book, an attempt to situate Qohelet within more orthodox belief. In my view, however, it forms a fitting conclusion. In 12:8 the narrator writes, "The end of the matter, all has been heard. Fear God and keep his commandments, for this is the whole duty of humankind." This forms a contrast, for example, with Baggini:

> Yet with a subject like the meaning of life, how can one ever feel that one has said enough or covered everything? Like the tourists who spend a weekend in Rome and say they've "done" the eternal city, there would be

---

[59] In the Middle Ages, however, Jewish philosophers paid close attention to Job.
[60] Leo Tolstoy, "A Confession," in *Exploring the Meaning of Life*, ed. Seachris, 380–387, 385.

something suspect about writing this book and concluding I had "done" the meaning of life.

The obvious truth at the source of this unease is that there is no last word on this subject.[61]

Baggini is right in that living the meaning of life is an ongoing project but his assertion that "there is no last word on this subject" forms a stark contrast with Eccl 12:8. The reason for the difference lies in the source of the answer to the question of the meaning of life. For Baggini, as with so many moderns, we must find it in ourselves. For the narrator of Ecclesiastes its source is God, and while God is inherently mysterious the narrator works with the view that God has spoken and revealed himself and revealed how to live according to the grain of creation. "Obedience" and "commandments" hardly sound to a modern ear like an adequate ending to a quest for the meaning of life but I suspect that this is largely because of our antipathy toward anything that challenges our autonomy. Patrick Miller gets at the richness of Torah and obedience in his description of the Ten Commandments as the ethos of the good neighborhood.[62] It is in such a neighborhood that this question is most fully answered, at least from the perspective of Ecclesiastes.

---

[61] Baggini, *What's It All About?*, Kindle Locations 1908–1910.
[62] Patrick Miller, *The Way of the Lord* (Grand Rapids, MI: Eerdmans, 2004, 2007), 51–67.

"Meaningless, Meaningless, Says Qohelet": Finding the Meaning of Life in the Book of Ecclesiastes

Tremper Longman III

1. Introduction

An interest in the question of the meaning of life seems like a modern luxury or even an elitist preoccupation. For much of early human history and for millions, even billions of people today, survival precludes interest in the question of the meaning of life.

But, in reality, the question of the meaning of life is not restricted to modern upper classes. The drive to survive suggests that life has value and meaning, and much ancient literature shows that such issues resonated with people in the past as well as in the present. The focus of this essay is on the biblical book of Ecclesiastes, dated with a high level of confidence to the postexilic period (after 539 BC), and perhaps even more precisely to the Greek period (post 333 BC).[1] The work is Jewish in origin and appears to come from a time period where the issue of the meaning of life was being questioned in that culture. That the meaning of life is a significant interest of the book is signaled by how often the Hebrew term *hebel*, traditionally and in my opinion rightly translated as "meaningless," occurs, over forty times.[2]

My intention in this chapter is to explore the book of Ecclesiastes to examine what it tells readers about the meaning of life. What makes life meaningful in the sense that we might find it worth living? Life is worth living if

---

[1] T. Longman III, "Determining the Historical Context of Ecclesiastes," in *The Words of the Wise are Like Goads: Engaging Qohelet in the 21st Century*, ed. M. J. Boda, et al. (Winona Lake, IN: Eisenbrauns, 2013).

[2] Arguments have relatively recently been marshaled to translate *hebel* as "transient," for which see D. C. Fredericks, *Coping with Transience: Ecclesiastes on the Brevity of Life* (Sheffield: JSOT Press, 1993). For a defense of the meaning "meaningless," see T. Longman III, *Ecclesiastes* (NICOT; Grand Rapids: Eerdmans, 1998), 61–5.

things fit together in the right way that leads to a sense of satisfaction and even human flourishing.

What is the relationship between the meaning (significance) of life and having a purpose (a reason or a goal) in life? Certainly if someone feels that life has purpose, it is likely that they will find life meaningful.[3] But can life be meaningful without a purpose in life? The relationship between meaning and purpose is contested, but our interest at the moment is with the perspective provided by the book of Ecclesiastes.

Admittedly, people will have different standards for what makes life worth living, but our interest here is to gain an understanding of the perspective of the author of the book of Ecclesiastes, who of course is trying to convince his readers that his perspective rings true and should be adopted and emulated by them. In this chapter, we will speak of Qohelet being unable to achieve his goal of finding the ultimate meaning of life, and his failure severely troubles him. He is not denying that there may be proximate meaning in life (wisdom is better than folly, 2:12–18), but he for one does not find that ultimately satisfying.

2. Qohelet and the frame narrator

To understand the book of Ecclesiastes it is vital to recognize that there are two voices in the book and not just one. The distinction between the two speakers is clear, though admittedly subtle. The main voice whom the author calls Qohelet (see below) speaks in the first person ("I Qohelet") beginning in 1:12 and ending in 12:7. The second speaker can be differentiated from Qohelet in that he speaks about Qohelet ("Qohelet, he ..."). The words of the second speaker are found at the beginning (1:1–11) and end (12:8–14) of the book.[4] Thus, his words frame Qohelet's, and this speaker is commonly referred to as the frame narrator,[5] though we will also call him the second wisdom teacher. This second wisdom teacher is talking to his son (see 12:12;

---

[3] The logotherapy developed by Victor Frankl would lend support to this statement (*Man's Search for the Meaning of Life* (Boston: Beacon Press, 2006 [orig. 1959]). He began to develop his distinctive approach to therapy in response to his observations in the concentration camps of World War II where people who had a sense of purpose in life survived longer under the horrifying rigors of the camp than those who "had nothing to live for."

[4] In 7:27, the frame narrator makes his presence known briefly ("Observe, this I have found:" *Qohelet said*, "one thing to another to find the sum of things..."), thus reminding the reader that there is a second party who narrates Qohelet's words. All translations from Ecclesiastes are from Longman, *Ecclesiastes*.

[5] To my knowledge, the one to first refer to the second voice as the "frame narrator" is M. V. Fox, "Frame-Narrative and Composition in the Book of Qohelet," *HUCA* 48 (1977): 83–106.

"Furthermore, of these, my son, be warned!"). Thus the dynamic of the book is a father who speaks to his son about Qohelet and the ideas he expresses in 1:12–12:7.

Accordingly, two questions are relevant for the interpretation of the book. First, what is the message of Qohelet, and, second, what is the message of the frame narrator? Since the second wise man's words frame Qohelet's the message of the book of Ecclesiastes flows from his words as they interact with Qohelet's ideas.[6]

2.1 Qohelet's message

Ecclesiastes 1:12 ("I, Qohelet, have been king over Israel in Jerusalem") marks the beginning of Qohelet's speech, having the form of a typically opening line of an ancient (fictional) autobiography.[7] His speech extends to 12:7. In 12:8 there is a shift to third-person speech about Qohelet.

The second wise man summarizes the final conclusion of Qohelet for his son in 12:8: "'Completely meaningless,' Qohelet said, 'Everything is meaningless.'" Qohelet has looked for meaning "under the sun" and has come up empty. He has concluded that life is difficult and the end for everyone is death. He has no belief in an afterlife. According to Qohelet, there are three factors that led to his conclusion that life has no meaning.

2.1.1 Death

The first factor is death. Death renders life meaningless. He concludes his speech with a reflection on death (12:1–7). In the first part (vv. 1–5), he uses a complex metaphor to describe the process of growing old. He likens the human body to a house and its four groups of inhabitants. The house and those who live in it slowly languish just like the body as it ages. In his scenario, a nice sunny day (representing one's youth) gives way to a dark, dreary time (representing old age; v. 2). In the house are four groups, two male and two female (v. 3), and each struggle: "the house guards tremble and the

---

[6] A second example of a biblical book that has multiple voices but only one authoritative voice is the book of Job, where we here from Job, the three friends, Elihu, and Yahweh, the latter of which, of course, is the authoritative voice (see T. Longman III, *Job* (BCOTWP; Grand Rapids: Baker, 2012)).
[7] T. Longman III, *Fictional Akkadian Autobiography* (Winona Lake, IN: Eisenbrauns, 1993), 39–48; A. Poebel, *Das appositionell bestimmte Pronomen der 1. Per. Sing. In den westsemitischen Inschriften und im Alten Testament*. AS 3 (Chicago: Oriental Institute, 1931).

landowners bend, and the women grinders cease because they are few, and those women who look through the window grow dim" (v. 3).

We might also see here a kind of allegory of the body, particularly noticeable with the women inhabitants.[8] The picture of grinders (women who grind the grain) ceasing because they are few surely meant to evoke a connection with physical decline, which in an ancient culture with no significant dental care and a coarse grain diet would lead to the loss of teeth. The women looking through the window growing dim suggests the loss of eyesight as one grows older. Though we cannot be as dogmatically precise, the trembling and bending of the male residents remind us of the bending of the back and the trembling of the hands that many older people experience. The other details of the description found in verses 4–5 confirm this approach to the passage (almond tree blossoming=the whitening of hair; the uselessness of caper berry [an aphrodisiac]=lessening sexual desire, etc.).

12:6–7 presents a second set of metaphors that communicate that death renders life meaningless. Precious items representing life (silver thread, golden bowl, jar, wheel) are destroyed and their usefulness comes to an end. Finally, in 12:7 ("and the dust returns to the earth as it was, and the spirit returns to God who gave it"), Qohelet describes death as the reversal of life as described in the primeval creation text (Gen. 2:7). Death rends the components of life and thus destroys it. Death is the end of the story for Qohelet.

Thus, in the light of death nothing in life has meaning. Qohelet, for instance, can find a relative value of wisdom over folly. After all, "the wise have eyes in their head, while fools walk around in darkness" (2:14a). However, "the same fate awaits them both" (2:14b). Since the wise will die just like fools, even wisdom is "meaningless." But why? Why does death render wisdom meaningless? According to Qohelet, the wise, like the fool, is "soon ... forgotten" (2:16). Qohelet looks to wisdom in order to provide a good reputation for himself, but this desire is impossible to achieve, at least a lasting reputation, due to death.

A little later Qohelet reflects how death renders work meaningless (2:18–23). Here work implies the positive consequences of work, most especially the "reward" that results from work well done. If one dies, they cannot enjoy the reward, but have to leave it "to an individual who did not work for it" (2:21). Thus, death thwarts the desires and goals that he has in his work, and the fact that someone else might enjoy the fruits of his difficult labor when he dies is particularly galling.

---

[8] J. F. A. Sawyer, "The Ruined House in Ecclesiastes 12: A Reconstruction of the Original Parable," *JBL* 94 (1974): 95–101.

2.1.2 Injustice

The second reason why life is meaningless is because there is no justice in this life. If one is not rewarded for good behavior in the afterlife, then for the world to work correctly at the very least the wise person should be blessed in this life. However, Qohelet's observations lead to a negative conclusion:

> But I have observed in my meaningless life: There is a righteous person perishing in his righteousness, and there is a wicked person living long in his evil. (7:15)

Since this is true, there is no reason to be wise or righteous:

> Do not be too righteous and do not be overly wise. Why ruin yourself? Do not be too wicked and do not be a fool. Why die when it is not your time? (7:16–17)

2.1.3 The right time

At the heart of biblical wisdom is timing. To be wise is to know the right time to say or do the right thing. The wise person feels and expresses the appropriate emotion at the right level that fits the occasion. In order to be a sage, a person needs to know how to discern the right time. The book of Proverbs has advice that often is at odds with each other, the most well-known example being 26:4–5:

> Don't answer fools according to their stupidity;
>   otherwise, you will become like yourself.
> Answer fools according to their stupidity;
>   otherwise, they will become wise in their own eyes.[9]

One must be able to read the situation and the people involved in order to know when one or the other of these proverbs is relevant.

In perhaps the best known passage in the book, Qohelet makes it clear that he knows that God has constructed the world so that:

> For everything there is a season,
>   and a time for every activity under heaven.

---

[9] Translations of Proverbs, comes from T. Longman III, *Proverbs* (BCOTWP; Grand Rapids: Baker, 2006).

> A time to be born and a time to die;
>> a time to plant and a time to uproot what has been planted.
> A time to kill and a time to heal;
>> a time to tear down and a time to build.
> A time to cry and a time to laugh;
>> a time of mourning and a time of dancing.
> A time to cast stones and a time to gather stones;
>> a time to embrace and a time to refrain from embracing.
> A time to seek and a time to give up as lost;
>> a time to keep and a time to thrown away.
> A time to tear and a time to sew;
>> a time to be silent and a time to speak.
> A time to love and a time to hate;
>> a time of war and a time of peace. (3:1–8)
>
> . . .

Indeed, "He (God) makes everything appropriate in its time. He also places eternity in their hearts" (3:11a).

When read out of its context, these words can appear to be comforting, but they were anything but comforting for Qohelet. Notice how he reacts to the fact that God has a proper time for everything. He begins by rhetorically asking, "What profit do people have from their toils?" (3:9), a question that presumes a negative answer. He then goes on to say "I observed the task that God has given to the human race to keep them occupied. He makes everything appropriate in its time. He also places eternity in their hearts. But still, no one can discover what God is doing from beginning to end" (3:10–11). Accordingly, Qohelet is not comforted, but rather frustrated by God creating the world so that everything has its appropriate time since God does not allow humans to discern the proper time. Thus, Qohelet denies that the world has meaning and he advocates a *carpe diem* approach to life.

2.1.4 Carpe diem ("seize the day")

In the previous section, we noted that Qohelet failed in his search for the meaning of life. He describes his attempt to find meaning in pleasure (2:1–11), wisdom or folly (2:12–17), work (2:18–23; 4:4–6), wealth (4:7–8; 5:10–6:9), and political power (4:13–16). Death, injustice, and the inability to discern the right time all conspire to rob life of purpose.

Qohelet thus promotes a *carpe diem* approach to life. Since life has no ultimate meaning, people should try to enjoy whatever pleasure they can in this life. Six times in the book Qohelet tells people to enjoy life the best they can:

> There is nothing better for people than to eat and drink and enjoy their toil. This too, I see, is from the hand of God. For who will eat and who will worry apart from him? For he gives wisdom, knowledge, and pleasure to the one who pleases him, but he gives to the one who is offensive the task of gathering wealth to be given to the one who pleases God. This too is meaningless and chasing the wind. (2:24–26)
>
> I know there is nothing better for them than to be happy and enjoy themselves during their lives. And everyone who eats, drinks, and enjoys their toil—that is a gift of God. I know that everything God does lasts forever. Nothing can be added to it or taken from it. God has acted, so that they might fear him. Whatever is, already has been. What will be has already been. God makes the same things happen over and over again. (3:11–15)
>
> So I observed that there is nothing better for people than for people to rejoice in their work, for that is their reward. For who can bring them to see what will happen after them? (3:22)
>
> Indeed, this is what I have observed to be good: that it is appropriate to eat, to drink, and to enjoy all the toil that one does under the sun the few days God has given to that person, for that is his reward. Furthermore, everyone to whom God gives wealth and possessions and allows them to eat of it and to accept their reward and to take pleasure in their toil—this is God's gift. Indeed, they do not remember much about the days of their lives for God keeps them so busy with the pleasure of their heart. (5:18–20)
>
> Then I commended pleasure, for there is nothing better for people under the sun except to eat and drink and to have pleasure. It will accompany them in their toil during the days of their life that God gives them under the sun. (8:15)
>
> Go, eat your food with pleasure, and drink your wine with a merry heart, for God has already approved your deeds. Let your clothes be white at all times, and do not spare oil on your head. Enjoy life with the wife whom you love all the days of your meaningless life, that is, all the meaningless days he has given you under the sun, for it is your reward in life and for all the toil that you do under the sun. All that your and finds to do, do with your power, for there is no action or thought or knowledge or wisdom in the grave where you are going. (9:7–10)

These six passages repeat the same basic message to which Qohelet returns again and again in the light of the absence of meaning in life. Since there is no greater purpose, the best that humans can hope for is enjoyment. He believes that this type of enjoyment or happiness comes from a good meal and drink, and in the final *carpe diem* he throws in the companionship provided by a wife. In addition, though one cannot find the meaning of life in work (or toil) finding pleasure in one's work according to the second passage also contributes to the enjoyment of life.

But what is the advantage of *carpe diem* in the light of the meaninglessness of life? We find the answer in the third passage listed above. After describing *carpe diem*, Qohelet concludes that such people (those who *carpe diem*) "do not remember much about the days of their life for God keeps them so busy with the pleasure of their heart" (5:20). In other words, finding solace in the little pleasures of life is a distraction from the harsh reality that life is difficult and then you die.

Today thoughtful people often ridicule people who avoid the big questions of life by watching TV or going to cocktail parties and engaging in "small talk." Qohelet, however, says that if there is no meaning in life, such distractions are beneficial. Indeed, he points out that those who are able to be distracted in this way have received a gift from God. After all, he says, one has to have the wherewithal to *carpe diem* and the disposition as well. In the passage that follows that quoted above, Qohelet goes on to bemoan those to whom "God gives wealth, possessions, and honor; they lack nothing that they desire. But God does not allow them to eat of it, but a stranger will eat of it. This is meaningless, and it is sickening evil" (6:2). Though he does not say it explicitly, one gets the distinct impression that Qohelet himself did not have the disposition to *carpe diem*. He looked at the world too realistically to allow himself the small luxury of diversion from a meaningless world.

2.2 Who is Qohelet?

Before moving on to consider the thought of the frame narrator, we should ask concerning the identity of Qohelet. Who is this person who has sought meaning/purpose but come up empty in the light of death, injustice, and the inability to discern the proper time? Who is this sage who has concluded that the best life offers are the distractions of "seizing the day?"

Traditionally, Qohelet was thought to be Solomon, the third and final king of a united Israel (965–931 BC).[10] Solomon never appears by name in the book, but several factors point toward an association with that well-known

---

[10] There are still a few, but very few, scholars who would suggest that Solomon was the author of the book. For one example, see W. C. Kaiser, Jr. *Ecclesiastes: Total Life* (Chicago: Moody, 1979).

monarch. The superscription ("The words of Qohelet, son of David, king in Jerusalem") could point to any of his descendants of his long-lived dynasty of twenty kings [only interrupted by Queen Athaliah] from his day until 586 BC, but it fits most naturally his immediate descendant, Solomon.[11] However, the distinctive connection with Solomon is made by the description of Qohelet as a wise man (1:13–18; 12:10, and throughout). In the historical books, Solomon is the only king whose wisdom is underlined (1 Kings 3–4).

However, while there are reasons to associate Qohelet and Solomon, there are also reasons not to identify Qohelet as Solomon or as a king. Most pointedly, there are a number of passages in Qohelet's speech that distance himself not only from Solomon, but also the kingship (1:12; 1:16a; 4:1–3; 5:8–9; 10:20).[12]

Qohelet associates himself with Solomon but does not identify himself as Solomon. We might also simply point out that if Qohelet actually was Solomon, then why not simply use the name Solomon rather than the nickname Qohelet? The nickname is yet another way of associating rather than identifying with Solomon.

The name Qohelet is derived from the Hebrew verb *qahal*, "to assemble," and is in the form of a feminine singular active participle (the form typical of a professional designation). The Hebrew thus means "the one who assembles a group." This verb connects with Solomon because it is a verb that is repeated in reference to Solomon as he dedicates the newly built temple (1 Kings 8:1, 2, 14, 22, 55). Thus again Qohelet is subtly associated with Solomon but not identified with him.

But why?

The association of Qohelet with Solomon serves an important role in making the point of the book. In the book of Ecclesiastes, Solomon sought, but failed to find meaning in wealth, wisdom, pleasure, and work. Solomon was a well-known past figure who had more wealth, more wisdom, and more pleasure than any other person. Thus, the message is that if Solomon could not find meaning in these things and indeed ended up a broken man who broke the kingdom, who are the readers of this book to say if only they had more money, more pleasure, more wisdom, then they would find meaning.

In the final analysis, who then is Qohelet?

---

[11] Contra J. Barbour [*The Story of Israel in the Book of Qohelet: Ecclesiastes as Cultural Memory* (Oxford: Oxford University Press, 2012)] who argues that Qohelet is a pastiche of all of Judah's kings. See T. Longman III, "Qoheleth as Solomon: 'For What Can Anyone Who Comes After the King Do?' (Ecclesiastes 2:12)," in *Reading Ecclesiastes Intertextually*, ed. K. Dell and W. Kynes (London: Bloomsbury, 2014), 42–56.

[12] For a full explanation, see comments in Longman, *Ecclesiastes*.

Qohelet is a wise man who searches for the meaning of life. In his search he takes the persona of Solomon and does a thought experiment as to whether one can find meaning "under the sun" (for the significance of which, see below). Solomon had more wealth, money, and pleasure than anyone else in ancient Israelite society and he ended life by turning away from God and destroying the kingdom. Thus, no one can live with the illusion of "if I only had more ..., then I would find meaning."

Of course, it is not even necessary that Qohelet himself is an actual person. The author of the book of Ecclesiastes (likely identified with the frame narrator) may be the one conducting the thought experiment and constructed the figure of Qohelet in order to carry out his purpose.

This way of thinking about Qohelet is consistent with the widely held view, held by this author,[13] that the book of Ecclesiastes was written during the postexilic period (Persian or maybe even the Greek period) in order to address questions contemporary to Jewish religion and society at that time.

2.3 The frame narrator's message

Qohelet, thus, comes to the conclusion that life has no ultimate meaning; therefore, *carpe diem*, grab whatever gusto one can out of life.

While, granted, Qohelet's thought encompasses the largest part of the book of Ecclesiastes, it is not the only voice that we hear. Indeed, it is not the voice that determines the message of the book. As mentioned above, a second wise man speaks to his son about Qohelet and his voice helps the son (with whom we the reader identify) frame the message of Qohelet in an appropriate manner.

While this second wise man's words open the book and introduce Qohelet's autobiographical reflections (1:1–11), it is the epilogue that closes the book that is most germane to our concerns. We will divide our discussion of the epilogue into two parts, the first concerns his evaluation of Qohelet:

> "Completely meaningless," Qohelet said. "Everything is meaningless." Furthermore, Qohelet was a wise man. He also taught the people knowledge. He heard, investigated, and put in good order many proverbs. Qohelet sought to find words of delight and he wrote honest words of truth. The words of the wise are like goads, and like firmly implanted nails are the masters of collections. They are given by a shepherd. Furthermore, of these, my son, be warned! There is no end to the making of many books, and much study wearies the body. (12:8–12)

---

[13] Longman, "Determining the Historical Context of Ecclesiastes."

The frame narrator thus begins by reiterating what he takes to be the final conclusion of Qohelet's thinking. Life has no ultimate meaning or purpose. Even so, he does not dismiss him or denigrate him. As a matter of fact, he goes on to compliment Qohelet.

He calls him a "wise man." However, we should not read too much into this attribution. In the book of Proverbs to call someone wise is the highest praise, but outside of that book a wise man or a sage is something of a professional designation. There are good sages and bad sages (see 2 Sam. 13:3). The effect would be the same as saying Qohelet was a professor, perhaps a philosophy professor.

He goes on to describe Qohelet as someone who "heard, investigated, and put in good order many proverbs." This too is a compliment, but a rather tepid one. In essence, he is saying that Qohelet was a good technician.

Finally by way of evaluation, he concludes with perhaps the most positive statement of all. Qohelet "sought to find words of delight and he wrote honest words of truth." One blinks at the statement that Qohelet's words might be ones that elicit delight ("life is difficult and then you die"), but perhaps the meaning is that his words are intellectually stimulating or perhaps they are well stated. Or one might even say that he "sought to find" words of delight, but failed.

While it is interesting to reflect on the first part of the statement, the more salient statement for our interests is the second part that Qohelet "wrote honest words of truth." Here, the frame narrator tells his son that he has exposed him to Qohelet's thinking because his words are true. When we turn to the last two verses of the epilogue (12:13-14), it will be clear that the second wise man has reached a different conclusion than Qohelet, so in what sense is it true?

At this point, we should remember that Qohelet has engaged in what we might call "under the sun" thinking. The phrase "under the sun" (1:14; 2:17, 18, 19, etc.) and its correlate "under heaven" (1:13; 2:3, etc.) occur throughout Qohelet's section of the book. He has, it is clear, sought to find the meaning of life "under the sun," which means roughly apart from God, or perhaps even apart from revelation. He has looked under the sun and found life meaningless.

Thus, it is more than probable that the second wise man is warning his son about "under the sun" thinking. In essence, he is saying, "My son, Qohelet is absolutely correct. Life under the sun is meaningless. One can only conclude that life is difficult and then one dies, so one must seize whatever joy one can manage in this present life."

But this is not the conclusion of the frame narrator's comments to his son. He goes on to say:

> The end of the matter. All has been heard. Fear God and keep his commandments, for this is the whole duty of humanity. For God will

bring every deed into judgment, including every hidden thing, whether good or evil. (12:13–14)

The second wise man turns his son's (and the reader's) attention away from Qohelet by announcing that he is finished speaking about him. He then turns to a positive statement about what is really important to remember, and there are three important components to his message: (1) fear God, (2) obey his commands, and (3) live in the light of the future judgment.

The admonition to "fear God" and its variant to "fear the Lord" is perhaps the central message of wisdom literature (see Prov. 1:7, 29; 2:5; 3:7; 8:13; 9:10, etc.; Job 1:1 and the picture of Job demonstrating fear of God at the end of the book [42:1–6]).[14] If one fears God, then they recognize that they are not the center of the universe. One who fears God obeys God. They are humble and not "wise in their own eyes." The father tells his son that it is not only important to fear God, but also to obey him by keeping God's commandments and he ends by reminding his son of the future judgment, a thought that will increase his fear of God and his willingness to keep his commandments.

Thus, the father tells his son to establish a right relationship with God ("fear") and maintain that relationship through obedience, and live in the light of the future judgment. One might call this instruction an "above the sun" perspective to contrast it with Qohelet's "under the sun" view of life.

But this threefold path to an "above the sun" life may well have a deeper resonance to its original audience than appears to modern readers at least at first sight. As we suggested above, the book was almost certainly written to a postexilic audience and likely a late postexilic audience. The book of Ecclesiastes may well have been composed as late as the Greek period (after Alexander's defeat of Persia in c. 330 BC).

By this time, the three-part Hebrew canon has already taken shape. Each part of the father's admonition to the son then would point him toward one section of the Tanak. When the son heard, "fear God" that would direct his attention toward the Writings (Ketubim) where fearing God was a major theme. The instruction to obey the commandments would certainly make the son think of the Torah, and finally, when the father urged the son to live in the light of the future judgment, the Prophets (Nebi'im) would come to mind. Thus, the final two verses, though brief, is likely a way of telling the

---

[14] It is true that Qohelet also speaks about "fear of God," but the context indicates something more akin to horror than to the type of submission that leads to obedience advocated by wisdom (see T. Longman III, "The 'Fear of God' in the Book of Ecclesiastes," *Bulletin of Biblical Research* 25 (2015): 13–22).

son (and the later readers of the book) to adopt an "above the sun" view of life shaped by the Law, Prophets, and Writings.

3. Busting idols: Ecclesiastes and the meaning of life

In the final analysis, what does the book of Ecclesiastes say about the meaning of life? Qohelet represents the person who tries to find the meaning or purpose of life apart from a robust relationship with God. He searches for meaning "under the sun" and comes up empty. Because of death, injustice in this life, and the inability to discern the proper time, there is no meaning in pleasure, wealth, work, relationships, status, or wisdom. The association between Qohelet and Solomon serves the purpose of informing the reader that not even the one who "had it all" could find meaning "under the sun." For this reason, the second wise man urges his son to adopt what we have called an "above the sun" perspective and put God first.

In essence, the book of Ecclesiastes is what we might call an idol buster. One creates an idol when one takes a created thing or person and makes it or her or him the most important thing in their life. If one tries to find the purpose of life in any created thing or person, it or they will let them down. Thus, the book reminds the reader that only God can bring true meaning and purpose to life.

3.1 *Contemptus mundi?*

Thus, the book of Ecclesiastes read as a whole, taking Qohelet's thought in the context of the second wise man's evaluation, urges the reader to find meaning in a proper relationship with God. Qohelet's sad failure to find meaning in wisdom, pleasure, wealth, or any other thing or person is an object lesson to readers not to follow his example.

But does that mean that anything and everyone other than God has no worth? That was the conclusion of Jerome (c. AD 347–420) whose commentary dominated thinking about the book of Ecclesiastes for the next thousand years. He suggested that the book of Ecclesiastes not only urged finding the meaning of life in a relationship with God, but also the disparagement of the world. His interpretation of the book has been called a *contemptus mundi* reading that lifted up the ascetic lifestyle of the monastic movement as the pinnacle of the spiritual life. We can see this, for instance, in a letter written to his disciple Paula, the mother of Blesilla, where he recommends that the daughter read Ecclesiastes to "gain the habit of despising the world and its vanities."[15]

Though Jerome's influence is not as pervasive as it was in the past, his reading of Ecclesiastes still finds some traction among a few lay interpreters. However, the book's point is simply that the ultimate meaning of life cannot be discovered in anything other than God. Ever since Luther and the Reformation, with its more robust appreciation of God's creation of the world, it has been suggested that, though not offering the meaning of life, wisdom, wealth, and so forth can indeed find a proper place in a person's life.[16]

3.2 Ecclesiastes from a New Testament perspective

The book of Ecclesiastes provides insight into the question of the meaning of life in and of itself. If one tries to find the meaning of life apart from making God one's Ultimate Concern, then life will have no meaning. If one's ultimate purpose in life is wealth, wisdom, or any other thing or person, life will be disappointing at best.

The Christian reader of the book, however, must finally read the book in the light of the fuller witness of the New Testament. Jesus himself informed his followers that the Old Testament (which he called "the Scriptures," "Moses and the Prophets," or "the Law of Moses, the Prophets and the Psalms") all anticipated his coming. Thus, the Christian reader of the Old Testament should read the Old Testament in the light of the revelation of the New Testament. When we so read the book of Ecclesiastes, what further insight is provided concerning its message?

This question brings us to Paul's remarkable and theologically rich comment in Rom. 8:18–25. He begins:

> I consider that our present sufferings are not worth comparing with the glory that will be revealed in us. For the creation waits in eager expectation for the children of God to be revealed. For creation was subjected to *frustration*, not by its own choice, but by the will of the one who subjected it . . .

Paul here speaks of the creation being subjected to frustration. The significance of his statement for our study of meaning in Ecclesiastes is that the

---

[15] Quoted in M. H. Pope, *Song of Songs* (AB 7C; Garden City, NY: Doubleday, 1977), 119.

[16] For an account of the history of interpretation, including the place of Luther's thought, see T. Longman III, "Ecclesiastes: History of Interpretation," ed. T. Longman III and P. Enns. *Dictionary of the Old Testament: Wisdom, Poetry and Writings* (Downers Grove, IL: InterVarsity Press, 2009), 140–49.

Greek word here translated frustration (*mataiotes*) is the same word used by the Greek Old Testament to translate the Hebrew word which we have translated "meaningless" (*hebel*) in the book of Ecclesiastes. Accordingly, Paul recognizes that the world is indeed meaningless. Who subjected it to such a state? None other than God himself. Paul utilizes the divine passive and readers would understand that he here is referencing the story of the Fall (Genesis 3), the story of primal human rebellion that led to the fracture of the relationship between God and humans, and the concomitant introduction of sin and death into the world (Rom. 5:12–21).

Why did Qohelet find only meaninglessness under the sun? Paul would answer that he was trying to find it in the world suffering from the curse of the Fall. No wonder he could not find meaning.

However, Paul does not end on such a dismal note. While Qohelet could not see beyond the fallen world, Paul goes on to proclaim that the one who subjected the creation to frustration (God) did so "in hope that the creation itself will be liberated from its bondage to decay and brought into the freedom and glory of the children of God" (Rom. 8:20b–21).

Unlike Qohelet, Paul looked at a frustrating/meaningless world and found hope because he did not stay mired "under the sun." Since he adopted what we have called an "above the sun" perspective, he knew that God was working toward the redemption of frustration.

Indeed, the message of the Gospel is the story of God's redemption of the world's frustration. Jesus subjected himself to the meaningless world in order to save us from meaninglessness. In another letter, Paul tells his readers that Jesus:

> Who, being in very nature God,
> > did not consider equality with God something to be used to his own advantage.
> rather, he made himself nothing
> > by taking the very nature of a servant,
> > being found in human likeness.
> And being found in appearance as a man,
> > he humbled himself
> > by becoming obedient to death –
> > > even death on a cross. (Phil. 2:6–8)

In a word, Jesus freed us from death, the thing that most rendered life meaningless according to Qohelet, by subjecting himself to it: "Christ redeemed us from the curse of the law by becoming a curse for us, for it is written 'Cursed is everyone who is hung on a pole'" (Gal. 3:13).

Jesus defeated death on the cross and thus death cannot render life meaningless. Jesus subjected himself to meaninglessness as he hung on the cross abandoned by the cheering crowds, his closest followers, and even God the father ("My God, my God, why have you forsaken me?" Matt. 27:46). At this moment he experienced the full effect of the meaningless world like Qohelet could not even imagine it. Though he died, he was raised, and in this great act, he made life meaningful.

4. Conclusion

The book of Ecclesiastes has maintained its relevance since it was first written precisely because the quest for the meaning of life has occupied humanity through the centuries. In Qohelet's conclusion that life has no ultimate meaning we can hear echoes of (post)modern voices that say the same, perhaps in Derrida's assertion that there is no Absolute Signifier or in the existentialism of the 60s. In his assertion of *carpe diem* can we hear a rough approximation to the idea that in the light of no meaning we ought to construct our own?

In any case, the message of the book of Ecclesiastes is that the meaning of life is not to be found in anything "under the sun." Life apart from God in a broken world cannot lead to satisfaction and human flourishing. The biblical narrative describes humanity's origins in a harmonious relationship with God and characterizes its original condition as "blessed" (Genesis 1–2). The meaning of life is discovered only when one has the proper attitude toward the true God and acts in obedience to his will. Again appealing to the opening chapters of Genesis, the loss of meaning and a sense of things fitting together occur as a result of disobedience and fracture in relationship with God (Genesis 3). Death, injustice, and the inability to discover the right time were consequences of human rebellion past and present. According to the biblical narrative, Old and New Testaments, the possibility of the recovery of the meaning of life, a sense of satisfaction that things fit together with the result of human flourishing (a "blessed" condition), comes about through the redemptive activity of God and, for the Christian, the reconciliation that comes through the death and resurrection of Christ.

Notes on Contributors

Craig G. Bartholomew (Ph.D., Bristol University) is H. Evan Runner Chair of Philosophy and Religion & Theology at Redeemer University College in Canada. He is also the principal of The Paideia Centre for Public Theology. He is the author of numerous books, including a recent commentary on Ecclesiastes (Baker Academic, 2009). He has edited over 10 volumes, and his journal articles have appeared in venues such as the *Calvin Theological Journal*, *Tyndale Bulletin*, and the *European Journal of Theology*, among many others.

John Cottingham (D.Phil., Oxford University) is Professor Emeritus of Philosophy at the University of Reading, Professorial Research Fellow at Heythrop College, University of London, and an Honorary Fellow of St. John's College, Oxford. He is an authority on early-modern philosophy, especially Descartes, and has published widely on moral philosophy and the philosophy of religion. His recent titles include *On the Meaning of Life* (Routledge, 2003), *The Spiritual Dimension* (Cambridge University Press, 2005), *Cartesian Reflections* (Oxford University Press, 2008), *Why Believe?* (Continuum, 2009), and *How to Believe* (Bloomsbury, 2015). He was from 1993 to 2012 editor of the international philosophical journal *Ratio*.

Terence Cuneo (Ph.D., Fordham University) is Professor of Philosophy at the University of Vermont. He has research interests in metaethics, early modern philosophy (esp. Thomas Reid), philosophy of religion, epistemology, and political philosophy. He has published numerous articles in top journals including *Philosophy and Phenomenological Research*, *Australasian Journal of Philosophy*, and *Noûs*. He is the author of *The Normative Web: An Argument for Moral Realism* (Oxford University Press, 2007), and *Speech and Morality: On the Metaethical Implications of Speaking* (Oxford University Press, 2014).

Trent Dougherty (Ph.D., University of Rochester) is Associate Professor of Philosophy at Baylor University. His main research interest is the normativity of rationality, especially the relationship between conceptions of epistemic rationality and practical rationality. He is the editor of *Evidentialism and Its Discontents* (Oxford University Press, 2011), author of *The Problem of Animal Pain: A Theodicy for All Creatures Great and Small* (Palgrave Macmillan, 2014), and numerous journal articles in venues such as *Philosophy and Phenomenological Research*, *Synthese*, *Religious Studies*, and *Faith and Philosophy*, among many others.

Stewart Goetz (Ph.D., University of Notre Dame) is the Ross Frederick Wicks Distinguished Professor in Philosophy and Religion at Ursinus College. He has written extensively on the freedom of choice and the nature of the self. His books include *Naturalism* (coauthored with Charles Taliaferro, Eerdmans, 2008), *Freedom, Teleology, and Evil* (Continuum, 2008), *The Soul Hypothesis* (coedited with Mark Baker, Continuum, 2011), *A Brief History of the Soul* (coauthored with Charles Taliaferro, Wiley-Blackwell, 2011), *The Purpose of Life: A Theistic Perspective* (Continuum, 2012), and *The Routledge Companion to Theism* (coedited with Charles Taliaferro and Victoria Harrison, Routledge, 2012). He has also authored numerous papers and reviews in philosophical journals such as *American Philosophical Quarterly*, *Christian Scholar's Review*, *Faith and Philosophy*, *Mind*, *Pacific Philosophical Quarterly*, *Philosophical Studies*, *Philosophy and Phenomenological Research*, *Philosophia Christi*, and *Religious Studies*. He is the senior editor of the Bloomsbury book series Bloomsbury Studies in Philosophy and Religion.

Tremper Longman III (Ph.D., Yale University) is the Robert H. Gundry Professor of Biblical Studies at Westmont College. He has authored or coauthored twenty books and written numerous articles. A number of these works are interdisciplinary. His *Literary Approaches to Biblical Interpretation* (Zondervan, 1987), *Complete Literary Guide to the Bible* (contributor and coeditor along with Leland Ryken, Zondervan, 1993), and numerous articles approach the study of the Bible through literary criticism. His interest in history and historiography is expressed in *A Biblical History of Israel* (coauthored with Iain Provan and Phil Long, Westminster John Knox, 2003). He has also written commentaries on Proverbs (Baker), Job (Baker), Song of Songs (Eerdmans), Ecclesiastes (Eerdmans), Daniel (Zondervan), Jeremiah and Lamentations (Baker), and Nahum (Baker). His study of ancient Near Eastern autobiography (*Fictional Akkadian Autobiography* (Eisenbrauns)) provides the cultural and literary background to the study of Ecclesiastes. Most recently, he has published "Determining the Historical Context of Ecclesiastes," in *The Words of the Wise Are Like Goads: Engaging Qohelet in the 21st Century*, edited by M. J. Boda, T. Longman III, C. G. Rata (Eisenbrauns, 2013).

Timothy Mawson (D.Phil., Oxford University) is Fellow and Tutor in Philosophy at St. Peter's College, Oxford. His research interests are in the philosophy of religion, philosophical theology, and moral philosophy. He is the author of two books, *Belief in God: An Introduction to the Philosophy of Religion* (Oxford University Press, 2005) and *Free Will: A Guide for the Perplexed* (Continuum, 2011). His articles have appeared in such journals as *Religious Studies, International Journal for Philosophy of Religion*, and the *European Journal for Philosophy of Religion*, among others.

Paul K. Moser (Ph.D., Vanderbilt University) is Professor of Philosophy at Loyola University in Chicago. He is the author of numerous books in epistemology and philosophy of religion, including *Philosophy after Objectivity* (Oxford University Press, 1993), *The Elusive God: Reorienting Religious Epistemology* (Cambridge University Press, 2009), and *The Severity of God: Religion & Philosophy Reconceived* (Cambridge University Press, 2013). He has edited fifteen volumes, and his articles have appeared in such journals as *The Canadian Journal of Philosophy*, *The Heythrop Journal*, *Analysis*, *The Philosophical Quarterly*, and *Philosophy and Phenomenological Research*, among many others.

Joshua W. Seachris (Ph.D., University of Oklahoma) is Program Director for Notre Dame's Center for Philosophy of Religion and Adjunct Professor of Philosophy at the University of Notre Dame. He is the editor of *Exploring the Meaning of Life: An Anthology and Guide* (Wiley-Blackwell, 2012) and has authored a number of articles on topics like the problem of evil, Confucius and virtue, the meaning of life, and death. His work has appeared in journals such as *Religious Studies, Asian Philosophy*, the *International Journal for Philosophy of Religion*, and *Ethical Theory and Moral Practice*, among others. He is currently working on a book manuscript on life's meaning (*What is the Meaning of Life? De-Mystifying Our Ultimate Question*).

Richard Swinburne is Emeritus Nolloth Professor of the Philosophy of the Christian Religion, University of Oxford, and Emeritus Fellow of Oriel College, Oxford. He is a Fellow of the British Academy. He is the author of over fifteen books including *The Coherence of Theism* (Oxford, 1977), *Faith and Reason* (Oxford University Press, 2005), *Revelation* (Oxford University Press, 2007), *The Resurrection of God Incarnate* (Oxford University Press, 2003), and *Mind, Brain, and Free Will* (Oxford University Press, 2013). He has edited several books, and has authored over 100 articles in journals such as the *European Journal for Philosophy of Religion, Religious Studies, Australasian Journal of Philosophy*, and *Mind*, among others.

Charles Taliaferro (Ph.D., Brown University) is Professor of Philosophy at St. Olaf College. He is the author or coauthor, editor or coeditor of twenty books, most recently *The Golden Cord: A Short Book on the Secular and the Sacred* (University of Notre Dame Press, 2012). With Stewart Goetz he is the coauthor of *A Brief History of the Soul* (Wiley-Blackwell, 2011) and coeditor of *The Routledge Companion to Theism* (Routledge, 2012). He has been a visiting scholar at Oxford, Princeton, NYU, and Columbia, and is the philosophy of religion area editor for Blackwell's *Philosophy Compass* and the Book Review Editor for *Faith and Philosophy*.

Nicholas Waghorn (Ph.D., University of Reading) is College Lecturer and Director of Studies, St. Benet's Hall, Oxford. His research interests are in the meaning of life, ontology (especially Nothing), metaphilosophy, and death. He is the author of *Nothingness and the Meaning of Life: Philosophical Approaches to Ultimate Meaning Through Nothing and Self-Reflexivity* (Bloomsbury, 2014).

Bibliography

Adams, Douglas. *The Restaurant at the End of the Universe*. London: Pan Books, 1984.
Adams, Robert Merrihew. "A Modified Divine Command Theory of Ethical Wrongness." In *Religion and Morality*, edited by G. Outka and J. P. Reeder, 318–347. Garden City, New York: Anchor, 1973.
Alexander, Jeffrey C. *The Dark Side of Modernity*. Cambridge: Polity, 2013.
Alfeyev, Hilarion. 2000. *The Spiritual World of Isaac the Syrian*. Kalamazoo. MI: Cisterian Publications.
Angeles, Peter. *Dictionary of Philosophy*. New York: Barnes and Noble, 1981.
Annas, Julia. *Intelligent Virtue*. Oxford: Oxford University Press, 2011.
Aristotle. *Nicomachean Ethics*, 2nd ed. Translated by Terrence Irwin. Indianapolis: Hackett, 1999.
Armstrong, David. "Naturalism, Materialism, and First Philosophy." *Philosophia* 8 (1978): 261–276.
Auerbach, Erich. *Mimesis*. Princeton, NJ: Princeton University Press, 2003.
Baggini, Julian. *What's It All About? Philosophy and the Meaning of Life*. Oxford: Oxford University Press, 2004.
Baier, Kurt. "The Meaning of Life." In *The Meaning of Life*, edited by E. D. Klemke, 81–117. New York: Oxford University Press, 1981.
Barbour, Jennie. *The Story of Israel in the Book of Qohelet: Ecclesiastes as Cultural Memory*. Oxford: Oxford University Press, 2012.
Barrett, Justin. *Why Would Anyone Believe in God?* New York: AltaMira Press, 2004.
Barrett, Justin. *Born Believers*. New York: Free Press, 2012.
Bartholomew, Craig. *Reading Ecclesiastes: Old Testament Exegesis and Hermeneutical Theory*. Analecta Biblica 139. Rome: Pontifical Biblical Institute, 1998.
Bartholomew, Craig. *Reading Proverbs with Integrity*. Cambridge: Groves, 2001.
Bartholomew, Craig and Michael W. Goheen. "Story and Biblical Theology." In *Out of Egypt: Biblical Theology and Biblical Interpretation*, vol. 5, Scripture and Hermeneutics Series, edited by Craig Bartholomew, Mary Healy, Karl Moller, and Robin Parry, 144–171. Grand Rapids, MI: Zondervan, 2004.
Beilby, James. *Naturalism Defeated? Essays on Plantinga's Evolutionary Argument against Naturalism*. Ithaca, NY: Cornell University Press, 2002.
Benatar, David, ed. *Life, Death, & Meaning: Key Philosophical Readings on the Big Questions*. Lanham, MD: Rowman & Littlefield Publishers, 2004.
Bergman, Michael. "Skeptical Theism and the Problem of Evil." In *Oxford Handbook to Philosophical Theology*, edited by Thomas Flint and Michael Rea, 374–399. Oxford: Oxford University Press, 2009.

Bering, Jesse. *The Belief Instinct: The Psychology of Souls, Destiny, and the Meaning of Life*. London: Brealing Publishing, 2010.

Blackburn, Simon. "Religion and Respect." In *Philosopher's without Gods: Meditations on Atheism and the Secular Life*, edited by Louise M. Antony, 179–193. Oxford: Oxford University Press, 2007.

Bloom, Harold, ed. *The Book of Job*. New York: Chelsea House, 1988.

Boff, Leonardo. *Passion of Christ, Passion of the Word*, 2nd ed. Maryknoll, New York: Orbis, 2001.

Bonhoeffer, Dietrich. *Ethics*. Edited by E. Bethge. London: SCM, 1955.

Boomershine, Thomas E. "Epistemology at the Turn of the Ages in Paul, Jesus, and Mark: Rhetoric and Dialectic in Apocalyptic and the New Testament." In *Apocalyptic and the New Testament: Essays in Honor of J. Louis Martyn*, edited by Joel Marcus and Marion L. Soards, 147–167. Sheffield, Eng.: Journal for the Study of the Old Testament Press, 1989.

Boyer, Pascal. *Religion Explained: The Evolutionary Origins of Religious Thought*. New York: Basic Books, 2002.

Brassier, Ray. *Nihil Unbound: Enlightenment and Extinction*. Basingstoke, UK: Palgrave Macmillan, 2007.

Bublia, J. *The Evolution of Religion: Studies, Theories, & Critiques*. Santa Margherita, CA: Collins Foundation Press, 2008.

Catechism of the Catholic Church, 2nd ed. Libreria Editrice Vaticana, 2000.

Chesterton, Gilbert K. "Orthodoxy." In *The Essential Gilbert K. Chesterton, Vol. 1: Non-Fiction*. Radford, VA: Wilder Publications, 2008.

Cottingham, John. *On the Meaning of Life*. London: Routledge, 2003.

Cottingham, John. *The Spiritual Dimension: Religion, Philosophy and Human Value*. Cambridge: Cambridge University Press, 2005.

Cottingham, John. "The Good Life and the 'Radical Contingency of the Ethical.'" In *Reading Bernard Williams*, edited by D. Callcut, 25–43. London: Routledge, 2008.

Cottingham, John. "Meaningful Life." In *The Wisdom of the Christian Faith*, edited by Paul K. Moser and Michael T. McFall, 175–196. Cambridge: Cambridge University Press, 2012.

Craig, William Lane. *Reasonable Faith, Christian Truth and Apologetics*, revised ed. Wheaton, IL: Crossway, 1994.

Crump, David. *Encountering Jesus, Encountering Scripture*. Grand Rapids: Eerdmans, 2013.

Cuneo, Terence. *Speech and Morality*. Oxford: Oxford University Press, 2014.

Cuneo, Terence. "Liturgy and the Moral Life." In *Character: New Directions from Philosophy, Psychology, and Theology*, edited by Christian Miller, 572–589. Oxford: Oxford University Press, 2015.

Cuneo, Terence. "Love and Liturgy." *The Journal of Religious Ethics* 43 (2015): 587–605.

Currie, Gregory. *Narratives & Narrators: A Philosophy of Stories*. Oxford: Oxford University Press, 2010.

Daley, B. E. *The Hope of the Early Church*. Cambridge: Cambridge University Press, 1991.
Davidson, Robert. *Courage to Doubt: Exploring an Old Testament Theme*. London: SCM, 1989.
Dershowitz, Alan. "Life is Not a Dramatic Narrative." In *Law's Stories: Narrative and Rhetoric in the Law*, edited by Peter Brooks and Paul Gewirtz, 99–105. New Haven: Yale University Press, 1998.
Descartes, René. *Meditationes de prima philosophia (Meditations on First Philosophy)*, Dedicatory Letter to the Sorbonne. 1641.
Dougherty, Trent. "Epistemological Considerations Concerning Skeptical Theism." *Faith and Philosophy* 25:2 (2008): 172–176.
Dougherty, Trent. "Further Epistemological Considerations Concerning Skeptical Theism." *Faith and Philosophy* 28:3 (2011): 332–340.
Dougherty, Trent. "Skeptical Theism." *The Stanford Encyclopedia of Philosophy* (Spring 2014 Edition). Edited by Edward N. Zalta. http://plato.stanford.edu/archives/spr2014/entries/skeptical-theism/.
Dougherty, Trent. "Skeptical Theism, Phenomenal Conservatism, and Probability." In *Skeptical Theism: New Essays*, edited by Trent Dougherty and Justin McBrayer. Oxford: Oxford University Press, 2014.
Dougherty, Trent and Paul Draper. "The Explanatory Argument from Evil." In *The Blackwell Companion to the Problem of Evil*, edited by Justin McBrayer and Daniel Howard-Snyder, 67–82. Oxford: Wiley-Blackwell, 2013.
Dworkin, Ronald. *Religion without God*. Cambridge, MA: Harvard University Press, 2013.
Eagleton, Terry. *The Meaning of Life*. Oxford: Oxford University Press, 2007.
Evans, C. Stephen. *Natural Signs and Knowledge of God: A New Look at Theistic Arguments*. Oxford: Oxford University Press, 2012.
Farmer, Herbert H. *Things Not Seen*. London: Nisbet, 1927.
Fehige, Christoph and Ulla Wessels, eds. *Preferences*. Berlin: Walter de Gruyter, 1998.
Fiddes, Paul S. *The Creative Suffering of God*. Oxford: Clarendon Press, 1988.
Fiddes, Paul S. *Past Event and Present Salvation*. London: Darton, Longman, and Todd, 1989.
Fiddes, Paul S. *The Promised End: Eschatology in Theology and Literature*. Oxford: Blackwell, 2000.
Fischer, John Martin. "Why Immortality Is Not So Bad." *International Journal of Philosophical Studies* 2 (1994): 257–270.
Flanagan, Owen. "What Makes Life Worth Living?" In *The Meaning of Life*, 2nd edn, edited by E. D. Klemke. New York: Oxford University Press, 2000.
Flannery, Austin, ed. *Vatican Council II: The Conciliar and Post Conciliar Documents*. Dublin: Dominican Publications, 1975.
Fox, Michael V. "Frame-Narrative and Composition in the Book of Qohelet." *HUCA* 48 (1977): 26–38.
Fox, Michael V. "Qohelet's Epistemology." *Hebrew Union College Annual* 58 (1987): 137–155.

Fox, Michael V. *A Time to Tear Down & A Time to Build Up: A Rereading of Ecclesiastes*. Grand Rapids, MI: Eerdmans, 1999.
Frankl, Victor. *Man's Search for Meaning*. Boston: Beacon Press, 2006.
Fredericks, D. C. *Coping with Transience: Ecclesiastes on the Brevity of Life*. Sheffield: JSOT Press, 1993.
Galston, W. A. *Liberal Pluralism: The Implications of Value Pluralism for Political Theory*. Cambridge: Cambridge University Press, 2002.
Girard, René. *Deceit, Desire, and the Novel: Self and Other in Literary Structure*. Translated by Y. Freccero. Baltimore, MD: Johns Hopkins University Press, 1965.
Goetz, Stewart, "Making Things Happen: Soul in Action." In *The Soul Hypothesis: Investigations into the Existence of the Soul*, edited by Mark Baker and Stewart Goetz, 99–117. New York: Continuum, 2011.
Goetz, Stewart. *The Purpose of Life: A Theistic Perspective*. London: Continuum, 2012.
Goetz, Stewart. "The Meaning of Life." In *The Routledge Companion to Theism*, edited by Charles Taliaferro, Victoria S. Harrison, and Stewart Goetz, 698–709. New York: Routledge, 2013.
Goetz, Stewart. *A Philosophical Walking Tour with C. S. Lewis: Why It Did Not Include Rome*. New York: Bloomsbury, 2015.
Goetz, Stewart and Charles Taliaferro. *Naturalism*. Grand Rapids, MI: William B. Eerdmans, 2008.
Greidanus, Sidney. *The Modern Preacher and the Ancient Text*. Grand Rapids: Eerdmans, 2000.
Hallo, William W., ed. *The Context of Scripture*. Volume 1. *Canonical Compositions from the Biblical World*. Leiden: Brill, 1997.
Harman, Gilbert. "Practical Reasoning." *The Review of Metaphysics* 29:3 (1976): 431–463.
Harrisville, Roy A. *Fracture: The Cross as Irreconcilable in the Language and Thought of the Biblical Writers*. Grand Rapids, MI: Eerdmans, 2006.
Hasker, William. *The Emergent Self*. Ithaca, NY: Cornell University Press, 2001.
Haybron, Daniel. *The Pursuit of Unhappiness: The Elusive Psychology of Well-Being*. New York: Oxford University Press, 2008.
Hays, Richard B. *The Conversion of Imagination: Paul as Interpreter of Israel's Scripture*. Grand Rapids, MI: Eerdmans, 2005.
Heschel, Abraham. *The Prophets*. New York: Jewish Publication Society of America, 1962.
Himmelfarb, Gertrude. *On Looking Into the Abyss: Untimely Thoughts on Culture and Society*. New York: Vintage, 1994.
Himmelmann, Beatrix, ed. *On Meaning in Life*. Boston: De Gruyter, 2013.
Hubbard, Moyer V. *New Creation in Paul's Letters and Thought*. Cambridge: Cambridge University Press, 1998.

Hutcheson, Francis. *An Inquiry into the Original of our Ideas of Beauty and Virtue; in Two Treatises. II. Concerning Moral Good and Evil*, 2nd ed. London, 1726.
Isaac of Nineveh [Isaac the Syrian]. *"The Second Part,"* Chapters IV-XLI, edited by Sebastian Brock. Corpus Scriptorum Christianonorum Orientalium 554, Scriptores syro 224. Louvain 1991.
Joyce, Richard. *The Evolution of Morality*. Cambridge, MA: MIT Press, 2006.
Kaiser, Jr., W. C. *Ecclesiastes: Total Life*. Chicago: Moody, 1979.
Kass, R. and A. Raftery. "Bayes Factors." *Journal of the American Statistical Association* 90:430 (1995): 773-795.
Kim, Jaegwon. *Physicalism, or Something Near Enough*. Princeton, NJ: Princeton University Press, 2005.
Kitcher, Phillip. *Life After Faith: The Case for Secular Humanism*. New Haven, CT: Yale University Press, 2014.
Klagge, James C. "From the Meaning of Life to a Meaningful Life." (Unpublished Manuscript).
Klemke, E. D., ed. *The Meaning of Life*, 2nd ed. New York: Oxford University Press, 2000.
Kwan, Kai-man. *The Rainbow of Experiences, Critical Trust, and God: A Defense of Holistic Empiricism*. London and New York: Continuum Press, 2011.
Landau, Iddo. "Why Has the Question of the Meaning of Life Arisen in the Last Two and a Half Centuries?" *Philosophy Today* 41 (1997): 263-269.
Levine, E. *The Aramaic Version of Qohelet*. New York: Sepher-Hermon, 1978.
Lewis, C. S. *The Screwtape Letters*. New York: Macmillan, 1961.
Lewis, C. S. *God in the Dock*. Grand Rapids, MI: Eerdmans, 1970.
Lewis, C. S. *Undeceptions: Essays on Theology and Ethics*. London: Bles, 1971.
Lewis, C. S. *Letters to Malcolm: Chiefly on Prayer*. New York: Harcourt, 2001.
Lewis, C. S. *The Great Divorce*. New York: Harper San Francisco, 2001.
Lewis, C. S. *Mere Christianity*. New York: Harper San Francisco, 2001.
Lewis, C. S. *Miracles*. New York: Harper Collins, 2001.
Lewis, C. S. *The Problem of Pain*. New York: Harper Collins, 2001.
Lewis, C. S. *The Weight of Glory and Other Essays*. New York: Harper Collins, 2001.
Lewis, C. S. *The Collected Letters of C. S. Lewis: Volume II; Books, Broadcasts, and the War, 1931-1949*, edited by Walter Hooper. New York: Harper San Francisco, 2004.
Lewis, C. S. *The Collected Letters of C. S. Lewis: Volume III; Narnia, Cambridge, and Joy, 1950-1963*, edited by Walter Hooper. New York: Harper San Francisco, 2007.
List, Christian and Philip Pettit. *Group Agency: The Possibility, Design and Status of Corporate Agents*. Oxford: Oxford University Press, 2011.
Lohfink, Norbert. *Qoheleth*. Translated by S. E. McEvenue. Continental Commentary. Minneapolis, MN: Fortress, 2003.

Longman III, Tremper. *Fictional Akkadian Autobiography: A Generic and Comparative Study*. Winona Lake, IN: Eisenbrauns, 1990.

Longman III, Tremper. *The Book of Ecclesiastes*, The New International Commentary on the Old Testament. Grand Rapids, MI: Eerdmans, 1998.

Longman III, Tremper. *Proverbs*. Baker Commentary on the Old Testament Wisdom and Psalms. Grand Rapids, MI: Baker, 2006.

Longman III, Tremper. "Ecclesiastes: History of Interpretation." In *Dictionary of the Old Testament: Wisdom, Poetry and Writings*, edited by T. Longman III and P. Enns, 140–149. Downers Grove, IL: InterVarsity Press, 2009.

Longman III, Tremper. *Job*. Baker Commentary on the Old Testament Wisdom and Psalms. Grand Rapids, MI: Baker, 2012.

Longman III, Tremper. "Determining the Historical Context of Ecclesiastes." In *The Words of the Wise are Like Goads: Engaging Qohelet in the 21st Century*, edited by Mark Boda et al., 89–102. Winona Lake, IN: Eisenbrauns, 2013.

Longman III, Tremper. "Qohelet as Solomon: 'For What Can Anyone Who Comes after the King Do?' (Ecclesiastes 2:12)." In *Reading Ecclesiastes Intertextually*, edited by K. Dell and W. Kynes, 42–56. London: Bloomsbury, 2014.

Longman III, Tremper. "The 'Fear of God' in the Book of Ecclesiastes." *Bulletin of Biblical Research* 25 (2015): 13–22.

Luper, Steven. *Invulnerability: On Securing Happiness*. Chicago and La Salle, IL: Open Court, 1996.

McDowell, John. *Mind and World*. Cambridge, MA: Harvard University Press, 1994.

MacIntyre, Alasdair. *After Virtue: A Study in Moral Theory*. 3rd ed. Notre Dame: University of Notre Dame Press, 2007.

Mackie, J. L. "Evil and Omnipotence." In *The Problem of Evil*, edited by Marilyn McCord Adams and Robert Merrihew Adams. Oxford: Oxford University Press, 1990.

Martin, Ralph P. *Reconciliation: A Study of Paul's Theology*. Atlanta: John Knox, 1981.

Martyn, J. L. "Epistemology at the Turn of the Ages: 2 Corinthians 5.16." In *Christian Christian History and Interpretation: Studies Presented to John Knox*, edited by C. F. D. Moule, R. R. Niebuhr, and W. R. Farmer, 269–287. Cambridge: Cambridge University Press , 1967.

Mawson, T. J. "Sources of Dissatisfaction with Answers to the Question of the Meaning of Life." *European Journal for Philosophy of Religion* 2:2 (2010): 19–41.

May, Rollo. *The Cry for Myth*. New York: Norton, 1991.

May, Todd. *A Significant Life: Human Meaning in a Silent Universe*. Chicago: University of Chicago Press, 2015.

Metz, Thaddeus. "Recent Work on the Meaning of Life." *Ethics* 112 (July 2002): 781–814.

Metz, Thaddeus. "New Developments in the Meaning of Life." *Philosophy Compass* 2 (2007): 196–217.
Metz, Thaddeus. "Imperfection as Sufficient for a Meaningful Life: How Much is Enough?" In *New Waves in Philosophy of Religion*, edited by Yujin Nagasawa and Erik Wielenberg, 192–214. New York: Palgrave Macmillan, 2009.
Metz, Thaddeus. *Meaning in Life: An Analytic Study*. Oxford: Oxford University Press, 2013.
Metz, Thaddeus. "The Meaning of Life." *Stanford Encyclopedia of Philosophy*. Edited by Edward N. Zalta. http://plato.stanford.edu/entries/life-meaning/.
Meyendorff, John. *The Orthodox Church*. New York: Pantheon Books, 1962.
Mill, J. S. *Utilitarianism*, Chapter 2, edited by M. Warnock. Collins, 1962.
Mill, J. S. *The Autobiography of John Stuart Mill*. New York: Signet Classics, 1964.
Miller, Patrick. *The Way of the Lord*. Grand Rapids, MI: Eerdmans, 2004.
Millgram, Elijah. *Practical Induction*. Cambridge, MA: Harvard University Press, 1997.
Millgram, Elijah, ed. *Varieties of Practical Reasoning*. Cambridge, MA: MIT Press, 2001.
Minear, Paul. *Christians and the New Creation: Genesis Motifs in the New Testament*. Philadelphia: Westminster, 1994.
Moser, Paul K. *The Elusive God*. Cambridge: Cambridge University Press, 2008.
Moser, Paul K. *The Evidence for God*. Cambridge: Cambridge University Press, 2010.
Moser, Paul K. *The Severity of God*. Cambridge: Cambridge University Press, 2013.
Moser, Paul K. "God and Evidence: A Cooperative Approach." *European Journal for the Philosophy of Religion* 5 (Summer 2013): 91–105.
Moser, Paul K. "God without Argument." In *Is Faith in God Reasonable?*, edited by Corey Miller and Paul Gould, 69–83. London: Routledge, 2014.
Mostert, Christiaan. "Theodicy and Eschatology." In *Theodicy and Eschatology*, edited by Bruce Barber and David Neville, 97–120. Adelaide, Australia: ATF Press, 2005.
Mother Mary and Kallistos Ware, eds. and trans. *The Lenten Triodion*. South Canaan, PA: St. Tikhon's Seminary Press, 2002.
Nagasawa, Yujin and Erik Wielenberg, eds. *New Waves in Philosophy of Religion*. New York: Palgrave Macmillan, 2009.
Nagel, Thomas. *Mortal Questions*. Cambridge: Cambridge University Press, 1979.
Nietzsche, Friedrich. *Zur Genealogie der Moral* (*On the Genealogy of Morals*). Translated by Douglas Smith (Oxford World Classics). Oxford: Oxford University Press, 2009.
Nietzsche, Friedrich. *Jenseits von Gut und Böse* (*Beyond Good and Evil*). Translated by W. Kaufmann. New York: Random House, 1966.
Nietzsche, Friedrich. *Die fröhliche Wissenschaft* (*The Joyful Science*), 1882.

Nussbaum, Martha. "Pity and Mercy." In *Nietzsche, Genealogy, Morality*, edited by R. Schacht, 139-167. Berkeley, CA: University of California Press, 1994.

O'Connor, Timothy. *Theism and Ultimate Explanation: The Necessary Shape of Contingency*. Malden, MA: Wiley-Blackwell, 2008.

O'Donovan, Oliver. *Resurrection and Moral Order: An Outline for Evangelical Ethics*, 2nd ed. Leicester: Apollos; Grand Rapids, MI: Eerdmans, 1994.

Palmer, G. E. H., Philip Sherard, and Kallistos Ware. "Introduction." In *The Philokalia*, vol. 1. 11-18, edited by G. E. H. Palmer, Philip Sherard, and Kallistos Ware. London: Faber and Faber, 1979.

Papineau, David. *Philosophical Naturalism*. Oxford: Blackwell, 1993.

Parfit, Derek. *On What Matters*, Vol. I. Oxford: Oxford University Press, 2011.

Pascal, Blaise. *Pensées*. Translated by Honor Levi. Oxford: Oxford University Press, 1657/1995.

Poebel, A. *Das appositionell bestimmte Pronomen der 1. Per. Sing. In den westsemitischen Inschriften und im Alent Testament*. AS 3. Chicago: Oriental Institute, 1931.

Pope, M. H. *Song of Songs*. AB 7C. Garden City, NY: Doubleday, 1977.

Prosch, Harry. "Preface." In *Meaning*, edited by Michael Polanyi and Harry Prosch. Chicago: University of Chicago Press, 1975.

Ratzinger, Joseph. *The Spirit of the Liturgy*. San Francisco: Ignatius Press, 2000.

Reppert, Victor. *C. S. Lewis's Dangerous Idea: In Defense of the Argument from Reason*. Downer's Grove, IL: IVP Academic, 2003.

Richardson, Brian. "Recent Concepts of Narrative and the Narratives of Narrative Theory." *Style* 34 (2000), 168-175.

Ricoeur, Paul. *Figuring the Sacred: Religion, Narrative, and Imagination*. Minneapolis, MN: Fortress, 1995.

Rosenberg, Alex. *An Atheist's Guide to Reality: Enjoying Life without Illusions*. New York: W. W. Norton & Company, 2011.

Rudrum, David. "From Narrative Representation to Narrative Use: Towards the Limits of Definition." *Narrative* 13:2 (May 2005): 195-204.

Rundle, Bede. *Why There is Something Rather than Nothing*. Oxford: Clarendon Press, 2006.

Russell, Bertrand, ed. "A Free Man's Worship." In *Mysticism and Logic*, 44-54. New York: Doubleday, 1903.

Russell, Bertrand, ed. "On History." In *The Basic Writings of Bertrand Russell*. London: Routledge, 2009.

Ryan, Marie-Laure. "Toward a Definition of Narrative." In *The Cambridge Companion to Narrative*, edited by David Herman, 22-35. Cambridge: Cambridge University Press, 2007.

Sacks, Jonathan. *The Great Partnership: Science, Religion, and the Search for Meaning*. New York: Schocken, 2011.

Sartre, Jean-Paul. *Nausea*. Translated by Lloyd Alexander. New York: New Directions, 1964.

Sartre, Jean-Paul. *Existentialism and Humanism*. Translated by Philip Mairet. Brooklyn, NY: Haskell House Publishers, 1977.
Sawyer, J. F. A. "The Ruined House in Ecclesiastes 12: A Reconstruction of the Original Parable." *Journal of Biblical Literature* 94 (1974): 95–101.
Schmemann, Alexander. *Introduction to Liturgical Theology*. Crestwood, NY: St. Vladimir's Seminary Press, 1966.
Schmemann, Alexander. *Great Lent*. Crestwood, NY: St. Vladimir's Seminary Press, 1969.
Schroeder, Timothy. "Desire." In *The Stanford Encyclopedia of Philosophy* (Spring 2014 Edition). Edited by Edward N. Zalta. http://plato.stanford.edu/archives/spr2014/entries/desire/ (accessed September 14, 2015).
Seachris, Joshua W. "The Meaning of Life as Narrative: A New Proposal for Interpreting Philosophy's 'Primary' Question." *Philo* 12 (Spring-Summer 2009): 5–23.
Seachris, Joshua W. "Death, Futility, and the Proleptic Power of Narrative Ending." *Religious Studies* 47 (2011): 141–163.
Seachris, Joshua W. "Meaning of Life: Contemporary Analytic Perspectives." *Internet Encyclopedia of Philosophy*. http://www.iep.utm.edu/mean-ana/, 2012.
Seachris, Joshua W., ed. *Exploring the Meaning of Life: An Anthology and Guide*. Malden, MA: Wiley-Blackwell, 2012.
Shemmer, Yonatan. "Desiring at Will and Humeanism in Practical Reason." *Philosophical Studies: An International Journal for Philosophy in the Analytic Tradition* 119:3 (2004): 265–294.
Shemmer, Yonatan. "Instrumentalism and Desiring at Will." *Canadian Journal of Philosophy* 35:2 (2005): 269–288.
Shoemaker, Sydney. "Desiring at Will (and at Pill): A Reply to Millgram." In *Preferences*, edited by Christoph Fehige and Ulla Wessels, 26–32. Berlin: Walter de Gruyter, 1998.
Sidgwick, Henry. *The Methods of Ethics*, 7th ed. New York: Dover Publications.
Silverstein, Matthew. "In Defense of Happiness: A Response to the Experience Machine." *Social Theory and Practice* 26 (2000): 279–300.
Spykman, Gordon J. *Reformational Theology: A New Paradigm for Doing Dogmatics*. Grand Rapids, MI: Eerdmans, 1992.
St. Augustine. *Confessions*. Translated by R. S. Pine-Coffin. London: Penguin, 1961.
St. Augustine. *The City of God against the Pagans*. Translated by R. W. Dyson. Cambridge: Cambridge University Press, 1998.
St. Augustine. *The Enchiridion on Faith, Hope and Love*. Translated by Thomas Hibbs. Washington, DC: Gateway Editions, 1999.
St. Isaac the Syrian. *On Ascetical Life*. Crestwood, NY: St. Vladimir's Seminary Press, 1989.
St. Isaac the Syrian. *The Ascetical Homilies of Saint Isaac the Syrian*. Translated by Dana Miller. Boston, MA. Monastery of the Holy Transfiguration, 1984.

St. John Chrysostom. *The Divine Liturgy of St. John Chrysostom*. Jordanville, NY: Holy Trinity Publications, 1999.

St. Thomas Aquinas. *Summa Theologica*. Translated by Fathers of the English Dominican Provinc. Christian Classics, 1981.

St. Thomas Aquinas. *Summa Contra Gentiles*. Translated by Anton Charles Pegis. Notre Dame: University of Notre Dame Press, 1991.

Strawson, Galen. "Realistic Monism: Why Physicalism Entails Panpsychism." In *Consciousness and Its Place in Nature: Does Physicalism Entail Panpsychism?* edited by Anthony Freeman. Charlottesville, VA: Imprint Academic, 2006.

Street, S. "A Darwinian Dilemma for Realist Theories of Value." *Philosophical Studies* 127 (2006): 109–166.

Stroud, Barry. "The Charm of Naturalism." In *Naturalism in Question*, edited by Mario De Caro and David Macarthur. Cambridge, MA: Harvard University Press, 2004.

Stump, Eleonore. *Wandering in Darkness*. Oxford: Oxford University Press, 2011.

Swinburne, Richard. *Responsibility and Atonement*. Oxford: Oxford University Press, 1989.

Swinburne, Richard. *The Resurrection of God Incarnate*. Oxford: Clarendon Press, 2003.

Swinburne, Richard. *Faith and Reason*, 2nd ed. Oxford: Oxford University Press, 2005.

Swinburne, Richard. *Was Jesus God?* Oxford: Oxford University Press, 2008.

Swinburne, Richard. *The Existence of God*, 2nd ed. Oxford: Oxford University Press, 2010.

Swinburne, Richard. *Is There a God?* revised ed. Oxford: Oxford University Press, 2010.

Taliaferro, Charles. *The Golden Cord: A Short Book on the Secular and the Sacred*. Notre Dame, IN: University of Notre Dame, Press, 2012.

Taliaferro, Charles and Jil Evans. *The Image in Mind: Theism, Naturalism, and the Imagination*. London: Continuum, 2013.

Taylor, Charles. *Sources of the Self: The Making of the Modern Identity*. Cambridge, MA: Harvard University Press, 1989.

Taylor, Richard. *Good and Evil*, Chapter 18. New York: Macmillan, 1970.

Taylor, Richard. *Metaphysics*. Saddle River, NJ: Prentice Hall, 1991.

Tennyson, Alfred. *In Memoriam*. 1850.

Tennyson, Alfred. *Ulysses*. 1842.

Thomson, Garrett. *On the Meaning of Life*. London: Wadsworth, 2003.

Tolkien, J. R. R. *The Return of the King: Being the Third Part of the Lord of the Rings*. Boston: Houghton Mifflin Company, 1965.

Trisel, Brooke Alan. "Futility and the Meaning of Life Debate." *Sorites* 14 (2002): 70–84.

Trisel, Brooke Alan. "Human Extinction and the Value of Our Efforts." *Philosophical Forum* 35:3 (2004): 371–391.

Van Inwagen, Peter. *God, Knowledge, and Mystery: Essays in Philosophical Theology*. Ithaca, NY: Cornell University Press, 1995.
Vatican II. *Dogmatic Constitution of the Church: Lumen Gentium*. Chicago: Pauline Books, 1965.
Velleman, J. David. "Narrative Explanation." *Philosophical Review* 112 (January 2003): 1–25.
Von Rad, Gerhard. *Wisdom in Israel*. Nashville, TN: Abingdon, 1972.
Vox, Michael V. *A Time to Tear Down & A Time to Build Up: A Rereading of Ecclesiastes*. Grand Rapids: William B. Eerdmans Publishing Company, 1999.
Waghorn, Nicholas. *Nothingness and the Meaning of Life: Philosophical Approaches to Ultimate Meaning through Nothing and Reflexivity*. London: Bloomsbury, 2014.
Ware, Timothy (Kallistos). *The Orthodox Church*, new ed. New York: Penguin, 1997.
Ware, Kallistos. "Forward." In *The Spiritual World of Isaac the Syrian*, edited by Hilarion Alfeyev, 9–13. Kalamazoo, MI: Cisterian Publications, 2000.
Ware, Kallistos. "The Meaning of the Great Fast." In *The Lenten Triodion*, edited and translated by Mother Mary and Kallistos Ware, 13–68. South Canaan, PA: St. Tikhon's Seminary Press, 2002.
Weber, Max. *From Max Weber*. Edited by H. Gerth and C. Wright Mills. New York: Oxford University Press, 1946.
Weber, Max. *Selections in Translation*. Edited by W. G. Bunciman. Cambridge: Cambridge University Press, 1978.
White, Nicholas. *A Brief History of Happiness*. Oxford: Blackwell, 2006.
White, Roger. "You Just Believe That Because …" *Philosophical Perspectives* 24 (2010): 573–615.
Wiggins, David. *Ethics*. London: Penguin, 2006.
Williams, Bernard. "The Makropulos Case: Reflections on the Tedium of Immortality." In *Problems of the Self*, 82–100. Cambridge: Cambridge University Press, 1973.
Williams, Bernard. *Ethics and the Limits of Philosophy*. London: Fontana, 1985.
Williams, Bernard. *Truth and Truthfulness*. Princeton, NJ: Princeton University Press, 2002.
Williams, John F. *Hating Perfection: A Subtle Search for the Best Possible World*, revised ed. Amherst, NY: Humanity Books, 2013.
Wisdom, John. "The Meanings of the Questions of Life." In *The Meaning of Life*, 3rd edn, edited by E. D. Klemke and Steven M. Cahn, 220–223. New York: Oxford University Press, 2008.
Wittgenstein, Ludwig. *Notebooks, 1914–16*, 2nd ed. Translated by G. E. M. Anscombe. Chicago: University of Chicago Press, 1979.
Wolf, Susan. "Meaningful Lives in a Meaningless World." *Quaestiones Infinitae* 14 (June 1997): 1–22.
Wolf, Susan. *Meaning in Life and Why It Matters*. Princeton: Princeton University Press, 2010.

Wolf, Susan. "The Meanings of Lives." In *Introduction to Philosophy: Classical and Contemporary Readings*, 5th edn, edited by John Perry, Michael Bratman, and John Martin Fischer, 794–805. New York: Oxford University Press, 2010.

Young, Julian. *The Death of God and the Meaning of Life*. London: Routledge, 2005.

Index

Adams, Douglas 126n. 8
Adams, Robert Merrihew 128n. 11
Alexander, Jeffrey C. 210n. 6
Alfeyev, Hilarian 185n. 1, 188n. 5
Angeles, Peter 209
Annas, Julia 72–3
Aristotle 134, 157, 225
Armstrong, David 62n. 10
Auerbach, Eric 221–2
Aurelius, Marcus 126
Averroes 132–3

Baggini, Julian 1n. 1, 10, 61, 64, 67, 77n. 42, 220–3, 229–30
Baier, Kurt 2–3, 100
Barbour, J. 239n. 11
Barrett, Justin 88, 95n. 18
Bartholomew, Craig G. 10, 23n. 21, 212nn. 10, 12, 13
Beilby, James 93n. 13
Benatar, David 1n. 1, 228
Bergmann, Michael 84n. 4
Bering, Jesse 95n. 19
Blackburn, Simon 137–43
Bloom, Harold 216n. 24
Boff, Leonardo 228
Bonhoeffer, Dietrich 221n. 34
Boomershine, Thomas E. 181n. 13
Brassier, Ray 211
Bruner, Jerome 4n. 4
Buber, Martin 216
Bublia, J. 94n. 16

Cahn, Steven 1n. 1
Calvin, John 87
Chesterton, G. K. 142–3, 225
Chrétien, Jean-Louis 226n. 52
Cottingham, John 1n. 1, 8, 15n. 9, 44n. 6, 125n. 6, 126n. 8, 219n. 30, 222, 224–5

Craig, William Lane 130–1
Crump, David 174n. 6
Cuneo, Terence 9–10, 197n. 25, 200n. 36, 204n. 45
Currie, Gregory 17n. 11

Daley, B. E. 159n. 12
Davidson, Robert 217n. 25
Dell, K. 239n. 11
Dershowitz, Alan 5n. 4
Descartes, René 133
Dooyeweerd, Herman 222
Dougherty, Trent 7, 84nn. 2, 4, 93n. 15
Draper, Paul 84nn. 2, 4
Dworkin, Ronald 138–43

Eagleton, Terry 1n. 1
Enns, P. 244n. 16
Evans, C. Stephen 88, 93, 96n. 20
Evans, Jil 139n. 6

Farmer, Herbert H. 173
Farmer, W. R. 181n. 13
Fiddes, Paul S. 24, 168n. 1, 172n. 4
Fischer, John Martin 65–7
Flanagan, Owen 76
Flannery, Austin 19n. 13
Fox, Michael 28n. 35, 213, 232n. 5
Frankl, Victor 232n. 3
Fredericks, D. C. 231n. 2

Galston, W. A. 53n. 11
Girard, René 226, 228
Goetz, Stewart 1n. 1, 7, 22n. 17, 63n. 13, 77nn. 35, 36
Goodenough, Ursula 218
Gould, Paul 175n. 7
Greidanus, Sidney 23–4

Hallo, William W. 212n. 11
Hare, John 224
Harman, Gilbert 102n. 5, 103n. 8, 104–5, 113
Harrisville, Roy A. 181n. 12
Haybron, Daniel 67n. 21
Hays, Richard B. 224n. 46
Heidegger, Martin 226
Henry, Michel 226n. 52
Hepburn, R. W. 5n. 5, 215n. 21
Heschel, Abraham 168n. 1
Himmelfarb, Gertrude 211
Himmelmann, Beatrix 1n. 1
Hubbard, Moyer V. 181n. 11
Hugh of St. Victor 87
Hutcheson, Francis 102–3

Jerome 243–4
Jesus (Christ) 23, 28, 31, 32, 156–9, 161, 168–9, 171–3, 180–2, 192–4, 198, 221, 227, 244–6
Job 28, 180, 212, 223, 229, 233n. 6, 242
Joyce, Richard 90n. 11

Kaiser Jr., W. C. 238n. 10
Kim, Jaegwon 62–3, 72
Kitcher, Philip 138–40, 143–6
Klagge, James 14–15
Klemke, E. D. 1n. 1, 209n. 2
Kuyper, Abraham 223
Kwan, Kai-man 145n. 12
Kynes, W. 239n. 11

Lacoste, Jean-Yves 226n. 52
Landau, Iddo 59
Lewis, C. S. 7, 61, 76–80, 90–1, 93n. 13
List, Christian 204n. 50
Lohfink, Norbert 214
Longman III, Tremper 10, 28n. 35, 225n. 50, 231nn. 1, 2, 232n. 4, 233nn. 6, 7, 235n. 9, 239nn. 11, 12, 240n. 13, 242n. 14

Luper, Stephen 106–7, 109, 113, 116n. 31, 117
Luther, Martin 244

McDowell, John 124
MacIntyre, Alasdair 217
Mackie, J. L. 74–5
Marcus, Joel 181n. 13
Marion, Jean-Luc 226n. 52
Martin, Ralph P. 171n. 3
Martyn, J. L. 181n. 13
Marx, Karl 50–1, 57, 91
Mawson, Timothy 6, 40n. 4
May, Rollo 25n. 28
May, Todd 1n. 1
Metz, Thaddeus 1n. 1, 14, 60, 76, 99–100, 117n. 32, 219n. 30
Meyendorff, John 204n. 49
Mill, J. S. 71–2, 80, 150–1
Miller, Christian 204n. 45
Miller, Corey 175n. 7
Miller, Patrick 230
Millgram, Elijah 102n. 4, 107–14, 116nn. 30, 31
Minear, Paul 181n. 11
Moser, Paul K. 9, 175n. 7, 176n. 8, 177n. 9, 180n. 10, 182n. 15
Moster, Christiaan 30

Nagel, Thomas 10, 72, 215n. 23, 216, 226–7
Nietzsche, Friedrich 124–5, 131, 222
Nozick, Robert 7, 61, 67–8, 70, 72, 76
Nussbaum, Martha 125n. 7

O'Connor, Timothy 26n. 31
O'Donovan, Oliver 223n. 44
Origen 160n. 15

Palmer, G. E. H. 187, 191
Papineau, David 62n. 10
Parfit, Derek 7, 60, 62
Pascal, Blaise 170

Index

Paul (Apostle) 28, 180–2, 224, 244–5
Pettit, Philip 204n. 50
Plantinga, Alvin 87
Poebel, A. 233n. 7
Polanyi, Michael 210
Pope Benedict XVI 27n. 33
Pope, M. H. 244n. 15
Prosch, Harry 210

Qohelet 10, 28, 30, 211–20, 223–9, 231–43, 245–6

Reppert, Victor 93n. 13
Richardson, Brian 17n. 11
Ricoeur, Paul 217–18, 226
Rookmaker, Hans 222
Rosenberg, Alex 62n. 10
Rudd, Anthony 4n. 4
Rudrum David 17n. 11
Rundle, Bede 26
Russell, Bertrand 140, 143, 181n. 14, 210
Ryan, Marie-Laure 17n. 11

St. Augustine 87, 160n. 16, 162, 225
St. Ephraim the Syrian 198–200
St. Isaac the Syrian 9, 10
St. Thomas Aquinas 96, 158n. 8, 161, 162n. 20, 190
Sartre, Jean-Paul 24, 37–53, 56–8
Savitt, Stephen 131n. 20
Sawyer, J. F. A. 234n. 8
Schmemann, Alexander 199n. 34, 203, 204n. 47
Schroeder, Timothy 105n. 11
Seachris, Joshua W. 1n. 1, 6, 14n. 4, 29n. 36, 32n. 42, 138, 209n. 2, 215, 226, 228–9
Shemmer, Yonatan 102–4, 109, 111–12, 116n. 30
Sherard, Philip 187, 191
Shoemaker, Sydney 109–11

Sidgwick, Henry 72, 80
Silverstein, Matthew 61, 68–71, 76
Soards, Marion L. 181n. 13
Spykman, Gordon J. 214
Stoics 126
Strawson, Galen 4n. 4, 72
Street, S. 90n. 11
Stroud, Barry 61
Stump, Eleonore 127n. 10
Swinburne, Richard 8, 83n. 1, 130n. 12, 153n. 4, 159n. 11, 162n. 21

Taliaferro, Charles 8, 63n. 13, 139n. 6
Taylor, Charles 217, 222
Taylor, Richard 93n. 13, 150n. 1
Tennyson, Alfred 131–2, 135n. 26
Thomson, Garrett 15n. 9
Tolstoy, Leo 229
Trisel, Brooke Alan 100

van Inwagen, Peter 86n. 5
Velleman, J. David 29–30
Von Rad, Gerhard 222

Waghorn, Nicholas 1n. 1, 7, 100n. 3, 111n. 25
Wallace, Mark 217–18
Ware, Kallistos 187, 191, 197n. 27, 204n. 46
Weber, Max 210
White, Nicholas 61
White, Roger 90n. 12
Wielenberg, Erik J. 221
Wiggins, David 124
Williams, Bernard 4n. 4, 29n. 37, 61, 64–5, 67, 124, 131
Williams, John 75–6
Wisdom, John 15n. 9
Wittgenstein, Ludwig 223
Wolf, Susan 1n. 1, 2, 14, 59–60, 152n. 3

Young, Julian 16n. 9, 24–5

www.ingramcontent.com/pod-product-compliance
Lightning Source LLC
Chambersburg PA
CBHW062122300426
44115CB00012BA/1781